KNOW YOUR ENGLISH

VOLUME 4

KNOW
YOUR ENGLISH

VOLUME 4

VOCABULARY AND PRONUNCIATION

S Upendran

Universities Press

Know Your English, Volume 4: Vocabulary and Pronunciation

UNIVERSITIES PRESS (INDIA) PRIVATE LIMITED

Registered Office
3-6-747/1/A & 3-6-754/1, Himayatnagar,
Hyderabad 500 029, Telangana, India.
e-mail: info@universitiespress.com; Web: www.universitiespress.com

Distributed by
Orient Blackswan Private Limited

Registered Office
3-6-752 Himayatnagar, Hyderabad 500 029, Telangana, India

Other Offices
Bengaluru / Bhopal / Chennai / Guwahati / Hyderabad / Jaipur /
Kolkata / Lucknow / Mumbai / New Delhi / Noida / Patna / Vijayawada

ISBN 978 81 7371 732 1

Illustrations
Arijit Dutta Chowdhury

Typeset in Life BT 10/12.3 *by*
OSDATA, Hyderabad

Printed at
Sriram Printing Press, Chennai 600 116

Published by
Universities Press (India) Private Limited
3-6-747/1/A & 3-6-754/1, Himayatnagar,
Hyderabad 500 029, Telangana, India
e-mail: info@universitiespress.com

501349
28062017

Preface

Which is more important – grammar, vocabulary or pronunciation? It depends on who – or is it whom? – one asks, I suppose. Way back in 1972, David Wilkins argued that vocabulary was much more important than grammar: "...without grammar very little can be conveyed, without vocabulary nothing can be conveyed." Makes one wonder why teachers of English in our country focus so much on grammar! Others, however, maintain that even if you have a rich vocabulary and demonstrate a sound knowledge of the rules of grammar, you will not be understood if your pronunciation is bad. In their opinion, bad pronunciation impedes communication.

This volume, the fourth in the *Know Your English* series, does not attempt to answer the thorny question of which component of language is the most important. As learners, we must constantly keep working on our grammar, fine-tune our pronunciation and continue to add to our existing 'wordrobe'. This book highlights some of the common words that we tend to mispronounce. Is 'sew' pronounced like the word 'so' or like the word 'sue'? In the sentence, 'I beat him', does 'beat' rhyme with 'met' or 'meat'? Is the 'th' in 'asthma' pronounced? How many syllables does 'develop' have – two or three? Is the 'scin' in 'scintillating' pronounced like the word 'skin' or 'sin'? Are the two words, 'desert' and 'dessert', pronounced similarly? Does one stress the first or second syllable in 'colleague'?

In addition, the book familiarises the reader with several hundred words and expressions that are used by native speakers of English in formal and informal contexts. Why does the Government merely provide 'band-aid solutions' to our problems? Are you a 'moofer'? If so, are you 'nomophobic'? What is the female equivalent of 'bachelor'? Do you plan on buying an 'uber-expensive' present for your parents? Do you have any 'qualms' about giving your best friend a 'regift'? Where will you find 'crow's feet' on the human body? Is your 'fathead' neighbour a 'foodaholic' or a 'connoisseur'? Did your favourite hero's latest film turn out to be a 'sleepfest'?

The 800-odd entries contained in this book are selections from the weekly column, *Know Your English*, published in *The Hindu*. Most entries provide information about the pronunciation of the word/expression, its meaning and, wherever possible, the etymology (origin of the word). In addition, each entry provides examples on how the word/expression is to be used. Information about pronunciation has been provided in two different ways – phonetic transcription; and for those unfamiliar with the symbols, I have adopted the style of explanation used in the KYE column. The *Oxford Advanced Learner's Dictionary, Merriam-Webster's Advanced Learner's Dictionary* and the *Online Etymology Dictionary* were consulted for information related to etymology. All explanations have been provided in as simple a manner as possible. Anyone who is 16 years of age or older will find this book useful.

I am grateful to the Editor of *The Hindu* for giving me permission to use the material from the column. Heartfelt thanks are also due to the members of my immediate family – especially my sister, Manaswini, for going through the manuscript and providing valuable suggestions and comments. I would also like to thank the readers of the column for their letters of appreciation and condemnation. Last, but not least, gratitude is due to my father, K. Subrahmanian, who started this column nearly 35 years ago. This set of four books would not have been possible without him.

S. Upendran

Contents

To
Achala and Ananya

180-degree turn

Meaning To do a complete turnaround; to make radical changes. Also possible to say, 'do a 180'.

Examples *Jeevan did a 180-degree turn and voted against the resolution.*

During the second debate, the candidate did a 180 on several key issues.

Origin When you make a 360-degree turn, you make a complete circle. You are back to square one; you return to where you started! If you wish to make radical changes in your thinking or behaviour, you need to make a 180-degree turn and not a 360-degree one.

A1

Meaning Something that is excellent or first rate. The expression can be used with people as well.

Examples *The car is over ten years old, but the engine is in A1 condition.*

As a teacher, Aishwarya is A1.

Origin Lloyd's, a British company that insured ships, coined the term. When rating a ship, the letters A, E, I, O and U were used to indicate the condition of the hull, and the numbers 1, 2, 3, etc. were used to indicate the state of the equipment (cables, anchor, and so on) on board. An A1 rating meant that both were in excellent condition.

Abecedarian /ei-bi:-si:-dʒə-riən/

Pronunciation — The first three syllables sound like the letters 'A', 'B' and 'C', and the fourth is pronounced like the word 'dare'. The word is pronounced 'a-b-c-**DARE**-ian'.

Meaning — Someone who is learning the letters of the alphabet; a novice – an individual who is learning the 'abc' of something. Anything that has been arranged alphabetically can also be called 'abecedarian'.

Examples — *The Wimbledon champion spent some time with the abecedarians of his club.*

I would like everything to be in abecedarian sequence.

Etymology — It comes from the Latin 'abecedarius', meaning 'alphabetical'.

Abnegate /æb-nɪ-geit/

Pronunciation — The first syllable rhymes with 'cab' and 'fab'; the following 'e' sounds like the 'i' in 'sit' and 'bit'. The final syllable sounds like the word 'gate'. One way of pronouncing the word is '**AB**-ni-gate'.

Meaning — To give up one's claims on something; to renounce. An additional meaning is 'to deny oneself the pleasures of something'.

Examples — *The ailing King was unwilling to abnegate his powers to his son.*

The young CEO said he was abnegating the luxuries of life.

Etymology — From the Latin 'abnegatus', meaning 'refuse or deny'.

Academic /æ-kə-dem-ik/

Pronunciation — The first 'a' is like the 'a' in 'pan' and 'fan', and the second is like the 'a' in 'china'. The 'e' is like the 'e' in 'set' and 'wet'. The word is pronounced 'a-ke-**DEM**-ic'. Most Indians tend to place the stress on the second syllable. Words that end in 'ic' usually have the stress on the syllable preceding it – e**lec**tric, fan**tas**tic, spe**ci**fic, etc.

Meaning — Related to education and educational institutions; a member of such an institution. Can also be used to mean 'theoretical'.

Examples — *As a student, Prahlad had no interest in academic matters.*

Since the series has already been lost, the final match will only be of academic interest.

Kunthala was perhaps the only academic in our family.

Etymology — The word comes from the Latin 'academicus', meaning 'of the Academy' – the garden where Plato taught his students.

Academic bulimia /æ-kə-dem-ik bʊ-lɪm-ɪ-ə/

Pronunciation — The 'u' in the second word is like the 'u' in 'put' and 'push' and the following syllable rhymes with 'rim' and 'dim'. The final 'ia' is like the 'ia' in 'India'. The word is pronounced 'bu-**LIM**-i-e'.

Meaning — A bulimic is someone who eats a lot of food, promptly goes to the bathroom and intentionally throws up. Just like the bulimic who throws up before he has digested his food, an academic bulimic vomits whatever he has memorized without having digested the contents.

Examples — *Do you think there's a solution to the problem of academic bulimia?*

Our educational system promotes academic bulimia.

Acerbic /ə-s͟ɜ:-bɪk/

Pronunciation The 'a' is like the 'a' in 'china', and the 'cer' sounds like the word 'sir'. The word is pronounced 'a-**SIR**-bik'.

Meaning Comments that are 'acerbic' are cruel, stinging or bitter tasting.

Examples *Ram's acerbic wit has made him many enemies.*

Despite the acerbic reviews, Usha's latest book has become a bestseller.

Etymology It comes from the Latin 'acerbus', meaning 'harsh'.

Acquiesce /æ-kwi-e͟s/

Pronunciation The 'a' sounds like the 'a' in 'ant' and 'sat', and the 'qui' is pronounced like the 'qui' in 'quit' and 'quick'. The final 'esce' is like the 'es' in 'yes' and 'mess'. The word is pronounced 'a-kwi-**ES**'.

Meaning To reluctantly agree or to accept something. One usually acquiesces 'in' or 'to' something.

Examples *The newly recruited officers acquiesced to the Minister's plans.*

When the plan failed, the officers acquiesced in the cover-up.

Etymology This formal word comes from the Latin 'acquiescere', meaning 'to become quiet'.

Acumen /æ-kju-mən/ /ə-kju:-mən/

Pronunciation The British and the Americans pronounce this word rather differently. The former pronounce the 'ac' like the 'ac' in 'pack' and 'back'. The 'u' is like the 'u' in 'put' and the final 'e' is like the 'a' in 'china'. They pronounce the word '**A**-kyu-men'. The Americans, on the other hand, pronounce the 'a' and the 'e' like the 'a' in 'china', and the second syllable like the word 'cue'. They pronounce the word 'e-**CUE**-men'.

Meaning Being extremely sharp, knowledgeable and capable of taking very quick decisions.

Examples *My cousin tells me that I have no business acumen.*

Rahul's political acumen helped his party win the election.

Etymology This rather formal word comes from the Latin 'acuere', meaning 'sharpen'.

Ad nauseam /æd nɒ-zɪ-æm/

Pronunciation The first word is pronounced like the word 'add'. The 'au' in 'nauseam' is like the 'au' in 'caught', 'taught' and 'naught', and the following 'se' is like the 'zi' in 'zip' and 'zinc'. The final syllable is pronounced like the word 'am'. The expression is pronounced 'add **NAU**-zi-am'.

Meaning When someone talks about something 'ad nauseam', he talks about it so much that it becomes extremely boring for the listeners.

Examples *She talked ad nauseam about the numerous prizes she had won.*

The Minister talked ad nauseam about his achievements.

Sashi went on ad nauseam about what a wonderful wife he has.

Etymology In Latin, the expression means 'to sickness'.

Adidas /ʌ-dɪ-da:s/ /ʌ-di:-da:s/

Pronunciation The first 'a' is like the 'u' in 'cut' and 'but' and the second is like the 'ar' in 'park' and 'dark'. The 'i' sounds like the 'i' in 'sit' and 'bit'. The Germans pronounce the word '**A** di daas'. The Americans make the second syllable rhyme with 'fee' and 'bee'. They pronounce the word 'a-**DEE**-das'.

Etymology: The founder of Adidas was a German named Adolf Dassler; he was nicknamed 'Adi' by his friends. When Dassler started his company in 1924, he decided to name it after himself. He combined his nickname 'Adi' with the first half of his surname 'Dassler' and came up with 'Adidas'!

Adieu /ə-dju:/

Pronunciation: The 'a' is like the 'a' in 'china', and the following 'dieu' sounds like the word 'due'. The word is pronounced 'e-**DUE**'.

Meaning: Goodbye.

Example: *The time has come to bid everyone adieu.*

Etymology: In French, 'à' means 'to' and 'dieu' means 'God'. The word is the shortened form of the French expression, 'à dieu (vous) commant', meaning 'I commend (you) to God'. The expression was used when taking leave of someone.

Adolescent /æ-də-les-ənt/

Pronunciation: The first syllable is pronounced like the word 'add' and the third like the word 'less'. The 'o' in the second and the 'e' in the final syllable are pronounced like the 'a' in 'India'. The word is pronounced 'ad-e-**LES**-ent'.

Meaning — A young person who is not a child, but one who has not matured into an adult. It is that awkward stage between childhood and adulthood.

Examples — *Mohan's adolescent daughter doesn't like her new school.*

Drinking has become a major problem among adolescents.

Puppy love is quite common among adolescents.

Etymology — From the Latin 'adolecentum', meaning 'growing near maturity, youthful'.

Adrenalin /ə-dren-ə-lɪn/

Pronunciation — The vowels in the first and third syllables are pronounced like the 'a' in 'china'. The 'e' is like the 'e' in 'pen' and 'den', and the final syllable rhymes with 'pin' and 'bin'. The word is pronounced 'e-**DREN**-e-lin'.

Meaning — A chemical substance the body produces when our emotions run high. Figuratively, the word is used to mean 'to make someone excited or angry'.

Examples *When I saw Nishant kicking the puppy, it got my adrenalin going.*

Aparna felt the rush of adrenalin through her body.

Etymology From the Latin 'adrenal', meaning 'near the kidneys'.

Aeon/Eon /iːɒn/ /iːən/

Pronunciation The first syllable sounds like the 'ee' in 'fee', 'feel' and 'feet', while the second is pronounced like the word 'on'. The word is pronounced '**EE**-on'. It is also possible to pronounce the vowel in the second syllable like the 'a' in 'china'.

Meaning A term used in geology to refer to a lengthy period of time – 'a unit of time that is equal to a thousand million years'. In everyday contexts, the word is frequently used to mean 'a long, long time'.

Examples *Sheba crossed the finish line aeons before we did.*

We've been waiting aeons to hear from Amjad.

Etymology The word comes from the Greek 'aion', meaning 'age'. It is also related to our Sanskrit 'aayu', meaning 'span of life'. The Americans spell it 'eon', while the British seem to prefer 'aeon'.

Affability /æ-fə-bɪ-lɪ-ti/

Pronunciation The first 'a' is pronounced like the 'a' in 'cat' and 'bat', while the second sounds like the 'a' in 'china'. The final 'bility' is like the 'bility' in 'ability', 'capability' and 'stability'. The word is pronounced 'a-fe-**BIL**-i-ti'.

Meaning A person who is 'affable' is very pleasant and friendly. Such a person is usually very courteous whenever he talks to someone.

Examples *Sujatha's mother is an extremely affable woman.*

Many students find the new teacher's affability very irritating.

Etymology The word comes from the Latin 'affabilis', meaning 'approachable, friendly'.

Aficionado /ə-fiʃ-jə-na:-dəu/

Pronunciation The 'a' in the first syllable and the 'o' in the third are like the 'a' in 'china'. The second syllable is pronounced like the word 'fish' and the 'i' that follows is like the 'y' in 'yes' and 'yet'. The second 'a' is like the 'a' in 'bath' and 'path', while the final 'do' rhymes with 'so', 'no' and 'go'. One way of pronouncing the word is 'a-fish-ye-**NAA**-doe'.

Meaning When you say that someone is an aficionado of something, what you mean is that the person is a great fan of it; he is very interested in a particular subject, and knows a great deal about it.

Examples *My boss says that his wife is an aficionado of Thai food.*

It was fairly obvious that the new CEO was a jazz aficionado.

Etymology The word comes from the Spanish 'aficionado', meaning 'amateur'. It was first used to refer to the lovers/devotees of bullfighting.

Agemate

Meaning Sometimes used in informal contexts to refer to people of the same age or about the same age.

Example *Vasantha had no agemate in the colony she was living in.*

Ailurophobia /ai-lu:-rə-f<u>əu</u>-biə/

Pronunciation The first syllable is pronounced like the word 'eye', and the following 'lu' sounds like the word 'loo'. The 'o' is like the 'a' in 'china'. One way of pronouncing the word is 'eye-loo-re-**PHO**-bia'.

Meaning — An irrational or morbid fear of cats.

Etymology — 'Ailouros' in Greek means 'cat'.

Airhead

Meaning — A stupid person; someone who speaks or acts unintelligently. The word is usually used with women, especially those who are good-looking, but considered to have nothing between their ears.

Examples — *Why did Sanjay choose to marry an airhead like Kiran?*

You can't rely on an airhead like Jyothi to help you.

Airplane talker

Meaning — Someone who sits or stands close to you and talks in a loud voice.

Examples — *Your friend Dileep is a total airplane talker.*

Some of our news anchors are airplane talkers. They seem to forget that they have a mike.

Origin — On planes, you may come across people who sit next to you and talk rather loudly because they do not want the noise of the engine to drown their voice. You are helpless because there is no escaping them.

Aisle /ail/

Pronunciation — The 'ai' is pronounced like the word 'I'; the 's' and the 'e' that follow are silent. In other words, 'aisle' is pronounced the same way as 'I'll' and 'isle'.

Meaning — The passage that is usually maintained or which exists between two rows of seats.

Examples — *There weren't enough chairs. So, we were forced to sit in the aisles.*

The steward kept walking up and down the aisle.

A.k.a

Meaning — Abbreviated form of 'also known as'.

Examples — *Vijay, a.k.a Goldie, has been missing since May.*

Samuel Clemens, a.k.a Mark Twain, was a brilliant writer.

Akimbo /ə-kɪm-bəu/

Pronunciation — The 'a' sounds like the 'a' in 'china'; the syllable that follows is pronounced like the name 'Kim'.

The final 'bo' rhymes with 'so' and 'no'. The word is pronounced 'e-**KIM**-bo'.

Meaning — To have your hands on your hips and the arms spread out, with the elbows pointing outwards. It is a posture that generally indicates impatience, hostility or contempt.

Examples — *The Principal stood, arms akimbo, glaring at the students.*

Standing behind the sofa with arms akimbo, Sheel told the painter what to do.

Etymology — From the Middle English 'kenebowe'.

Albeit /ɒl-bi:-ɪt/

Pronunciation — The first syllable is pronounced like the word 'all', the second like the word 'bee' and the final syllable like the word 'it'. This rather old-fashioned word is pronounced 'all-**BEE**-it'.

Meaning — It is mostly used in formal contexts to mean 'although'.

Examples — *The Government was making progress, albeit slowly.*

Renu tried, albeit unsuccessfully, to jog 20 miles.

Etymology — It comes from the phrase 'all be it', meaning 'although it be'.

Alibi

/æ-lɪ-bai/

Pronunciation — The 'a' in the first syllable is like the 'a' in 'cat', 'bat' and 'sat', while the 'i' in the second is like the 'i' in 'sit' and 'bit'. The final syllable is pronounced like the word 'by'. The word is pronounced '**A**-li-by'.

Meaning — The evidence one provides to prove that one was somewhere else when a criminal activity took place.

Examples — *The husband has a cast-iron alibi. He was not in the country when his wife was murdered.*

I was watching TV at home. I guess that's not much of an alibi.

Etymology — It comes from the Latin 'alibi', meaning 'elsewhere'.

All-nighter

Meaning — An informal word to refer to an activity or event that will last all night. It can also be used to refer to someone who stays awake all night.

Examples — *I'm told that Mala is an all-nighter. No wonder she is so grumpy in the morning.*

Tonight's study session is going to be an all-nighter. I'm going to stay awake by drinking lots of coffee.

Alma mater /æl-mə <u>ma:</u>tə/

Pronunciation The first 'a' in 'alma' is like the 'a' in 'cat' and 'sat', while the second is like the 'a' in 'china'. The 'a' in 'mater' is like the 'a' in 'bath' and 'path', and the final 'er' is like the 'a' in 'china'. One way of pronouncing the word is 'al-me **MAA**-te'.

Meaning Used to refer to the school, college or university that one has graduated from. Sometimes, schools and colleges have their own songs; these official songs can also be called 'alma mater'.

Examples *Usha is planning to visit her alma mater next month.*

Princeton is Achala's alma mater.

Etymology It comes from the Latin 'alma', meaning 'nourishing', and 'mater', meaning 'mother'. The expression literally means 'bountiful mother'.

Alumnus /ə-<u>lʌm</u>-nəs/

Pronunciation The vowels in the first and third syllables are like the 'a' in 'china', and the second syllable rhymes with 'rum' and 'come'. The word is pronounced 'e-**LUM**-nes'.

Meaning A former student of a school or college.

Examples *Like you, Manjit, I too am an alumnus of Stephen's.*

Ajay claims to be an alumnus of IIT Madras.

Etymology From the Latin 'alumnus', meaning 'pupil'.

Alzheimer's /ælts-hai-məz/

Pronunciation The 'al' is like the 'al' in 'pal' and 'shall', and the following 'z' like the 'ts' in 'pants' and 'shorts'. 'Heimer' rhymes with 'timer' and 'primer'. The final 's' sounds like the 'z' in 'zip' and 'zap'. The word is pronounced '**ALTS**-hime-erz'.

Meaning A brain disease which results in memory loss, speech loss, etc. Such people will be unable to think clearly.

Example *Geetha's father has been diagnosed with Alzheimer's.*

Etymology The disease is named after the German neurologist, Alois Alzheimer.

Amour-propre /a:mur prəu/

Pronunciation The 'a' in 'amour' is like the 'a' in 'ask', 'bath' and 'path', and the 'ou' sounds like the 'u' in 'put', 'full' and 'pull'. The second word is

	pronounced like the word 'pro'. One way of pronouncing this expression is 'aamur **PRO**'.
Meaning	Self-esteem or self-respect.
Example	*Whatever you do, don't offend Kavitha's amour-propre.*
Etymology	A French expression that literally means 'love of oneself'.

Angst /æŋkst/

Pronunciation	The 'ang' sounds like the 'ank' in 'bank' and 'sank'; the final 'st' is like the 'st' in 'step' and 'stink'. The word consists of only one syllable and is pronounced '**ANKST**'.
Meaning	Refers to the feeling of frustration, unhappiness or insecurity that we experience from time to time; worrying about something trivial.
Examples	*Don't worry about it too much. I'm sure it's just teenage angst.* *His daughter's short skirt and unkempt hair caused him considerable angst.*
Etymology	In German, it means 'fear' or 'anxiety'.

Annus horribilus /æn-əs <u>hə-ri:</u>-bə-ləs/

Pronunciation	The first syllable of 'annus' is pronounced like the name 'Ann', while the vowel in the second is

like the 'a' in 'china'. The first 'i' in 'horribilus' is like the 'ee' in 'fees', 'bees' and 'cheese'. All the other vowels are like the 'a' in 'china'. The expression is pronounced 'ann-es he-**REE**-be-les'.

Meaning A Latin expression, meaning 'horrible year'. The opposite is 'annus mirabilis', meaning 'year of wonders'.

Example *According to experts, 2009 was an annus horribilus for the corporate sector.*

Ante-mortem

Meaning Before death; the opposite of 'post-mortem'.

Examples *According to the coroner, the victim's injuries were post-mortem and not ante-mortem.*

Their ante-mortem dental records were used to identify the crash victims.

Etymology From the Latin 'ante', meaning 'before', and 'mortem', meaning 'death'.

Antsy

Meaning To be nervous or restless.

Examples *Aravind becomes rather antsy before exams.*

Sitting in the locker room, the two finalists looked antsy.

Apartheid /ə-pa:-tait/ /ə-pa:-teit/

Pronunciation — The first two syllables are pronounced like the word 'apart'. The last syllable can rhyme with 'fight' or 'fate'. The word can be pronounced 'e-**PAR**-tight' or 'e-**PAR**-tate'.

Meaning — Discriminating against people on grounds of race.

Examples — *During the days of apartheid, people of colour had no rights.*

Sheba experienced the social apartheid that exists in most prestigious institutions.

Etymology — The word comes from Afrikaans, and means 'separateness' or 'apartness'; it refers to the racial segregation that was practised in South Africa till 1992. Nowadays, the word is frequently used to refer to blatant discrimination of any kind – not necessarily racial. People talk about 'gender apartheid', 'cultural apartheid' and 'sexual apartheid'.

Aplomb /ə-plɔm/

Pronunciation — The 'a' is like the 'a' in 'china', and the following 'o' sounds like the 'o' in 'hot', 'pot' and 'cot'. The final 'b' is silent. The word is pronounced 'e-**PLOM**'.

Meaning — When you do something with aplomb, you do it in a relaxed manner, and with a great deal of confidence. The word is mostly used in formal contexts.

Examples — *The young couple handled the difficult situation with aplomb.*

The ageing champion faced his young opponent with aplomb.

Etymology — It comes from the French 'à plomb', meaning 'balanced, being upright'.

Apropos /æ-prə-peu/

Pronunciation — The 'a' sounds like the 'a' in 'act', cat' and 'hat'. The first 'o' is like the 'a' in 'china', and the second rhymes with 'no' and 'so'. The 's' is silent. The word is pronounced 'a-pre-**PO**'.

Meaning — The word is usually used to introduce a new subject, one that is connected to what you were talking about earlier. When you say that something is 'apropos', you mean that it is suitable or appropriate.

Examples — *I received a call from Priyanka last night – apropos of which, did you send her the paintings?*

Frankly, I don't think her outfit was apropos for the occasion.

	The Vice Chancellor's remarks were very apropos.
Etymology	It comes from the French 'à propos', meaning 'to the point'.

Archives	/a̲:-kaivz/
Pronunciation	The first syllable 'arch' rhymes with the words 'dark', 'bark' and 'park', and the final 'ive' rhymes with 'five', 'hive' and 'drive'. The word is pronounced '**AA**-kivz', with the stress on the first syllable.
Meaning	An archive is a collection of documents or records which contains historical information. It is also used to refer to the place where such documents are kept.
Examples	*I need more background information. So I plan to visit the library archives tomorrow.* *I found some interesting documents in the family archives.*
Etymology	From the Greek 'ta arkheia', meaning 'public records'.

ASAP	/e̲i̲-sæp/
Pronunciation	Each letter can be pronounced individually. It is also possible to pronounce it as a word – '**A**-sap'.

Meaning Abbreviated form of 'as soon as possible'.

Examples *We need to have this room cleaned asap.*

Malini, you need to see a doctor asap.

Askance /əs-kæns/ /əs-ka:ns/

Pronunciation The 'a' in the first syllable is like the 'a' in 'china', while the 'a' in the second can be pronounced either like the 'a' in 'can' and 'pan' or like the 'a' in 'dance' and 'ask'. The word can be pronounced 'es-**CANS**' or 'es-**KAANS**'.

Meaning To look at someone or something with disapproval or distrust. In most cases, you do not look at the person/object directly; you choose to glance at him/it sideways.

Examples *My father-in-law looked askance at my crumpled clothes.*

Raju looks askance at politicians. He believes they are all crooks.

Assuage /əs-weidʒ/

Pronunciation The first 'a' is like the 'a' in 'china', and the following 'uage' is pronounced like the word 'wage'. The word is pronounced 'es-**WAGE**'.

Meaning — Make something less unpleasant or less severe; reducing its strength.

Examples — *The President tried to assuage the fears his neighbour had about a potential war.*

Nothing you do will assuage Anand's desire for power.

The committee failed to assuage the fears of the workers.

Etymology — From the French 'assuager', meaning 'soften' or 'pacify'.

Asthma /æs-mə/ /æz-mə/

Pronunciation — The first syllable is pronounced like the word 'ass', and the following 'th' remains silent. The final 'a' is like the 'a' in 'china'. The word is pronounced '**ASS**-me'. Americans tend to say '**AZ**-me'.

Meaning — A respiratory condition which causes difficulty in breathing.

Examples — *While he was trekking, Vinay had an asthma attack.*

If you have asthma, you shouldn't visit Georgia during spring.

Etymology — It comes from the Greek 'asthma', meaning 'short breath, panting'.

Auspices /ɒs-pɪ-sɪz/

Pronunciation The 'au' is like the 'aw' in 'pawn', 'fawn' and 'dawn'; the following syllable sounds like the 'spi' in 'spill' and 'spin'. The final 's' is like the 'z' in 'zip' and 'zing'. The word is pronounced '**AW**-spi-siz'.

Meaning When you say that a meeting was held under the auspices of an organisation, it means that it had the help and support of the organisation. The word is normally used in formal contexts.

Examples *Several relief camps have been set up under the auspices of the United Nations.*

The marathon was held under the auspices of the World Wildlife Fund.

Etymology From the Latin 'auspicium', meaning 'observer of birds'. In the past, people tried to predict future events by observing the behaviour and flight patterns of birds.

Auteur /əu-tɜː/

Pronunciation The 'au' sounds like the 'o' in 'go', 'so' and 'no', while the 'eur' is like the 'ir' in 'birth', 'bird' and 'first'. The word is pronounced 'o-**TIR**'.

Meaning — We know that all well-known directors have a distinctive style of making movies. It is possible to watch a couple of scenes from a film and guess who the director is. Dictionaries define this distinctive style, which enables a director to keep creative control over his work, as 'auteur'. This is just one of the meanings of the word.

Example — *It surprised many that the big budget film wasn't being directed by a noted auteur.*

Etymology — In French, the word means 'author'.

Awry /ə-rai/

Pronunciation — The 'aw' is like the 'a' in 'china', and the 'ry' rhymes with 'my' and 'by'. The word is pronounced 'e-**RAI**'.

Meaning — The word has several meanings. When things go awry, they don't go the way you had planned. When something is not in its normal or proper position, it is said to be awry. It is somewhat crooked.

Examples — *When things go awry around the house, poor Mala is blamed.*

The plans went awry because the Chief Guest arrived two hours late.

Etymology In Old English, 'a' meant 'on' and 'wry' meant 'twisted to one side'.

Bachelorette /bætʃ-lə-ret/

Pronunciation The first syllable is pronounced like the word 'batch', and the vowel that follows is like the 'a' in 'china'. The final syllable rhymes with 'set' and 'bet'. The word is pronounced 'batch-le-**RET**'.

Meaning A female bachelor; a young, unmarried woman.

Examples *The bachelorettes were requested to leave the room.*

Sheba introduced me to her bachelorette friends.

Etymology From the French 'bachelette', meaning 'young girl'.

Bad-mouth someone

Meaning To deliberately say uncomplimentary things about a person in order to damage his reputation. Used in informal contexts.

Examples *Because of the intense competition, cinema stars often tend to bad-mouth one another.*

Bhalla continues to bad-mouth his former boss.

Ballpark estimate/figure

Meaning Used in informal contexts in American English to mean 'an approximate figure' or 'a rough estimate'. The word 'ballpark' is used in American English to refer to a stadium.

Examples *There must have been a hundred people at Sujatha's party. That's just a ballpark estimate.*

How much do you think it'll cost to go on a cruise? Give me a ballpark figure.

Band-aid solution

Meaning A temporary solution to a problem; something that has been put together rather hastily. It is a stop-gap arrangement that does not attempt to solve the underlying problem.

Examples *Our politicians are only interested in a band-aid solution to the water problem.*

I can provide a band-aid solution to your problem.

Bang on

Meaning: Absolutely correct; exactly. Mostly limited to informal contexts.

Examples: *Achala's criticism of the new policy was bang on.*

Many of Satish's predictions about the market were bang on.

Baton

/bæt-ɔn/ /bə-ta:n/

Pronunciation: The British pronounce the first syllable like the word 'bat' and the second like the word 'on'. They pronounce the word '**BAT**-on'. The Americans, on the other hand, pronounce the 'a' like the 'a' in 'china' and the 'o' like the 'a' in 'father', 'path' and 'bath'. They pronounce the word 'be-**TAAN**'.

Meaning: The stick that is handed off by one runner to another in a race. The word can also be used to refer to the stick used by a music conductor.

Examples: *The runner dropped the baton as he neared the finish line.*

The conductor waved the baton menacingly at the trumpet player.

Etymology: The word comes from the Latin 'bastum', meaning 'stick'.

Beat (past tense) /biːt/

Pronunciation The past tense of 'beat' is not pronounced like the word 'bet'. It rhymes with the words 'meat', 'heat' and 'neat'.

Examples *The teacher beat the children every day.*

The last time our teams met, we beat them.

Beau /bəu/

Pronunciation It is pronounced like the word 'bow' – the weapon you use to shoot arrows with.

Meaning Boyfriend or lover. The word is considered old fashioned.

Examples *The fashion model made a grand entrance, hand-in-hand with her latest beau.*

Radha's current beau has an excellent sense of humour.

Etymology It comes from the French 'beau', meaning 'beautiful'.

Beau geste /bəu ʒest/

Pronunciation The first word rhymes with 'foe' and 'doe'. The 'g' in 'geste' is pronounced like the 's' in 'pleasure', 'leisure' and 'measure'. The 'este' that follows is like the 'est' in 'best', 'west' and 'nest'. The expression is pronounced 'bo **ZEST**'.

Meaning It literally means 'beautiful gesture'. The expression is mostly used to refer to a noble, but meaningless gesture; a generous gesture which doesn't really change the outcome of anything.

Examples *When they heard that I'd been dropped, the other team members said they would talk to the Manager. But their beau geste didn't really change anything.*

Giving the bankrupt farmer two more weeks to repay his loan is nothing more than a beau geste. Why don't you just write off the loan?

Etymology In French, 'beau' means 'beautiful' and 'geste' means 'action'.

Becomes you

Meaning To suit someone; usually used as a compliment.

Examples *The blue saree she is wearing becomes her.*

Don't try to be a stand-up comedian in class. It doesn't become you.

Behemoth /bɪ-hiː-mɔθ/

Pronunciation — The first 'e' is like the 'i' in 'sit' and 'pit' and the second like the 'ee' in 'cheese', 'bees' and 'fees'. The final syllable is pronounced like the word 'moth'. One way of pronouncing the word is 'bi-**HEE**-moth'.

Meaning — Anything that is big and powerful.

Examples — *The superstar drove his behemoth truck to the premiere.*

A corporate behemoth bought over Uday's small company.

Etymology — From the Hebrew 'b'hemah', meaning 'beast'. The word was originally used to refer to a giant animal.

Beleaguered /bɪ-liː-gəd/

Pronunciation — The first 'e' is like the 'i' in 'big', 'pig' and 'dig'. The following 'leaguer' is pronounced like the word 'league'. The 'r' is silent and the final 'e' is like the 'a' in 'china'. The word is pronounced 'bi-**LEE**-ged'.

Meaning — To be troubled or pestered by someone or something; to face many difficulties and have harsh comments directed at you.

Examples — *The Prime Minister spoke in defence of his beleaguered government.*

The beleaguered CEO has made up his mind to quit.

Etymology — It comes from the Dutch 'belegeren', meaning 'camp around'. In the past, one way of capturing an enemy fort was to surround it and wait till the occupants surrendered – very often because they would run out of food and water. When the word 'beleaguered' was borrowed into English in the 16th century, it originally meant 'surrounded by enemies'.

Belly-up

Meaning — Used in informal contexts to mean 'to fail or be defeated'. 'Belly' is another word for stomach.

Examples — *If the bank doesn't give Mayank a loan, his company will go belly-up.*

The former champion went belly-up in the first round.

Origin — When a fish dies, it usually floats belly up.

Besiege /bɪ-si:dʒ/

Pronunciation — The 'e' in the first syllable sounds like the 'i' in 'it', 'bit' and 'sit', and the following 'ie' sounds like the 'ee' in 'fees', 'bees' and 'cheese'. The final 'ge' is like the 'j' in 'jam', 'juice' and 'jump'. The word is pronounced 'bi-**SEEJ**'.

Meaning — The word has several meanings. When soldiers, for example, besiege a town, they surround it. They prevent people and supplies from entering or leaving the town. When a person is besieged, he is surrounded by other people. The word can also be used to mean 'to make many requests or complaints about something'.

Examples — *The moment Sachin walked out of the stadium, he was besieged by reporters.*

The radio station was besieged with telephone calls from angry women.

Etymology — 'Siege' comes from the Latin 'sedere', meaning 'to sit', and 'be' means 'on all sides'. When a fort was 'besieged', the invading soldiers used to sit around it – thus preventing those inside from escaping.

Bête noire /bet nwa:/

Pronunciation — The 'bête' is pronounced like the word 'bet', and the 'o' in 'noire' is like the 'w' in 'wet', 'was' and 'will'. The final 'ire' sounds like the 'a' in 'path', 'bath' and 'ask'. One way of pronouncing the word is 'bet **NWAA**'.

Meaning	When you say that something is your bête noire, you mean it is something that you avoid or detest. The object or person is a great source of annoyance.
Examples	*The new Vice Chancellor is the bête noire of all feminists on campus.* *Madhu's particular bête noire is a sink full of dirty dishes.*
Etymology	The word is of French origin, and it literally means 'black beast'.

Between jobs

Meaning	A polite way of saying that someone is unemployed. The individual is looking for a job.
Examples	*I understand that Divyashree is between jobs.* *If I am not careful, I may soon be between jobs.*

Big cheese

Meaning	Used in informal contexts to mean 'an important individual in a company or an organisation; someone who is highly influential'.
Examples	*Renu is a big cheese in the diamond industry.*

Do you think I'll be able to meet the big cheese?

Origin According to some scholars, the expression comes from the Hindi 'bada cheez' (big thing).

Billet-doux /bɪ-lei du:/

Pronunciation The 'bi' in 'billet' sounds like the 'bi' in 'bit' and 'bin', and the following 'llet' is pronounced like the word 'lay'. The 'doux' sounds like the word 'do'. This French expression is pronounced 'bi-lay **DO**'.

Meaning A love letter. The plural is 'billets-doux'.

Examples *When he was in college, Rahul wrote at least three billets-doux a week to his girlfriend.*

Dilip received an anonymous billet-doux.

Etymology In French, 'doux' means 'sweet' and 'billet' means a 'note' or 'document'. The expression literally means 'sweet note'.

Bite someone's head off

Meaning To react angrily to what someone has said or done; very often, the other person thinks there was no real need for such an outburst.

Examples — *My boss will bite my head off if I ask him for a raise.*

The last time I enquired about her children, Sumana bit my head off.

For a change, I walked out of Javed's office without having my head bitten off.

Blasé

/bla:-zei/ /bla:-zei/

Pronunciation — The 'a' is pronounced like the 'a' in 'flask' and 'blast', and the 's' that follows is like the 'z' in 'zip' and 'zoo'. The final 'e' is like the 'ay' in 'bay' and 'may'. Some people pronounce the word 'blaa-**ZAY'**, while others pronounce it **'BLAA**-zay'.

Meaning — To remain indifferent about something that others are very excited about. Of course, this impression that you create that you are bored and not excited, could be just an act!

Examples — *When Shyam's parents heard that he had won two million dollars, they were excited. But Shyam himself was very blasé about it.*

Unlike her father, Sushmita is very blasé about parties.

Bharath goes to America so often that he is blasé about it.

Etymology — From the French 'blaser', meaning 'to satiate'.

Blinkers

Meaning: The leather patches fixed next to the horse's eyes are called 'blinkers'. They compel the animal to look straight ahead; it cannot see what is to its right or left. When you say that an individual wears blinkers, it means he has a limited view of something. He does not have a complete understanding of the situation.

Examples: *Satish prefers not to know about his friend's drug problems. He wears blinkers when it comes to that.*

The company refuses to tell us what the problem is. We have a feeling of having blinkers put on us.

Mohan has blinkers on when it comes to politics.

Blithe /blaið/

Pronunciation: The 'i' is pronounced like the 'y' in 'my', 'by' and 'fly', and the following 'th' sounds like the 'th' in 'this', 'those' and 'there'. The final 'e' is silent. The word is pronounced **'BLYTH'**.

Meaning: A rather formal word, meaning 'happy and carefree'. It can also mean 'showing a lack of due concern' for someone or something.

Examples *Nataraj is one of those blithe spirits who cannot remain in one place for long.*

Most Indians show a blithe disregard for traffic rules.

Etymology From the Old English 'blipe', meaning 'joyous, cheerful'.

Blockbuster

Meaning This is a word usually associated with a highly successful movie or book.

Examples *Have you seen the latest blockbuster from Bollywood?*

They are predicting that Kundan's new book will be a blockbuster.

Origin The word was first used during the Second World War to refer to bombs. 'Blockbuster' was Air Force slang for a powerful bomb that was capable of destroying an entire city block.

Blonde moment

Meaning To behave like a typical blonde – to become scatterbrained and do something silly.

Examples *Keep an eye on Meera, will you? She has a blonde moment now and then.*

I don't know why I said what I did. I must have had a blonde moment.

Origin

For several decades now, 'blonde' has become synonymous with stupidity. Women with blonde hair are always seen as being beautiful, but without an iota of intelligence – the 'dumb blonde'.

Bludgeon /blʌdʒ-ən/

Pronunciation

The first syllable rhymes with the words 'judge', 'grudge' and 'budge', and the final 'eo' sounds like the 'a' in 'china'. The word is pronounced '**BLUJ**-en'.

Meaning

A club or a heavy stick that can be used as a weapon. When used as a verb, the word means 'to repeatedly hit someone with a heavy object'. It can also be used to mean 'to force someone into doing something'.

Examples

Several young men were seen walking around with bicycle chains and bludgeons.

The young girl was bludgeoned to death in broad daylight.

The students bludgeoned the teacher into putting off the test.

Blunted

Meaning — The word has several meanings, and one of them is 'to make less sharp or forceful'.

Examples — *The dead cockroaches floating in the vegetable soup blunted our appetite.*

The bad weather has blunted my enthusiasm for early morning walks.

There's so much cricket being played these days that it has blunted my enthusiasm for the game.

Bon voyage /bɔn vɔi-ja:ʒ/

Pronunciation — The 'o' in 'bon' is like the 'o' in 'hot' and 'got', while the 'o' in 'voyage' is like the 'oy' in 'boy' and 'toy'. The 'a' sounds like the 'ar' in 'dark' and 'park', and the final 'ge' is like the 's' in 'pleasure' and 'measure'. It is pronounced 'bon-voy-**AAJ**'.

Meaning — A French expression, meaning 'have a good journey'.

Examples — *He gave her a bouquet and wished her bon voyage.*

I hope you have a great time. Bon voyage.

Bona fide /bəu-nə <u>fai</u>-di/

Pronunciation — The 'o' is pronounced like the 'o' in 'so', 'no' and 'go', and the following 'a' is like the 'a' in 'china'. The 'i' in 'fide' sounds like the 'y' in 'my' and 'by', and the final 'e' is like the 'i' in 'sit', 'bit' and 'hit'. The word is pronounced 'bo-ne **FY**-di'.

Meaning — Real, genuine.

Examples — *They say your favourite star's latest movie is a bona fide hit.*

If you ask me, she's a bona fide expert.

Etymology — This Latin expression literally means 'in good faith'. The opposite is 'mala fide'.

Bonfire

Meaning — A fire lit to celebrate an occasion or to burn rubbish.

Examples — *The children sat around the bonfire and sang.*

In summer, we light a bonfire and burn all the leaves.

Etymology — The word 'bonfire' was originally 'bonefire'. During the Middle Ages, thousands of people would die of the plague. In order to prevent the disease from spreading, dead bodies were thrown into a big fire; such fires were referred to as 'bonefires'. So, to begin with, the word 'bonfire' was not associated with anything pleasant.

Bonhomie /bɔ-nə-mɪ/ /ba:-nə-mɪ:/

Pronunciation There are two ways of pronouncing the word. One way is to rhyme the first syllable with 'con' and 'don'. The second 'o' sounds like the 'a' in 'china', and the final 'ie' sounds like the 'i' in 'bit', 'kit' and 'sit'. The word, in this case, is pronounced **'BO**-ne-mi'. Some people pronounce the first 'o' like the 'a' in 'bath', 'path' and 'ask' and the final 'ie' like the 'ee' in 'feel', 'peel' and 'heel'. They pronounce the word 'baa-ne-**MEE**'. In either case, the 'h' remains silent.

Meaning The word is mostly used in formal contexts to mean 'happy, good-natured friendliness'.

Examples *The cheerful bonhomie displayed by the rival candidates surprised everyone.*

Jai's bonhomie won the hearts of all those who came in contact with him.

Etymology The word comes from the French 'bon', meaning 'good', and 'homme', meaning 'man'.

Bonkers /bɔŋ-kəz/

Pronunciation: The first syllable rhymes with 'song' and 'long' and the 'er' is like the 'a' in 'china'. The final 's' sounds like the 'z' in 'zoo' and 'zip'. The word is pronounced '**BONK**-erz'.

Meaning: Informal word, meaning 'silly, stupid, crazy'.

Examples: *She must be bonkers to marry a guy like Aravind.*

The kids are driving everyone at home bonkers.

You're bonkers to ask for such a big raise.

Etymology: It comes from 'bonk', meaning 'to hit someone on the head'.

Boomerang (v) /buː-mə-ræŋg/

Pronunciation: The first syllable is pronounced like the word 'boo' and the third like the word 'rang'. The 'e' sounds like the 'a' in 'china'. The word is pronounced '**BOO**-me-rang'.

Meaning: When something boomerangs, the result is the exact opposite of what you wanted it to be.

Examples: *The media's attempt to discredit the Minister boomeranged. Now, people are more suspicious of the media than of the Minister.*

	Whenever I try to play a practical joke on someone, it always boomerangs.
Etymology	From an Aboriginal language in Australia.

Boondoggle /bu:n-dɔgl/

Pronunciation	The first syllable rhymes with 'moon', 'soon' and 'noon'; the second sounds like the word 'dog'. The final 'e' is silent. It is pronounced '**BOON**-dogl'.
Meaning	A white elephant; something that wastes a lot of public money and does not achieve anything significant. The word can also be used to refer to complicated official activities that are a waste of time.
Examples	*Many of our development programmes turn out to be million-dollar boondoggles.* *The newspaper has brought to light another one of those Government boondoggles.*

Bootlegger

Meaning	Someone who brews and sells illicit liquor. Nowadays, it is used to refer to someone who makes copies of CDs, DVDs and software and sells them illegally.

Examples — *Prakash was caught bootlegging Windows 2000 CDs.*

Amrit bought a bootleg CD of last night's concert.

My friend Ramesh bootlegs DVDs in Chor Bazaar.

Origin — Bootleggers brewed whiskey on the outskirts of towns and cities. As it was illegal to sell whiskey in the open market, the dealers had to find ingenious ways of bringing the bottles into towns and cities. A method they employed was to hide the bottles inside the tall boots they wore. Since they hid the bottles in their boots, they began to be called 'bootleggers'!

Boulevard /bʊ-lə-vaːd/

Pronunciation — The 'boul' is pronounced like the word 'bull' and the following 'e' is like the 'a' in 'china'. The final syllable rhymes with 'yard' and 'card'. The word is pronounced '**BULL**-e-vaad'.

Meaning — A street or a road lined with trees on both sides. In the US, any broad road.

Example — *My wife and I enjoy walking along the boulevard.*

Etymology — It comes from the Dutch 'bolwerc', meaning 'bulwark', a wall that is built for protection.

Bouquet /bu:kei/

Pronunciation: The 'ou' is like the 'oo' in 'cool', 'pool' and 'fool', and the following 'quet' sounds like the name 'Kay'. The word is pronounced 'boo-**KAY**'.

Meaning: An attractive arrangement of flowers.

Examples: *The students presented her with a bouquet.* *Bouquets have become really expensive.*

Etymology: It comes from the French 'bouquet', meaning 'little wood'.

Bourgeois /buəʒ-wa:/

Pronunciation: The 'bour' rhymes with 'pure', 'sure' and 'cure'; the 'g' sounds like the 's' in 'pleasure', 'measure' and 'leisure'. The sound that follows is like the 'w' in 'what', 'why' and 'wait'. The final vowels sound like the 'ar' in 'bar', 'par' and 'car'. The word is pronounced '**BUEZ**-waa'.

Meaning: Often used disapprovingly to refer to the middle class – people who are only interested in material possessions.

Examples: *Karthik has become rather bourgeois since he returned from the States.*

If you ask me, there are several advantages in marrying a bourgeois like Dilip.

Etymology — Derived from the Old French 'bourjois', meaning 'town dweller'.

Bowl /bəul/

Pronunciation — The word rhymes with 'soul', 'pole' and 'goal'. The word 'bowl' that we use in cricket and the dish from which we drink soup are both pronounced the same way.

Etymology — From the Old English 'bolla', meaning 'cup' or 'pot'.

Braggadocio /bræ-gə-dəu-ʃɪ-əu/

Pronunciation — The first syllable is pronounced like the word 'brag'; the 'a' in the second is like the 'a' in 'china'. The 'o' in the third and final syllables sounds like the 'o' in 'no', 'so' and 'go'. The 'ci' is like the 'shi' in 'ship' and 'shin'. The word is pronounced 'brag-e-**DOE**-shi-o'.

Meaning — Someone who brags about himself a lot; a vain individual who talks about his achievements in a rather proud manner. Most of the time, it is only empty boasting. A literary word, mostly used in formal contexts.

Examples *Tarun came across as a braggadocio who deliberately tried to make others uncomfortable.*

According to reporters, the Chairman's braggadocio at the meeting was a sign of weakness, not strength.

Etymology The word comes from the name of a boastful character (Braggadocchio) in Edmund Spenser's poem, *Faerie Queene*.

Break the bank

Meaning To spend a lot of money on something; to exhaust one's savings or resources.

Examples *It'll hardly break the bank if you buy her a dozen roses.*

My uncle is planning to send his son to study in the US. He says it'll break the bank to do it.

I don't like to spend money. But I guess an occasional movie and dinner won't break the bank.

Origin The 'bank' in this expression refers to a child's piggy bank.

Breakfast /brek-fəst/

Pronunciation The first syllable rhymes with 'neck, 'peck' and 'deck'. The 'a' in the second syllable 'fast' is like the 'a' in 'china'. The word is pronounced '**BREK**-fest'.

Example *Chinthan didn't have breakfast this morning.*

Etymology It is derived from 'break' and 'fast'.

Bric-a-brac /brɪk-ə-bræk/

Pronunciation The first syllable sounds like the word 'brick' and the third rhymes with 'sack' and 'back'. The 'a' is like the 'a' in 'china'. The word is pronounced '**BRICK**-e-brack'.

Meaning Small ornamental objects that people collect, and which are of little value.

Examples *Bala clutters his office table with a lot of bric-a-brac.*

My cousin Ananya's house is filled with bric-a-brac.

Etymology It comes from the French 'à bric et à brac', meaning 'at random, any old way'.

Bromance /brəu-mæns/

Pronunciation The first syllable rhymes with 'pro' and 'grow', and the 'a' in the second is like the 'a' in 'man', 'van' and 'can'. One way of pronouncing the word is '**BRO**-mans'.

Meaning — A close but asexual relationship between two men.

Examples — *Ram and Keshav – the office bromance everyone is talking about.*

People are unable to understand the bromance between Bala and Prahlad. They have nothing in common.

Etymology — It is a combination of 'brother' and 'romance'.

Brontophobia /brɔn-tə-fəu-biə/

Pronunciation — The first 'o' sounds like the 'o' in 'song' and 'wrong', while the second is like the 'a' in 'china'. The word is pronounced 'bron-te-**FOE**-bia'.

Meaning — Fear of thunder and thunderstorms. A person who suffers from this phobia is a 'brontophobe'.

Examples — *Sachin had to share a room with a brontophobe during a thunderstorm.*

I am told that Prakasham suffers from brontophobia.

I wouldn't take Meera out on a night like this. She is brontophobic.

Etymology — The Greek word for thunder is 'bronto'.

Brouhaha

/bru:-ha:-ha:/ /bru:-ha:-ha:/

Pronunciation The 'brou' is pronounced like the word 'brew'; the 'a' in the following two syllables sounds like the 'a' in 'art', 'part' and 'cart'. The British put the stress on the first syllable, while the Americans place it on the second.

Meaning Normally used in informal contexts to mean 'a commotion or an angry complaint about something'.

Examples *The brouhaha over the new version of the song is getting interesting.*

There is a report on the recent brouhaha over the non-payment of the bonus.

Etymology This word, which became popular after the Second World War, comes from the French 'brouhaha', meaning 'noisy chattering'.

Brown-noser

Meaning A flatterer/sycophant who does everything possible to keep those in power happy.

Examples *I understand my neighbour excels in the art of brown-nosing.*

My boss keeps brown-nosers at a distance.

Brownie points

Meaning: To do something because you think people will praise you for it. Doing something to please someone influential.

Examples: *Some students want to score brownie points by doing odd jobs for their teachers.*

Sachin tries to earn brownie points by giving his boss' wife roses on her birthday.

Mala tried to earn brownie points with her brother-in-law by offering to proof-read his two-hundred-page manuscript.

Origin: In the United States, Girl Scouts/Guides in the age group of seven to ten are called Brownies. The points that a girl earns for doing a good deed are called 'Brownie points'. This is one theory behind the origin of the expression.

Brusque /bru:sk/ /brʌsk/

Pronunciation: The British tend to pronounce the 'u' like the 'oo' in 'cool' and 'pool'; the Americans rhyme the word with 'tusk' and 'musk'. The word can be pronounced **'BROOSK'** or **'BRUSK'**.

Meaning: To speak harshly; to behave rudely.

Examples: *Officials in most Government offices tend to be brusque.*

I'm not going to be put off by your brusque replies.

Etymology The word comes from the Italian 'brusco', meaning 'sour' or 'sharp'. The word was also used to refer to a prickly plant.

Bucket list

Meaning A wish list; a list of things a person wishes to do before he dies, i.e., before he actually 'kicks the bucket'.

Examples *I have one more thing to add to my bucket list.*

"Don't worry, Dad! Finding a job is definitely on my bucket list."

	I took my mother to see the Taj last weekend. That's one more thing she can strike off her bucket list.
Origin	The expression comes from the title of a Hollywood film starring Jack Nicholson and Morgan Freeman.

Budget

Meaning	A detailed plan that informs someone how much an organisation or a person will earn and how much it/he will spend in the given time. The word can be used as a noun and a verb.
Examples	*Reema has been asked to draw up a budget for her department.* *We have budgeted 25 lakhs for computers this year.*
Etymology	From the Latin 'bulga', meaning 'leather bag'. Originally, the word referred to anything that was made of leather: wallets, knapsacks, bags, etc. With the passage of time, 'budget' began to be used to refer to the contents of a bag, rather than the bag itself.

Buffet

/bu-fei/ /bə-fei/

Pronunciation: The British prefer to pronounce the 'u' like the 'u' in 'put' and 'push' and the 'et' like the 'ay' in 'bay' and 'day'. They pronounce the word '**BU**-fay'. The Americans pronounce the 'u' like the 'a' in 'china'. They pronounce the word 'be-**FAY**'.

Meaning: A buffet is a meal where you serve yourself.

Example: *We should go to the new restaurant and have their buffet lunch.*

Etymology: It comes from the French 'bufet', meaning 'bench' or 'stool'.

Bullish

Meaning: Being very confident about something; sometimes, even aggressively so.

Examples: *Ravi Shastri was bullish about India's chances of defeating Australia in the World Cup.*

The whole country was in a bullish mood after we had won six games in a row.

Our CEO is very bullish about the success of the new product.

Origin — A term used in the stock market. A 'bullish' market is one where the market is doing well – the prices of shares are rising.

Bumf /bʌmf/

Pronunciation — The 'bum' is pronounced like the word 'bum' and the following 'f' sounds like the 'f' in 'fish' and 'fill'.

Meaning — It is used in informal contexts to refer to any printed material – flyers, promotional materials from companies, manuals, official documents, etc. – that is unwanted or uninteresting to read.

Examples — *Padmaja went to the industrial exhibition and came home with a lot of bumf.*

The Government is calling it a study, but if you ask me, it is nothing more than publicity bumf.

Etymology — 'Bumf', also spelt 'bumph', is the combination of two words, 'bum' and 'fodder'. It was originally the slang term for toilet paper.

Burgeon /bɜ:-dʒən/

Pronunciation — The first syllable rhymes with 'fur' and 'purr', and the following 'g' sounds like the 'j' in 'jam', 'juice' and 'jump'. The final 'eo' is like the 'a' in 'china'. The word is pronounced '**BER-**jen'.

Meaning — When 'burgeon' is used in relation to plants, it means 'to put out leaves; sprout'. In everyday context, the word can be used to mean 'to grow or flourish'.

Examples — *After winning the first set, the champion's confidence began to burgeon.*

There is a burgeoning demand for bicycles.

Etymology — It comes from the Old French 'bourgeonner', meaning 'to put out buds'.

Burlesque /bɜ:-lesk/

Pronunciation — The 'ur' sounds like the 'ur' in 'fur' and 'purr', and the 'lesque' rhymes with 'desk'. The word is pronounced 'bur-**LESK**'.

Meaning — A burlesque is a parody; it is something written or enacted, and its aim is to make people laugh, usually by reducing something serious to a farce. When used as a verb, it means 'to make ridiculous'.

Example — *Prodipta is the lead actor in a musical burlesque written by her husband.*

Etymology — The word comes from the Italian 'burla', meaning 'joke, fun, mockery'.

Buy(ing) a lemon

Meaning: In American English, it means 'being tricked into buying something worthless or something that fails to work properly'. In British English, lemon means 'a silly person'.

Examples: *Rajeev bought a second-hand car last month. It's turned out to be a real lemon.*

I felt such a lemon when I tripped over the carpet.

Many of the students think that the Dean is a bit of a lemon.

Buzz-kill

Meaning: Used in informal contexts to refer to a wet blanket; someone who prevents others from enjoying themselves. Can be used with things as well.

Examples: *Please don't invite our boss to the party. He is a definite buzz-kill.*

Running a marathon in this weather? Sounds like a definite buzz-kill.

Origin: One of the meanings of 'buzz' is excitement. A 'buzz-kill' is someone who kills the excitement.

Cabal /kə-bæl/ /kə-ba:l/

Pronunciation: The first vowel is pronounced like the 'a' in 'china', while the second is pronounced like the 'a' in 'cat' and 'bat' or like the 'ar' in 'bar' and 'far'. In both cases, the stress is on the second syllable.

Meaning: The word is mostly used in the context of politics to refer to a small group of people who work secretly to usurp power – either by overthrowing the existing government or by installing a puppet regime.

Examples: *The cabal of dissidents within our party ensured we lost the election.*

The cabal has been plotting to have the CM assassinated.

Origin: From the Hebrew 'cabalah', referring to the mystical interpretation of the Hebrew scripture. It is also seen as an acronym for the five people who plotted against Charles II of England. Their names were Clifford, Arlington, Buckingham, Ashley and Lauderdale.

Cachet /kæ-ʃei/ /kæ-ʃei/

Pronunciation: The 'a' is like the 'a' in 'cat', 'bat' and 'sat', and the final 'et' is like the 'ay' in 'say', 'bay'

	and 'may'. The 'ch' is like the 'sh' in 'should', 'sheep' and 'ship'. The British put the stress on the first syllable, while the Americans tend to stress the second.
Meaning	A special mark put on articles of very high value. When used with a person, it refers to the special quality that an individual has which wins him the respect and admiration of others.
Examples	*Balu's success as a movie producer has won him a certain cachet in the industry.* *Driving a BMW or a Benz has a certain cachet.*
Etymology	From the French 'cacher', meaning 'to press'.

Cacophony /kə-kɒ-fə-nɪ/

Pronunciation	The 'a' and the second 'o' sound like the 'a' in 'china'. The second syllable is pronounced like the word 'cough'. The word is pronounced 'ke-**KOF**-e-ni'.
Meaning	Harsh sounding; a mixture of loud, unpleasant sounds.
Examples	*I couldn't sleep because of the cacophony of noises from the street.* *The teacher was greeted with a cacophony of screams.*

The cacophony of car horns could be heard a kilometre away.

Etymology — From the Greek 'kakos', meaning 'bad', and 'phone', meaning 'sound'. The opposite is 'euphony'.

Cajole /kə-dʒəul/

Pronunciation — The first vowel is like the 'a' in 'china', and the syllable that follows rhymes with 'pole', 'hole' and 'mole'. The word is pronounced 'ke-**JOLE**'.

Meaning — To flatter or make false promises to get someone to do/give you what you want. The word, at times, has a negative connotation.

Examples — *Vimal cajoled Jayanthi into investing in his company.*

The young couple cajoled Dharmender into selling his vintage car.

Etymology — From the French 'cajoler', meaning 'to coax'.

Canard /kə-na:d/ /kæ-na:d/

Pronunciation — The 'a' in the first syllable of this rather formal word can be pronounced like the 'a' in 'china' or like the 'a' in 'cat' and 'bat'. The 'ar' in the second syllable sounds like the 'ar'

	in 'park', 'dark' and 'mark'. The word can be pronounced 'ke-**NAAD**' or 'ka-**NAAD**'.
Meaning	A false piece of information deliberately spread by someone in order to confuse or deceive others.
Examples	*In India, there is a widespread canard that all politicians are corrupt.* *The Prime Minister has accused the media of spreading canards.*
Etymology	It comes from the French 'canard', meaning 'duck'.

Capish /kə-pi:ʃ/

Pronunciation	The 'a' is like the 'a' in 'china' and the 'i' sounds like the 'ee' in 'feel', 'peel' and 'kneel'. The word is pronounced 'ke-**PEESH**'.
Meaning	Mostly used in informal contexts to mean 'do you understand?'.
Examples	*I am not going to help Jai. You capish?* *You need to be a lot more careful. Capish?*
Etymology	From the Italian 'capisce', meaning 'understand'.

Caption /kæp-ʃən/

Pronunciation The first syllable is pronounced like the word 'cap'. The 'tion' sounds like the 'tion' in words like 'solution', 'position' and 'exhibition'. The word is pronounced **'KAP**-shen'.

Meaning The text under a picture in newspapers, magazines, etc.

Examples *We want you to write captions for these beautiful pictures.*

I wanted you to come up with funny captions.

Etymology It comes from the Latin 'capere', meaning 'take' or 'seize'. The heading of a legal document is also referred to as 'caption'.

Captious /kæp-ʃəs/

Pronunciation The first syllable is pronounced like the word 'cap', and the 't' that follows sounds like the 'sh' in 'ship', 'sheet' and 'shoe'. The final 'iou' sounds like the 'a' in 'china'. The word is pronounced '**CAP**-shes'.

Meaning To raise objections about trivial matters. A captious critic is someone who takes pleasure in criticising people or things no matter how trivial the fault may be.

Examples *The captious critic wasted our time objecting to the font size and colour.*

Mohan, a captious teacher, wasn't popular among the students.

Etymology 'Caption' and 'captious' are related.

Carte blanche /ka:t bla:nʃ/

Pronunciation The first word is pronounced like the word 'cart'. The 'a' in 'blanche' is like the 'ar' in 'dark' and 'park', and the 'che' sounds like the 'sh' in 'ship' and 'sheep'. One way of pronouncing the word is 'cart **BLAANSH**'.

Meaning When you give someone 'cart blanche', you give them total freedom to do whatever they want; you are giving them a blank cheque.

Examples *The children were given carte blanche to buy whatever they wanted with their money.*

The captain was not given carte blanche to choose the players he wanted.

It's not a wise idea to give carte blanche to someone who has so little experience.

Etymology A French expression, meaning 'white card'. The term was first used in the military. In a war, the commander of the losing army was made to put his signature on a blank sheet of paper. By doing this, he was allowing the victorious army the freedom to dictate the terms of surrender.

Cast-iron stomach

Meaning — The ability to eat or drink anything – good or bad – and digest it.

Examples — *When I went to Vietnam, my host asked me if I would like to try snake soup. Since I don't have a cast-iron stomach, I said no.*

My cousin Karthik has a cast-iron stomach.

Origin — Anything made of cast iron was considered extremely strong.

Cataclysm /kæ-tə-kli-zəm/

Pronunciation — The first syllable is pronounced like the word 'cat', and the 'a' and the 'y' that follow are like the 'a' in 'china'. The 's' sounds like the 'z' in 'zoo', 'zip' and 'zebra'. This rather literary word is pronounced '**CAT**-e-kliz-em'.

Meaning — Large-scale destruction brought about by natural causes – earthquakes, floods, etc. A social movement which brings about sweeping changes can also be called 'cataclysm'.

Examples — *Ravi's new book deals with some of the cataclysmic events of the 18th century.*

According to scientists, the virus could result in worldwide cataclysm.

Etymology — It comes from the Greek 'kataklysmos', meaning 'flood'.

Categorical inaccuracy

Meaning — Politically correct term for lying – especially by those who are in power.

Examples — *Some people believe that there were several categorical inaccuracies in President Bush's speech.*

The Prime Minister's statement was a categorical inaccuracy.

Catnap

Meaning — To sleep or doze for a very short period of time during the day; usually not more than fifteen minutes.

Examples — *After reading the paper, my father catnaps for ten minutes.*

I read somewhere that taking a catnap in the afternoon is good for health.

Several people in my office have a catnap during their lunch break.

Origin — From the belief that cats take short naps during the day – this, however, is not always true.

Cavalcade /kæ-vəl-keid/

Pronunciation — The 'a' in the first syllable sounds like the 'a' in 'cat', 'bat' and 'rat', while the 'a' that follows is like the 'a' in 'china'. The final syllable rhymes with 'made', 'fade' and 'paid'. The word is pronounced '**KA**-vel-kade'.

Meaning — A procession of people on horses, in cars, carriages, etc.

Examples — *While I was waiting at the bus stop, I saw a cavalcade of limousines zoom past.*

The parade included a cavalcade of army men on motorcycles.

The Prime Minister's cavalcade was caught in the traffic jam.

Etymology — Both 'cavalcade' and 'cavalry' come from the Latin 'caballus', meaning 'horse'.

Caveat /kæ-vɪ-æt/ /kei-vɪ-æt/

Pronunciation — The 'a' in the first and third syllables is pronounced like the 'a' in 'hat', 'bat' and 'cat'. The 'e' sounds like the 'i' in 'it', 'kit' and 'bit'. The word is pronounced '**KA**-vi-at'. Some people pronounce the 'a' in the first syllable like the 'ay' in 'say', 'day' and 'may'. They pronounce the word '**KAY**-vi-at'.

Meaning — Used in formal contexts to mean 'warning' or 'caution'; a proviso.

Examples — *She agreed to the divorce with one caveat – that he would never see the children again.*

I think we can go ahead with the plan, but with certain caveats.

Etymology — The word comes from the Latin 'cavere', meaning 'let him beware'. The expression 'caveat emptor' means 'buyers beware'. In other words, it is the buyer's responsibility to ensure that the product is in good condition.

C'est la vie /sei-la:-<u>vi:</u>/

Pronunciation — There are different ways of pronouncing this French expression. One way is to pronounce the 'c'est' like the word 'say'. The 'a' in 'la' is like the 'a' in 'bath', 'path' and 'pass', while the 'ie' in 'vie' sounds like the 'ee' in 'bees', 'fees' and 'geese'. The expression is pronounced 'say la **VEE**'.

Meaning — It means 'such is life' or 'that's life'. It is mostly used to downplay your sense of disappointment.

Examples — *I can't go to the exhibition with you tomorrow because my mother-in-law is arriving in the morning. C'est la vie.*

It was a good match. Our team lost in the tiebreaker. C'est la vie.

Etymology — A French expression, meaning 'that's life'.

Chagrin /ʃæ-grɪn/

Pronunciation — The 'ch' is like the 'sh' in 'ship' and 'sheet', and the vowel that follows is like the 'a' in 'cat', 'sat' and 'mat'. The second syllable sounds like the word 'grin'. The word is pronounced '**SHA**-grin'.

Meaning — Feeling of embarrassment or annoyance.

Examples — *Much to Saurav's chagrin, he was out for a duck.*

Mohan appeared chagrined when his boss informed him that he hadn't been promoted.

Etymology — From the French 'chagrin', meaning 'anxiety, melancholy'.

Chaperone /ʃæ-pə-rəun/

Pronunciation — The 'ch' is like the 'sh' in 'ship' and 'sheep', and the 'a' that follows sounds like the 'a' in 'fat', 'mat' and 'cat'. The 'e' is pronounced like the 'a' in 'china', and the final 'rone' rhymes with 'bone', 'cone' and 'phone'. The word is pronounced '**SHA**-pe-rone'.

Meaning — Someone who accompanies a young person to a social event to ensure that he/she doesn't get into trouble.

Examples — *Whenever my neighbour's kids go to a party, they always ask Sujatha to be their chaperone.*

Vinita's father was willing to chaperone the kids to the zoo.

Etymology — From the French 'chaperon', meaning 'protector'. In the old days, a chaperone was usually an elderly woman who escorted a young, unmarried woman to a social event.

Chary /tʃɜə-rɪ/ /tʃe-rɪ/

Pronunciation — The British and the Americans pronounce the word in very different ways. The former pronounce the 'char' like the word 'chair' and the following 'y' like the 'i' in 'sit' and 'bit'. The Americans pronounce it like the word 'cherry'. No matter how you pronounce 'chary', the stress is on the first syllable.

Meaning — Mostly used in formal contexts to mean 'cautious' or 'wary'; unwilling to take action because one is afraid of the consequences. The word is usually followed by 'about' or 'of'.

Examples *Like most men, Rakesh was chary of expressing his true feelings.*

Ananya is chary about asking people for help.

Etymology From the Old English 'cearig', meaning 'sorrowful' or 'anxious'.

Cheerless

Meaning Gloomy and depressing; the opposite of cheerful.

Examples *It was a damp and cheerless morning.*

Arun lives in a bare, cheerless apartment.

Chef d'oeuvre /ʃei-dʒ:vrə/

Pronunciation The 'ch' is like the 'sh' in 'sheep' and 'ship', and the 'e' that follows sounds like the 'ay' in 'bay' and 'way'. The 'f' is silent, and the 'oeu' is like the 'ir' in 'bird' and 'birth'. The final 'e' sounds like the 'a' in 'china'. The word is pronounced 'shay **DE**-vre'.

Meaning An artist's or a writer's crowning glory, his masterpiece.

Examples *The critics may not agree, but I think Venkat's first novel was his chef d'oeuvre.*

This painting is her chef d'oeuvre.

Etymology — This word of French origin literally means 'chief work'.

Chequebook diplomacy

Meaning — Any foreign policy in which a country dangles money, in the form of economic aid and investment, to win diplomatic favour. Another expression that has more or less the same meaning is 'dollar diplomacy'.

Examples — *China denies using chequebook diplomacy in Africa.*

The Americans are using chequebook diplomacy to use our neighbour's airfields.

Origin — The expression was coined in 1990 during the First Gulf War, when Saddam Hussein invaded Kuwait. Instead of sending troops, Germany and Japan gave a lot of money towards the war effort against Saddam.

Cherry pick

Meaning — To look at various items on display and select the best or the most valuable among them.

Examples — *A brilliant student like Anil can cherry-pick the university he wants to go to.*

	Either you buy everything or nothing at all. You'll not be allowed to do any cherry picking.
Etymology	People who are hired to pluck cherries from trees are told to pick only those that are ripe; the unripe ones are not to be touched.

Chew someone out

Meaning	To scold someone; mostly limited to informal contexts.
Examples	*Usha chewed me out for forgetting her birthday.* *When the students walked in late, Lina gave them a good chewing-out.*

(He's) Chicken

Meaning	Often used with people in informal contexts to mean someone who is not brave; a coward or a scared individual.
Examples	*My boss was too much of a chicken to fight with the Chairman.* *When I was young, I was too chicken to climb trees.* *When Gopal refused to pet the monkey, I knew he was chicken.*

Chill out

Meaning: To relax; to be calm and not get upset about things. It is also possible to say 'chill'.

Examples: *Most people like to chill (out) during weekends.*

The argument was turning nasty. So I told the guys to chill (out).

Sheba took the week off to chill (out).

Chimera

/kai-miə-rə/

Pronunciation: The 'ch' is like the 'k' in 'king', 'key' and 'kiss', and the following 'i' is like the 'y' in 'by' and 'my'. The 'e' is like the 'ea' in 'fear', 'dear' and 'ear'; the final 'a' is like the 'a' in 'china'. One way of pronouncing the word is 'ky-**MIE**-re'.

Meaning: A formal word used to refer to a crazy or a wild idea; something that is extremely unlikely to come true.

Examples: *The idea that cricket is a gentleman's game is just a chimera.*

Expecting honesty from our politicians continues to be as much a chimera as ever.

Etymology: The original 'chimera' was a fire-breathing monster with a lion's head, a goat's body and a dragon's tail.

Chock-a-block /tʃɒk ə blɒk/

Pronunciation The 'o' in the two words sounds like the 'o' in 'sock', 'knock' and 'lock'. The 'a' is like the 'a' in 'china'. The British put the main stress on 'block'.

Meaning The expression is mainly used in informal contexts to mean 'completely full; tightly packed'. It is usually followed by 'with'.

Examples *The cupboard was chock-a-block with hundred-rupee notes.*

I wouldn't go there now. The place will be chock-a-block with tourists.

On Friday evening, Ashok's house was chock-a-block with guests.

Etymology An expression used by sailors. When two pulley blocks were so close together (chock) that they could not move, they were said to be 'chock-a-block'.

Chutzpah /huts-pə/

Pronunciation The 'ch' is like the 'h' in 'hat', 'had' and 'hiss', and the following 'utz' rhymes with the 'uts' in 'puts'. The final 'ah' sounds like the 'a' in 'china'. The word is pronounced '**HUTS**-pc'. Sometimes, the word is spelt 'hutzpah'.

Meaning	To be extremely confident, sometimes even arrogantly so. An individual who is not afraid to speak his mind – at times embarrassing all those around him.
Examples	*Uma had the chutzpah to tell her boss to stop interfering in her work.* *Such was his chutzpah that he asked his new boss if he could take her daughter to a movie.*
Etymology	It comes from the Yiddish 'khutspe', meaning 'impudent' (not showing respect to others). In English, the word is always used to show approval.

Ciao /tʃau/

Pronunciation	The 'c' is pronounced like the 'ch' in 'church' and 'chips', and the following 'iao' rhymes with the 'ow' in 'how', 'cow' and 'now'.
Meaning	Greeting, meaning 'hello/goodbye'.
Examples	*I'm getting late. I'll call you later. Ciao.* *I've got to get going. Ciao.*
Etymology	From the Italian greeting 'ciao', meaning 'hello/goodbye'.

Cinephile /sɪ-nɪ-fail/

Pronunciation — 'Cine' rhymes with 'mini' and 'Binny', and the third syllable sounds like the word 'file'. The word is pronounced '**SIN**-i-file'.

Meaning — Someone who loves or is a great fan of the cinema.

Examples — *Satish is an avid cinephile.*

Bhavani claims to be a cinephile, but she hasn't really seen too many movies.

All the local cinephiles meet at the Club on Friday nights.

Circa /sɜː-kə/

Pronunciation — The first syllable is pronounced like the word 'sir'. The second 'c' sounds like the 'k' in 'kiss', 'kill' and 'kid', while the 'a' is like the 'a' in 'china'. The word is pronounced '**SIR**-ke'.

Meaning — Used in formal contexts with dates to mean 'approximately'.

Examples — *The play was written circa 1350.*

A few scholars claim he was born circa 300 BC.

Etymology — It comes from the Latin 'circa', meaning 'around, about the time of'.

Cleptopenia /klep-ta:-pɪ-nɪ-je/

Pronunciation The first syllable rhymes with 'step' and 'pep' and the second sounds like 'tar'. The 'pen' is pronounced like the word 'pin'. One way of pronouncing the word is 'klep-**TAA**-pi-nie'.

Meaning Stealing pens unconsciously.

Example *Hide your pens. Uday has cleptopenia.*

Owner: "You are the right person for the job. Is there anything I need to know before I hire you?"

Young girl: "Yes, sir! I've been diagnosed with cleptopenia."

Etymology From the Greek 'kleptein', meaning 'steal', and the Latin 'penna', meaning 'feather'. In the past, feathers were used as writing instruments.

Clerk /kla:k/ /klɜ:k/

Pronunciation There are two ways of pronouncing the word. The British make the word rhyme with 'park', 'dark' and 'shark', while the Americans make it rhyme with 'work', 'shirk' and 'lurk'.

Meaning Someone employed in an office to look after routine administrative duties.

Examples *Rahul is a clerk in some government office.*

For a change, the clerk was quite friendly.

Etymology The word comes from the Latin 'clericus', meaning 'priest'; in the past, a 'clerk' belonged to the 'cleric'. Kings and nobles frequently hired this person as their scribe and accountant. With the passage of time, 'clerk' began to be used to refer to anyone – not necessarily a priest – who could read and write and maintain accounts.

Clock-watcher

Meaning Someone who keeps looking at the clock instead of doing his work.

Examples *Most people in my Dad's office are clock-watchers.*

Niraj becomes a clock-watcher during the Physics class.

There is no place for clock-watchers on my team.

Clotheshorse

Meaning Someone who is obsessed with clothes; willing to spend lots of money on them.

Examples *Unlike my friend Gayathri, I'm not a clotheshorse.*

Amarnath is likely to become a bit of a clotheshorse, like his father.

Etymology This word originally referred to a wooden rack used for hanging wet clothes.

Clutch player

Meaning People who perform exceedingly well in tense and critical situations – when the game is on the line. The opposite is 'choker'.

Examples *Laxman and Dravid were good players to have in the clutch.*

The captain, as expected, turned to his clutch bowler.

Etymology	The player clutches or takes complete control of the game. The expression was first used in baseball.

Coffee-table book

Meaning	Normally hardbound, relatively large in size, and containing many illustrations/photographs. It is rather expensive and designed to be pleasing to the eye.
Example	*The coffee-table book I'd wanted to buy was expensive.*
Etymology	These books are usually left on coffee tables.

Cognoscente /kɔg-nə-ʃen-tɪ/

Pronunciation	The first syllable rhymes with 'fog' and 'dog', while the second 'o' sounds like the 'a' in 'china'. The 'sc' is pronounced like the 'sh' in 'sheep' and 'ship'. The syllable itself rhymes with 'bent' and 'sent', and the final 'e' sounds like the 'i' in 'bit' and 'hit'. One way of pronouncing the word is 'cog-ne-**SHEN**-ti'.
Meaning	A connoisseur; a formal word used to refer to someone who is well informed about the fine arts or about a particular field. The singular form is spelt 'cognoscenti'.

Examples *Prahlad, the music cognoscenti, explained the subtler points of the raga.*

The cognoscenti in the commentary box hailed Sharma's bowling performance.

Etymology From the Italian 'cognoscente', meaning 'knowing man'.

Collage /kɔ-la:ʒ/ /kə-la:ʒ/

Pronunciation The 'o' is like the 'o' in 'hot', 'pot' and 'cot', and the following 'a' is like the 'a' in 'bath', 'path' and 'cart'. The final 'ge' sounds like the 's' in 'measure', 'treasure' and 'pleasure'. Some people pronounce the 'o' in the first syllable like the 'a' in 'china'. The word can be pronounced 'ko-**LAAJ**' or 'ke-**LAAJ**'.

Meaning A picture created by sticking various types of materials – paper, cloth, metal, wood – onto a hard surface. A collection of different things can also be called a collage.

Examples *Vinita spent the afternoon making a collage.*

The group played an interesting collage of old Tamil songs.

Etymology It comes from the Old French 'coller', meaning 'to glue'.

Collateral damage

Meaning — Civilians killed or injured during a military operation; people killed/injured other than the intended target.

Examples — *The General maintained that there was no collateral damage.*

The children who were caught in the crossfire were collateral damage.

Origin — Military jargon used since the 1960s.

Colleague /kɔ-li:g/

Pronunciation — The 'o' sounds like the 'o' in 'hot' and 'cot', and the second syllable is pronounced like the word 'league'. The word is pronounced '**CO**-league'.

Meaning — A person you work with in an office/organisation.

Examples — *Your new colleague, John, was a classmate of mine in college.*

Bhindra is really looked up to by all his colleagues.

My colleagues made sure that the project was completed on time.

Etymology From the Latin 'collega', meaning 'partner in office'.

Comb for

Meaning To desperately search for someone or something, hoping to find it.

Examples *I combed the office for the document all morning. Unfortunately, I couldn't find it.*

The film star combed the entire house for the missing diamond necklace that her husband had given her.

The police combed the neighbourhood for the escaped convicts.

Comb-over

Meaning Growing one's hair long in order to hide one's bald spots.

Examples *Hemant has a comb-over. Why doesn't he buy himself a wig?*

That's the ugliest comb-over I've seen in my life.

Origin It's called a comb-over because what these men usually do is to allow the hair on one side of the head to grow long. They then proceed to comb it over the top of their head to hide their baldness.

Come clean

Meaning Unburden oneself; to be completely honest. To tell someone everything about the wrong that you have done.

Examples *Sujatha refused to come clean with her problems.*

The Minister refused to come clean about his ill gotten gains.

Come out with all guns blazing

Meaning To enter the field with a lot of energy; to put one's effort into an activity.

Examples *The Australian team came out with all guns blazing.*

The angry students entered the Principal's office with all guns blazing.

Let's hope that the Indian team comes out with all guns blazing in the next two games.

Comestibles /kə-mes-tə-b(ə)lz/

Pronunciation The 'o' and the 'i' are pronounced like the 'a' in 'china'; the first 'e' is pronounced like the 'e' in 'bed', 'fed' and 'led'. The final 's' sounds

	like the 'z' in 'zip' and 'zoo'. The word is pronounced 'ke-**MES**-te-blz'.
Meaning	A formal word for an item of food or anything that can be eaten. Some dictionaries list it as being old fashioned.
Examples	*There were no comestibles inside the fridge.* *The comestibles they had on display looked very inviting.*
Etymology	From the Latin 'comedere', meaning 'to eat up'.

Comeuppance /kʌm-ʌp-əns/

Pronunciation	The first syllable is pronounced like 'come', and the second like the word 'up'. The 'a' is like the 'a' in 'china'. It is pronounced 'come-**UP**-ens'.
Meaning	The well-deserved punishment that one receives.
Examples	*Jai is mean to everyone. He will get his comeuppance soon.* *In every movie, the villain gets his comeuppance in the end.*
Etymology	One of the meanings of 'come up' is 'to appear before a judge'.

Comfortable /kʌm-fə-tə-bəl/

Pronunciation — The first syllable is pronounced like the word 'come', and the remaining vowels sound like the 'a' in 'china'. The word is pronounced '**COME**-fe-te-bl'. Indians tend to lengthen the second vowel and pronounce the word 'come-**FERT**-e-bel'.

Meaning — The word has many meanings. One of them is 'to be relaxed'.

Examples — *Vindhya isn't very comfortable talking to strangers.*

Rocky looked very comfortable sitting in his new chair.

Etymology — From the Anglo-French 'conforter', meaning 'to comfort'.

Comfy /kʌm-fɪ/

Pronunciation — The first syllable is pronounced like the word 'come' and the following 'y' sounds like the 'i' in 'sit', 'bit' and 'kit'. The word is pronounced '**COME**-fi'.

Meaning — Used in informal contexts to mean 'comfortable'.

Examples *The chair that Kshema was sitting on looked comfy.*

I hope you find the rooms comfy.

Commentate /kɒ-mən-teit/

Pronunciation The 'o' in the first syllable is like the 'o' in 'pot', 'cot' and 'got'. The 'e' in the second is like the 'a' in 'china', and the final syllable rhymes with 'date', 'gate' and 'hate'. The word is pronounced '**CO**-men-tate'.

Meaning To provide a running commentary; to report on a live event for the electronic media.

Examples *Please leave me out of it. I don't wish to commentate.*

Usha has been asked to commentate on this evening's match.

Etymology It comes from the word 'commentator'.

Comstockery /kəm-sta:-kə-rɪ:/

Pronunciation The first vowel and the 'e' in 'ery' are like the 'a' in 'china'. The 'o' in the second syllable is like the 'ar' in 'dark', 'park' and 'mark', and the final 'y' sounds like the 'ee' in 'fees', 'bees' and 'knees'. One way of pronouncing the word is 'kem-**STOK**-e-ree'.

Meaning — Heavy censorship of anything considered immoral or obscene in the arts – literature, painting, etc.

Etymology — Anthony Comstock, a US Postal Inspector, succeeded in 1875 in getting the 'Comstock Law' passed by Congress. This law made it illegal for people to send obscene materials through post. For Comstock, obscene materials included pamphlets relating to birth control and medical books on human anatomy. It was this ridiculous censorship that made George Bernard Shaw coin the word 'comstockery'.

Conduit /kɔn-dju:-ɪt/

Pronunciation — The first syllable is pronounced like the word 'con' and the following 'du' like the word 'dew'. The final syllable sounds like the word 'it'. One simple way of pronouncing the word is '**KON**-dew-it'.

Meaning — A pipe or a passage which allows wires or water to pass through. The word can also be used to refer to a channel that carries something from one place to another or from one person to another – it could be information, money, etc.

Examples — *Villages near the border have always been a conduit for the sale of illegal drugs.*

Jai is the conduit between the arms dealers and the Ministry of Defence.

Etymology It comes from the Old French 'conduit', meaning 'pipe'.

Conglomerate /kən-glɔ-mə-rət/ /kən-glɔm-rət/

Pronunciation There are different ways of pronouncing this word. The British tend to pronounce the first 'o', the first 'e' and the 'a' like the 'a' in 'china'. The 'o' in the second syllable sounds like the 'o' in 'cot', 'hot' and 'not', while the final 'e' remains silent. One way of pronouncing the word is 'ken-**GLO**-me-ret'. Some people drop the vowel in the third syllable and pronounce the word 'ken-**GLOM**-ret'.

Meaning Frequently used in the world of business to refer to several small companies coming together to form a relatively large business. The products or services offered by these small independent companies are usually varied.

Examples *According to this article, Reliance is one of the biggest conglomerates in India.*

Nandini's aim is to build a media conglomerate by 2020.

Etymology The word comes from the Latin 'conglomerare', meaning 'to roll together' or 'wind into a ball'.

Conk out /kɔŋk/

Pronunciation The word rhymes with 'honk' and 'plonk'.

Meaning If a machine conks out, it stops working. When a person conks out, he falls asleep.

Examples *Geeta's car conked out when she was on her way to the university.*

Rishi conked out while he was watching the movie.

Buy a new iron before this thing conks out.

Origin The nose was informally referred to as 'conk'. The expression originally meant 'a punch on the nose'.

Conniption /kə-nɪp-ʃən/

Pronunciation The 'o' in the first syllable and the 'io' in the last are pronounced like the 'a' in 'china'. The second syllable rhymes with 'tip', 'sip' and 'dip'. The word is pronounced 'ke-**NIP**-shen'.

Meaning To become extremely upset or angry. When you have a conniption, you throw a fit. The word is used in informal contexts.

Examples *When Shalini told her father that she was marrying Teja, he had a conniption fit.*

Every time I try to sport a beard, my mother has conniptions.

Etymology — No one is really sure about the etymology of the word. Some believe that it is a corruption of 'captious'.

Connoisseur /kɔn-ə-s͟ɜː/

Pronunciation — The first syllable is pronounced like the word 'con', and the final syllable like the word 'sir'. The 'oi' in the second sounds like the 'a' in 'china'. One simple way of pronouncing the word is 'con-e-**SIR**'.

Meaning — An expert; someone who knows a great deal about and has an appreciation of some of the finer things in life – dance, painting, food and theatre.

Examples — *My friend Raghu is a connoisseur of Carnatic music.*

They tell me that Mukund's wife is a wine connoisseur.

Etymology — It comes from the French 'conoistre', meaning 'to know'.

Conscientiously /kɔn-ʃɪ-en-ʃəs-lɪ/

Pronunciation — The first syllable sounds like the word 'con', and the 'sc' and the 'ti' sound like the 'sh' in 'ship' and 'shin'. The 'e' is pronounced like the 'e' in 'set' and 'bet', and the final 'ou' like the 'a' in 'china'. The word is pronounced 'con-shi-**EN**-shes-li'.

Meaning — It means 'putting a lot of effort into your work'. A conscientious person takes care to do things properly.

Examples — *Vikram is very conscientious, and I'm certain he will finish his dissertation on time.*

The Minister said that he had been carrying out his duties conscientiously.

Etymology — From the Latin 'conscientia', meaning 'knowledge within oneself'.

Control freak

Meaning — Someone who is obsessed with being in control of everything – the situation and the people around him. Determined to get others to do what he wants.

Examples — *Vinay is difficult to work with because he's a control freak.*

Don't let Anita's looks fool you. She'll have her way. She's a control freak.

Even at the age of 85, my grandfather remains a control freak.

Controversy /kɔn-trə-vɜ:-si/ /kən-trɔ-və-si/

Pronunciation There are two ways of pronouncing the word. One way is to pronounce the first and third syllables like the words 'con' and 'verse', respectively. The 'o' in the second syllable sounds like the 'a' in 'china'. In this case, the word is pronounced '**KON**-tre-ver-si'. Some people, however, pronounce the first 'o' like the 'a' in 'china' and the second like the 'o' in 'don' and 'con'. They pronounce the word 'ken-**TRO**-ver-si'.

Meaning A public disagreement between two parties; a quarrel.

Examples *If you introduce this rule, it will create a lot of controversy.*

Every book he writes becomes a subject of controversy.

Etymology From the Latin 'controversia', meaning 'turned in an opposite direction'.

Convalesce /kɔn-və-les/

Pronunciation The first syllable is pronounced like the word 'con', and the 'a' sounds like the 'a' in 'china'. The final 'lesce' is pronounced like the word 'less'. The word is pronounced 'con-ve-**LESS**'.

Meaning	The period of time one spends trying to recuperate after a serious illness or accident. In some countries, 'nursing homes' are referred to as 'convalescent homes'.
Examples	*After the surgery, Mahesh spent nearly six months convalescing.* *Atul wrote his bestseller while he was convalescing.*
Etymology	It comes from the Latin 'con', meaning 'together', and 'valescere', meaning 'to grow strong'.

Copycat

Meaning	Someone who copies or apes others; since there is nothing original about this individual, the word is mostly used to show disapproval.
Examples	*The police say that the copycat serial killer has murdered 15 people so far.* *"I'm the original", said the star. "The rest are mere copycats."*
Origin	In the past, the cat was associated with everything evil – often, it was used as a term of contempt. Shakespeare used it in this negative sense in *All's Well That Ends Well*: "A pox upon him for me, he is more and more a

Cat". Anyone who copied others was therefore contemptuously referred to as a 'copycat'.

Cornucopia /kɒn-jʊ-kəup-iə/

Pronunciation The first syllable sounds like the word 'corn' and the second like the word 'you'. The 'cop' is pronounced like the word 'cope'. The 'i' is like the 'i' in 'bit' and 'sit' and the final 'a' like the 'a' in 'china'. The word is pronounced 'corn-yu-**CO**-pi-e'.

Meaning The word is used in English to mean 'abundant' or 'a great supply of'.

Examples *The new supermarket offers a cornucopia of fresh fruit and vegetables.*

You have a cornucopia of options to choose from.

Etymology It comes from the Latin 'cornu copiae', meaning 'horn of plenty'. According to Greek mythology, when Zeus, the king of the gods, was a child, he was taken care of by a goat named Amalthea. One day, while he was playing with the goat, Zeus accidentally broke off one of her horns. From this horn came an unending supply of food. Traditional paintings of 'cornucopia' show a horn with lots of fruit and nuts next to it.

Cost a bomb

Meaning: Used in informal contexts to mean 'very expensive, cost a fortune'.

Examples: *Mahidhar's new car cost him a bomb.*

The mistakes that Gurunath made cost the company a bomb.

In summer, vegetables cost a bomb.

Costermonger /kɔs-tə-mʌŋ-gə/

Pronunciation: The first syllable is pronounced like the word 'cost' and the 'er' in the second and final syllables is like the 'a' in 'china'. 'Mong' rhymes with 'sung', 'rung' and 'lung'. The word is pronounced '**KOST**-e-mong-e'.

Meaning: Mainly used in British English to refer to someone who sells fresh fruit, vegetables, fish, etc. on the street.

Etymology: 'Monger' means 'seller or trader'; 'coster' is a corruption of the old English word 'costard', meaning 'apple'. A 'costardmonger' was someone who sold apples on the street.

Cosy/Cozy up to /kəu-zɪ/

Pronunciation 'Cosy' rhymes with 'nosey'.

Meaning An informal expression, meaning 'to try to be liked by others by being friendly with them or by being nice to them'. It is often used to show disapproval.

Examples *Raju doesn't like people cozying up to him.*

Everyone knows that Chamundi cozies up to people in power.

Country cousin

Meaning A cousin who lives in the countryside. He is unsophisticated and rather naive about the ways of the world; often a source of embarrassment.

Examples *My country cousins are paying us a visit next month.*

Every year, we get together with our country cousins at my grandmother's house.

Coup de grace /ku:-də-gra:s/

Pronunciation The 'oup' in 'coup' sounds like the 'oo' in 'pool', 'cool' and 'stool'; the final 'p' is silent.

The 'e' in 'de' is like the 'a' in 'china', and the final 'grace' is pronounced like the word 'grass'. The expression is pronounced 'koo-de-**GRASS**'.

Meaning A deathblow given to an individual or an animal who/which has been very badly injured. Nowadays, the expression is used to refer to an action that puts an end to something.

Examples *Lee administered the coup de grace by dismissing Tendulkar and Dravid in the same over.*

An unfortunate car accident dealt the coup de grace to his acting career.

Etymology This is a French expression which means 'stroke of grace' or 'stroke of mercy'. It was first used to refer to any kind of mercy killing.

Cowed into

Meaning To be frightened or intimidated into doing something.

Examples *The students were cowed into submission by the police.*

The women were cowed into silence by their husbands.

Crèche /kreʃ/ /kreiʃ/

Pronunciation — The first 'e' can be pronounced like the 'e' in 'set' and 'bet' or like the 'ay' in 'bay' and 'say'. The 'che' is like the 'sh' in 'ship' and 'sheet'. The word can be pronounced '**KRESH**' or '**KRAYSH**'.

Meaning — A nursery where babies are looked after while their parents are away at work.

Examples — *The company that Suchitra works for has a crèche.*

Julu and Vandana are thinking of starting a crèche.

Etymology — From the Old French 'crèsche', meaning 'crib, manger'.

Criticaster /krɪ-tɪ-kæs-tə/ /krɪ-tɪ-kæs-tə/

Pronunciation — 'Criti' rhymes with 'pretty' and 'gritty', and the syllable that follows sounds like the word 'cast'. The final 'er' is like the 'a' in 'china'. The word can be pronounced '**KRI**-ti-cast-e' or 'kri-ti-**CAST**-e'.

Meaning — An old-fashioned word for a petty or a minor critic.

Examples — *I wouldn't pay much attention to what that criticaster has to say.*

A few criticasters argued that the music in the film was bad.

Etymology It is a combination of 'critic' and the Latin suffix 'aster', meaning 'one who plays'. The word literally means 'one who plays a critic'.

Crowdsource

Meaning Refers to the practice of outsourcing something to a whole lot of people – sometimes obtaining their services for no fee at all.

Examples *To find out what features young people wanted in their cars, our company crowdsourced on Facebook.*

Crowdsourcing enables people to gather a lot of information very quickly.

Etymology The word is a combination of 'crowd' and 'outsourcing'.

Crow's feet

Meaning The lines that appear by the side of someone's eyes; the singular is 'crow's foot'.

Examples *Joan uses a lot of make-up to hide the crow's feet around her eyes.*

There were signs of crow's feet at the corners of Suresh's eyes.

Origin — The lines are called 'crow's feet' because they look like the feet of crows!

Crummy /krʌm-ɪ/

Pronunciation — 'Crum' rhymes with 'from' and 'drum' and the final 'y' is like the 'i' in 'bit', 'sit' and 'kit'. The word is pronounced '**KRUM**-i'.

Meaning — Informal word for 'worthless' or 'of very poor quality'. It can also be used to mean 'to feel unwell'.

Examples — *Hemant lives in a crummy little apartment opposite the station.*

I've been feeling crummy all morning.

Etymology — The word is believed to have come from 'crumb' and 'y'. 'Crumby' originally meant 'something that could crumble easily'.

Cuckoo /kʊ-ku:/

Pronunciation — The first 'u' is like the 'u' in 'put' and 'full', while the second is like the 'oo' in 'pool' and 'fool'. The word is pronounced '**KU**-koo'.

Meaning — A bird; when used with people, it means 'crazy' or 'eccentric'.

Examples — *I'm not allowing you to marry a cuckoo like Rahul.*

Sitting in my office all day sometimes drives me cuckoo.

Cul de sac

/kʌl dɪ sæk/ /kʌl dɪ sæk/

Pronunciation: The first word rhymes with 'gull' and 'dull', while the vowel in the second is like the 'i' in 'sit' and 'bit'. The final word sounds like the word 'sack'. The expression can be pronounced '**KUL** di sack' or 'kul di **SACK**'.

Meaning: It is a street that is open at one end only; in other words, the street has an entrance but no exit. Americans call it a 'dead end street' or a 'blind alley'.

Examples: *They live in a huge house in a quiet cul de sac.*

By the time the thief realized he had entered a cul de sac, it was too late.

Etymology: A French expression, meaning 'bottom of the sack'.

Cult figure

Meaning: An individual who is very popular among a particular group of people.

Examples: *After his death, James Dean became a cult figure.*

Sachin Tendulkar is a cult figure among school children in India.

Culture vulture

Meaning: Someone who is excessively interested in the arts.

Examples: *In the beginning, everyone thought Sheba was a culture vulture.*

My neighbours watch only highbrow television programmes. They're real culture vultures!

Curmudgeon /kə-mʌ-dʒən/ /kɜː-mʌ-dʒən/

Pronunciation: The 'u' in the first syllable and the 'eo' in the last syllable are pronounced like the 'a' in 'china'. The second syllable rhymes with 'judge' and 'budge'. The word is pronounced 'ke-**MU**-jen'. Some people pronounce the 'ur' in the first syllable like the 'ur' in 'burn' and 'burst'.

Meaning: An old-fashioned word to refer to someone who is bad tempered. Usually used with men.

Examples: *Randhir decided to resign because he couldn't put up with his new boss, a terrible old curmudgeon.*

Not Uncle Raju again! Why do you have to invite that curmudgeon every weekend?

Cyberchondriac /sai-bə-<u>kɔn</u>-drɪ-æk/

Pronunciation: The first syllable is pronounced like the word 'sigh' and the following 'e' is like the 'a' in 'china'. The third syllable is pronounced like the word 'con' and the final 'a' is like the 'a' in 'act', 'pact' and 'fact'. The word is pronounced 'sigh-be-**CON**-dri-ak'.

Meaning: Someone who reads about ailments and diseases on the Internet and imagines that he has them too. He frequently visits the doctor, complaining about his imaginary ailments.

Examples: *Ever since his surgery, Ashok has become a cyberchondriac.*

They tell me that my boss' wife is a cyberchondriac.

Cyber hoarding

Meaning: A hoarder is someone who collects large amounts of something – rice, wheat, sugar, etc. – and hides them in a safe place. A cyber hoarder collects meaningless things and stores them on his computer – emails, photographs, documents, etc. Although he may never look at any of these items, he will not delete them. He will go on accumulating a lot of junk.

Examples *Cyber hoarding is something I don't believe in. As soon as I've answered an email, I delete it.*

My cousin Mala is a cyber hoarder.

Cynophobia /sai-nə-fəu-biə/

Pronunciation The first syllable 'cyn' sounds like the word 'sign' and the following 'o' sounds like the 'a' in 'china'. The word is pronounced 'sign-e-**PHO**-bie'.

Meaning Refers to the irrational fear of dogs.

Examples *According to this article, cynophobia is quite common among children.*

Amarnath doesn't have cynophobia. He hates all animals.

Etymology 'Cyno' in Greek means 'dog', and we all know what 'phobia' means.

Cynosure /sɪ-nə-zjuə/ /sai-nə-ʃuə/

Pronunciation There are different ways of pronouncing this word. One way is to pronounce the 'cyn' like the word 'sin', and the following 'o' like the 'a' in 'china'. The 's' is like the 'z' in 'zip' and 'zoo', and the final 'ure' sounds like the 'ure' in 'pure' and 'cure'. The word is pronounced '**SIN**-e-zyue'. Others pronounce the 'y' like the 'y' in 'my' and 'by', and the third syllable like the word 'sure' – '**SIGH**-ne-sure'.

Meaning — A person who is the centre of attraction; everyone is drawn to this individual. The word can be used with both objects and people.

Examples — *At the banquet, Aparna was the cynosure of all eyes.*

The young couple didn't even realise that they were the cynosure of all eyes.

Etymology — This rather literary word, which is mostly used in formal contexts, comes from the Greek 'kunosoura', meaning 'dog's tail' – a term used to refer to Ursa Minor, the constellation which contains the pole star. In the old days, sailors used this star as a guide to determine in which direction they were sailing.

Daddy of them all

Meaning — Used in informal contexts to mean 'the best example of something'.

Examples — *I have met many bad cooks in my life, but Uma is the daddy of them all!*

We've had some pretty heavy downpours this year. But last night's thunderstorm was the daddy of them all.

Dais /dei-ɪs/

Pronunciation The first syllable is like 'day', and the following 's' sounds like the 's' in 'sink' and 'sit'. The word is pronounced '**DAY**-is'.

Meaning A dais is a raised platform behind which a speaker stands when giving a talk.

Examples *When the shooting started, the man took cover behind the dais.*

The speaker was so short he had to stand in front of the dais.

The club decided to give the dais a new coat of varnish.

Etymology From the Old French 'dais', meaning 'platform'.

Danseuse /dɔn-sɜ:z/

Pronunciation One way of pronouncing the word is to pronounce the first syllable like the word 'don' and the second like the word 'sirs'. The word is pronounced 'don-**SIRS**'.

Meaning A female ballet dancer.

Examples *Don't say anything to upset her. She is our star danseuse.*

The young danseuse displayed the poise of a veteran.

Etymology — From the French 'danseuse', meaning 'female dancer'. The male counterpart is called 'danseur'. In India, 'danseuse' is used to refer to a woman who is an exponent of any style of classical dance – Bharatnatyam, Kuchipuddi, Kathak, etc.

De rigueur /də rɪ-gɜː/

Pronunciation — The 'e' in 'de' is like the 'a' in 'china', and the 'i' in 'rigueur' sounds like the 'i' in 'sit', 'bit' and 'hit'. The final 'eur' is like the 'ir' in 'bird', 'first' and 'thirst'. The word is pronounced 'de ri-**GIR**'.

Meaning — Something which according to etiquette or fashion is absolutely essential; something necessary if you wish to be considered part of the 'in' crowd.

Examples — *When you go for an interview, jeans and T-shirt are hardly de rigueur.*

In the early 1970s, Rajesh Khanna made the kurta de rigueur.

Etymology — This French expression literally means 'of strictness'.

Dead from the neck up

Meaning Someone with no brains; an informal expression used to refer to an individual who is stupid.

Examples *There are days when I'm pretty convinced that some of my cousins are dead from the neck up.*

Unlike most politicians, our local MP isn't dead from the neck up.

Dead-tree media

Meaning The traditional print media – newspapers, magazines, journals, books, etc. – that are printed on paper. The opposite of 'dead-tree media' is 'electronic media' and 'electronic publishing'.

Examples *My cousin is very keen on working for the dead-tree media.*

Unlike me, my father prefers to read the dead-tree edition of any book.

Deal fell through

Meaning When a deal, plan or agreement 'falls through', it fails; you fail to complete it successfully.

Examples *Last year I was planning to visit Sikkim, but at the last minute, the plan fell through.*

My aunt and uncle were planning to buy our neighbour's house. But for some reason, the deal fell through.

Debacle

/dei-ba:-kl/

Pronunciation The first syllable sounds like the word 'day', and the following 'a' is like the 'a' in 'path', 'father' and 'ask'. The final 'cle' is like the 'cle' in 'uncle' and 'buckle'. The word is pronounced 'day-**BAA**-kl'.

Meaning A fiasco or complete failure.

Examples *After the debacle of his first film, no director showed any interest in Ravi.*

The series in England turned out to be a debacle for the star batsman.

Etymology The word comes from the French 'débâcler', meaning to 'unbar' or 'free'. Originally, it was used to refer to the flooding that sometimes resulted when the river ice cracked and melted during spring. In English, the word is not used to refer to any natural calamity.

Debris

/deb-ri:/ /dei-bri:/

Pronunciation There are different ways of pronouncing this word. One way is to pronounce the 'e' in the first syllable like the 'e' in 'set', 'bet' and 'get', and the following 'i' like the 'ee' in 'bees', 'fees' and 'knees'. The word can be pronounced 'de-**BREE**'. Others pronounce the first syllable like the word 'day'. They pronounce the word 'day-**BREE**'.

Meaning It is normally used to talk about pieces torn from a large object – for example, from an aeroplane. The small pieces that remain after something has been destroyed.

Examples *They found only debris. There were no survivors.*

The lake, which was once known for its beauty, was now littered with debris.

The detectives went through the debris very carefully.

Etymology From the Old French 'débriser', meaning 'to break down'.

Debut

/dei-bju:/ /de-bju:/

Pronunciation The first syllable 'de' sounds like 'day' and the second syllable rhymes with 'few', 'dew' and 'new'. The vowel in the first syllable can also be pronounced like the 'e' in 'set', 'bet' and 'wet'. The word can be pronounced '**DAY**-byuu' or 'de-**BYUU**'.

Meaning — To make one's appearance in public for the first time as an artist, player, performer, etc.

Examples — *Ramani's debut album will be released next week.*

Mayank made his debut at the ripe old age of 62.

Shashi is making her debut tonight.

Etymology — From the French 'début', meaning 'first appearance'.

Debutante

/deb-jʊ-ta:nt/ /dei-bjʊ-ta:nt/

Pronunciation — The 'e' sounds like the 'e' in 'set', 'wet' and 'get' or like the 'ay' in 'day' and 'bay'. The vowel that follows sounds like the 'u' in 'pull', 'full' and 'put', and the final 'tante' is pronounced like the word 'aunt'. The word can be pronounced '**DEB**-yu-taant' or '**DAY**-byu-taant'.

Meaning — A young woman making her debut or her first appearance as a player. It can also refer to a girl belonging to the upper class who makes an appearancc at a number of social events for the first time.

Examples *The Indian team includes the twenty-one-year-old debutante, Ananya.*

The performance of the two debutantes was encouraging.

Etymology From the French 'débutante', meaning 'a female performer making her début'.

Decrepit /dɪ-kre-pɪt/

Pronunciation The 'e' in the first syllable and the 'i' in the final syllable are pronounced like the 'i' in 'bit', 'fit' and 'hit'. The second syllable rhymes with 'prep'. One way of pronouncing the word is 'di-**KREP**-it'.

Meaning Can be used with things and people to mean 'old' and 'run down'. When used with people, it has a negative connotation.

Examples *Mohan spends half an hour every morning trying to start his decrepit scooter.*

The decrepit old woman was toying with her dentures.

The authorities finally tore down the decrepit building.

Etymology It comes from the Latin 'decrepitus', meaning 'very old, infirm'.

Deep pockets

Meaning — Someone who is extremely rich.

Examples — *Some of our MPs have very deep pockets, I am told.*

If the school is keen on improving its facilities, then the management must find some deep pockets to finance the project.

They become politicians to make their pockets deeper!

Déjà vu

/dei-ʒa: vu:/

Pronunciation — The 'dé' is pronounced like the word 'day', and the following 'j' is like the 's' in 'pleasure' and 'leisure'. The 'à' is like the 'ar' in 'barn', 'cart' and 'harm', and the final 'vu' rhymes with 'who' and 'boo'. The word is pronounced 'day-ja **VOO**'.

Meaning — The feeling of having already experienced in the past the sequence of events that are happening to you now. Having the feeling of reliving the past.

Examples — *As Amrit walked into the committee room, she had a strange sense of déjà vu.*

When I ran into Shyamraj at the club, I had a feeling of déjà vu.

Sunila's new play had a strong sense of déjà vu about it.

Etymology — From the French 'déjà vu', meaning 'already seen'.

Delhi belly

Meaning — Diarrhoea; upset stomach that foreign visitors usually experience in India.

Examples — *After eating at the roadside stall, Pat and Mike suffered a severe case of Delhi belly.*

Susan couldn't do any sightseeing because of a bad case of Delhi belly.

Demarche

/<u>dei</u>-maːʃ/

Pronunciation — The first syllable is pronounced like the word 'day', and the second like the word 'mar'. The final 'che' sounds like the 'sh' in 'ship', 'sheet' and 'shin'. The word is pronounced '**DAY**-maash'. Some people put the stress on the second syllable.

Meaning — A formal diplomatic representation which one country makes to another, stating its official position on a particular subject. The word can also be used to refer to the written statements or protests presented to public officials by private citizens.

Example — *We will once again deliver a demarche to the Government of Pakistan.*

Etymology — From the French 'démarche', meaning 'walk, gait'.

Deplane

Meaning — To get off a plane; to disembark. Mostly used in the US.

Examples — *After a long flight, most passengers were eager to deplane.*

Ananya and I were one of the last people to deplane.

Dereliction /de-rə-lik-ʃən/

Pronunciation — The 'e' in the first syllable is like the 'e' in 'set', 'bet' and 'get', while the 'e' in the second is like the 'a' in 'china'. The final two syllables rhyme with the words 'fiction' and 'diction'. The word is pronounced 'de-re-**LICK**-shen'.

Meaning — Failure to do one's duty; wilful negligence. The word can also be used to mean 'in bad condition'; it is normally used in reference to abandoned buildings.

Examples — *The students are taking the Principal to court for dereliction of duty.*

What you and your friends did was a grave dereliction of duty.

The hotel was in a state of dereliction. The new owner wanted to renovate it.

Etymology — It comes from the Latin 'de', meaning 'entirely', and 'relinquire', meaning 'abandoned or left behind'. The word was first used to refer to ships that were stranded.

Derring-do /de-riŋ-du:/

Pronunciation — The 'e' in 'derring' is like the 'e' in 'set', 'bet' and 'wet' and the following two syllables are pronounced like the words 'ring' and 'do', respectively. The word is pronounced 'de-ring **DOO**'.

Meaning — An old-fashioned word meaning 'daring, displaying courage against overwhelming odds'; mostly used to refer to the daring actions performed by heroes in stories.

Examples — *The title suggested it would be a tale of derring-do. It turned out to be a soppy love story.*

The movie was fun; full of heroic derring-do.

Etymology — The original expression, as used by Chaucer, was 'dorrying don', meaning 'daring to do'. Through a series of copying and printing errors, it became 'derring-do'.

Desert

/de-zət/ /dɪ-zɜːt/

Pronunciation: When used as a noun, the vowel in the first syllable sounds like the 'e' in 'set', 'wet' and 'bet', while the following 's' is like the 'z' in 'zip' and 'zoo'. The 'er' sounds like the 'a' in 'china'. The word is pronounced '**DE**-zet'. When used as a verb, the first vowel sounds like the 'i' in 'pit' and 'sit' and the 'er' like the 'ir' in 'shirt' and dirt'. The verb is pronounced 'di-**ZERT**'.

Meaning: A large area covered mostly with sand. When used as a verb, it means 'to abandon someone'.

Examples: *Rohit plans to walk across the Sahara desert.*

When she lost all her money, most people deserted her.

Desk jockey

Meaning: Anyone whose job involves sitting behind a desk most of the time. Mostly used in informal contexts.

Examples: *Zaheer's father is a desk jockey in the new pharmaceutical company.*

After having worked in the field for 20 years, I have no wish to be reduced to a desk jockey.

Dessert /dɪ-z̲ɜ̲:̲t̲/

Pronunciation — Same as the verb form of 'desert'.

Meaning — The sweet eaten after the main meal.

Examples — *What would you like to have for dessert?*

For dessert, we had vanilla ice cream with gulab jamun.

Etymology — It comes from the French 'desservir', meaning 'clear the table'.

Desultory /d̲e̲-səl-trɪ/ /d̲e̲-zəl-trɪ/

Pronunciation — One simple way is to pronounce the first syllable like the 'de' in 'desk' and 'den', and the following 'u' like the 'a' in 'china'. The 'tory' sounds like the 'try' in 'entry' and 'gentry'. Some people pronounce the 's' like the 'z' in 'zip' and 'zoo'. The word can be pronounced '**DE**-sel-tri' or '**DE**-zel-tri'.

Meaning — Aimless, displaying a total lack of interest; jumping from one topic to another. The word can also be used to mean 'without a clear plan or purpose'.

Examples — *Govind's desultory presentation put the audience to sleep.*

The conversations we had at the party were at best desultory.

Etymology — It comes from the Latin 'deseltorius', meaning 'hasty' or 'superficial'. It originally referred to an acrobat in a circus who jumped from one horse to another while the animals were galloping.

Deus ex machina /dei-əs eks mæ-kɪ-nə/

Pronunciation — The 'de' in 'deus' is pronounced like the word 'day', and the following 'u' and the final 'a' in 'machina' are like the 'a' in 'china'. The 'ex' is pronounced like the letter 'x'. The 'mach' in 'machina' rhymes with 'pack', 'back' and 'sack', and the 'i' is like the 'i' in 'bit', 'kit' and 'pit'. One way of pronouncing the word is 'day-es ex **MACK**-i-ne'.

Meaning — The sudden and unexpected appearance of someone and his miraculous ability to solve all problems; the expression is usually used to show disapproval.

Example — *The main characters survive thanks to deus ex machina.*

Etymology — The expression comes from the world of Greek drama and it literally means 'God from the machine'. In Greek drama, gods (deus) usually made an appearance in the final act and magically sorted out the problems of the main characters. The actor playing God was suspended from a contraption (machina) to give the illusion that he was floating.

Develop /dɪ-ve-ləp/

Pronunciation: The first syllable is like the 'di' in 'dip' and 'dim' and the 'vel' rhymes with 'well' and 'bell'. The final 'o' is like the 'a' in 'china'. The word is pronounced 'di-**VE**-lep'. Many of us pronounce the word '**DEV**-lep'.

Etymology: It comes from the Old French 'desveloper', meaning 'to unwrap'.

Dichotomy /dai-kɔ-tə-mɪ/

Pronunciation: The 'di' is pronounced like the word 'die', and the following 'chot' like the word 'cot'. The 'o' that follows is like the 'a' in 'china', and the final 'y' is like the 'i' in 'kit' and 'bit'. The word is pronounced 'die-**COT**-e-mi'.

Meaning: Used in formal contexts to mean that there is a big difference between the two things being compared. They are so different that they seem to be the complete opposite.

Examples: *Like most politicians, there is a dichotomy between what Raj says and what he does.*

What most students don't realise is that there is a dichotomy between theory and practice.

Etymology The word comes from the Greek 'dikhotomia', meaning 'cutting in two'.

Diddly-squat

Meaning Slang expression, meaning 'absolutely nothing'.

Examples *After all the work I did, I got paid diddly-squat.*

Kishore knows diddly-squat about chemistry.

Diem /di:-em/ /dai-em/

Pronunciation The vowel in the first syllable can be pronounced like the 'ee' in 'seed' and 'weed' or like the 'y' in 'my', 'by' and 'guy'. The 'e' is like the 'a' in 'china'. Most people pronounce the word '**DEE**-em'.

Meaning Day.

Etymology It comes from the Latin 'diem', meaning 'day'. The word is used in English in certain fixed expressions like 'carpe diem' and 'per diem'. Of the two, 'per diem' is much more common in India, especially in Government circles. It means 'per day'; when employees of the government are sent on official duty to other places, they are paid a daily allowance. This is called per diem, and it is given to an individual to meet his daily expenses. 'Carpe diem' means 'seize the day'.

Dies non

/dai-i:z nɔn/

Pronunciation — The 'di' is pronounced like the word 'die' and the following 'es' is like the word 'ease'. The second word is pronounced like the word 'non'. The word is pronounced 'die-ease **NON**'.

Meaning — Days when no legal business can be done; days the court does not work.

Etymology — It is the shortened form of the Latin 'dies non juridicus'. 'Dies' means 'day', 'non' means 'not' and 'juridicus' means 'judicial'.

Differently abled

Meaning — A politically correct term for someone who is either physically or mentally challenged.

Examples — *Our new chemistry teacher is differently abled.*

We need to build a ramp. How will the differently abled get in?

Origin — The United States Democratic Committee coined the term in the 1980s in order to view people who were physically challenged in a positive light.

Dilettante /dɪ-lə-taːn-tei/ /dɪ-lə-tæn-tɪ/

Pronunciation The first syllable rhymes with 'bill' and 'chill', and the vowel in the second is like the 'a' in 'china'. The 'a' can be pronounced like the 'a' in 'cat' or like the 'a' in 'ask'. The word can be pronounced 'di-le-**TAN**-ti' or 'di-le-**TAAN**-tay'.

Meaning Someone who tries to cultivate an interest in the arts without really making the necessary commitment.

Examples *I wouldn't take him too seriously. He is a musical dilettante.*

He often refers to his writings as the musings of a dilettante.

The critics, as expected, did not take the young dilettante poet seriously.

Etymology It comes from the Latin 'delectare', meaning 'to delight'.

Discombobulate /dɪs-kəm-bɔb-jʊ-leit/

Pronunciation The first syllable rhymes with 'miss' and 'kiss' and the third with the words 'rob' and 'mob'. The 'o' in the second syllable sounds like the 'a' in 'china' and the final 'bulate' rhymes with the 'culate' in 'calculate' and 'matriculate'. The word is pronounced 'dis-kem-**BOB**-yu-late'.

Meaning — To be thoroughly confused or upset. Mainly used in American English.

Examples — *The letter from the Minister completely discombobulated the Chairman.*

I told Murthy not to let the heat of the argument discombobulate him.

Discomfit /dɪs-kʌm-fɪt/

Pronunciation — The first syllable rhymes with 'miss' and 'kiss'. The following two syllables are pronounced like the words 'come' and 'fit', respectively. The word is pronounced 'dis-**COME**-fit', with the stress on the second syllable.

Meaning — To make someone rather uneasy or embarrassed. The verb can also be used to mean 'to ruin someone's plans'.

Examples — *Ramesh was discomfited by Sujatha's comments.*

The constant telephone calls discomfited him in his attempt to finish the project.

Etymology — From the French 'desconfit', meaning 'to be utterly defeated' or 'frustrated'. Since 'discomfit' sounded a lot like 'discomfort', the meaning of the word gradually changed. Nowadays, the word is mostly used to mean 'to disconcert or embarrass'.

Dishevelled /dɪ-ʃe-vəld/

Pronunciation: The 'i' in the first syllable is like the 'i' in 'bit', 'sit' and 'hit', while the following 'sh' sounds like the 'sh' in 'sheep', 'ship' and 'shoot'. The 'evel' rhymes with 'devil' and 'level'. One way of pronouncing the word is 'di-**SHEV**-ld'.

Meaning: To look a complete mess, untidy. In American English, the word is spelt 'disheveled'.

Examples: *Some of the bowlers in our cricket team always look dishevelled.*

Ishant always comes to work looking rather dishevelled.

Etymology: It comes from the French 'dishevely', meaning 'bare headed'.

Disorientated /dɪs-ɒ-rɪ-en-teit-ɪd/

Pronunciation: The second, third and fourth syllables together are pronounced like the word 'orient'. The final syllables rhyme with 'dated' and 'slated'. The word is pronounced 'dis-**O**-ri-en-tate-id'.

Meaning: To confuse someone; to cause someone to lose their sense of direction. Has the same meaning as 'disoriented'.

Examples *The smoke in the apartment left Dev disoriented/disorientated, and he had a tough time making his way out.*

The sudden change of plans left many of the teachers disoriented/disorientated.

Disparage /dɪs-pæ-rɪdʒ/

Pronunciation The first syllable rhymes with 'miss' and 'kiss', and the third with 'fridge' and 'bridge'. The vowel in the second is like the 'a' in 'fact' and 'pact'. The word is pronounced 'dis-**PA**-rij'.

Meaning To ridicule someone; to speak in a manner that makes it plain to the listener that he is not highly thought of. The word is mostly used in formal contexts.

Examples *I would like to submit my resignation now. I have no wish to be disparaged by the Board.*

Please refrain from making disparaging comments about my favourite teacher.

Etymology From the Old French 'desparagier', meaning 'to marry someone below your status or rank'.

Diva /diː-və/

Pronunciation The 'i' is like the 'ee' in 'fees' and 'bees', and the 'a' like the 'a' in 'china'. The word is pronounced '**DEE**-ve'.

Meaning — A distinguished woman singer; a lady performer who sings any form of popular music – jazz, rock, pop, Carnatic. The word is also used to refer to a woman celebrity who thinks no end of herself and is, therefore, very difficult to please.

Examples — *The well-known pop diva, Madonna, will be performing at the show.*

I'd be careful if I were you. She has a reputation of being a bit of a diva.

Etymology — It comes from the Latin 'diva', meaning 'goddess' or 'divine'. Initially, it was only used with women who sang in operas, but nowadays it is used with everyone.

Divorce /dɪ-vɒs/

Pronunciation — The 'i' sounds likes the 'i' in 'fit', 'hit' and sit' and the syllable that follows rhymes with 'force', 'Morse' and 'course'. The word is pronounced 'di-**VORCE**'. Indians tend to pronounce it as '**DIE**-vorce'.

Meaning — To legally end a marriage. It can also be used to refer to the separation of two things.

Examples — *Ram is thinking of asking for a divorce.*

There's divorce between what he says and what he does.

Etymology From the Latin 'divortium', meaning 'separation or dissolution of marriage'.

Divorcée /dɪ-vɒ-si:/ /dɪ-vɒ-sei/

Pronunciation The first two syllables are pronounced like the word 'divorce'. The British pronounce the final 'ée' like the 'ee' in 'see' and 'bee', while the Americans pronounce it like the 'ay' in 'bay' and 'pay'. The word can be pronounced 'di-vor-**SEE**' or 'di-vor-**SAY**'.

Meaning A divorcée is a woman who is divorced; a man who is divorced is called a divorcé. Both words are pronounced the same way, and both have an accent mark on the 'e' after the 'c'.

Example *Shekar didn't know that Deepa was a divorcée.*

The divorcée had everyone talking about her.

Etymology From the French 'divorcée', meaning 'divorced woman'.

Dodo /dəu-dəu/

Pronunciation Both the vowels in the word rhyme with the words 'no', 'go' and 'so'. The word is pronounced '**DOE**-doe'.

Meaning	When used with people, it means that you think he/she is silly or foolish.
Examples	*I felt like a dodo when I slipped on the banana peel.* *Every time I talk to Sujatha, I feel like a dodo.*
Etymology	From the Portuguese 'doudo', meaning 'simpleton' or 'fool'. Originally used to refer to a flightless bird, now extinct.

Domestic engineer

Meaning	A politically correct term for a homemaker – could be a man or a woman. Sounds a lot more impressive than 'housewife' or 'househusband', doesn't it? The politically correct term for the garbage man is 'sanitation engineer' and for the man who fills petrol in your vehicle is 'petroleum transfer engineer'.
Examples	*Janani worked for a software company for nearly 10 years. Now she is content being a domestic engineer.* *If Rahul is eating at the Taj, it means that the domestic engineer is out of town.*

Doozy /du:zɪ/

Pronunciation	The 'oo' in the first syllable is like the 'oo' in 'cool', 'fool' and 'pool', and the 'y' is like the 'i'

in 'pit', 'bit' and 'kit'. The word is pronounced '**DOO**-zi'.

Meaning — A slang term for something that is extraordinarily good or bad; unique. The word can also be spelt 'doozie'.

Examples — *The annual day programme was a real doozy this year. Many people walked out after half an hour.*

You should see Vikram's black eye. It's a real doozy.

Dossier /d<u>ɔs</u>-ɪ-ei/ /d<u>ɔs</u>-ɪ-ə/

Pronunciation — The first syllable rhymes with 'toss', 'boss' and 'cross'. The following 'i' is like the 'i' in 'sit', 'knit' and 'kit', and the final 'er' sounds like the 'ay' in 'bay', 'hay' and 'gay'. The word is pronounced '**DOS**-i-ay'. It is also possible to pronounce the final 'er' like the 'a' in 'china'.

Meaning — A file containing information about a person or about something important.

Examples — *I'm sure we have a dossier on our main political rival.*

We were ordered to hand the dossier of evidence over to the police.

Etymology — From the French 'dossier', meaning 'a bundle of papers'.

Double entendre /du:-bəl a:n-ta:n-drə/

Pronunciation The first word in this French expression is not pronounced like the English 'double'. The 'ou', in fact, sounds like the 'oo' in 'pool', 'fool' and 'cool'. There is no corresponding sound for the 'en'. The closest we can get is to pronounce the 'e' in the first and second syllables of 'entendre' like the 'a' in 'ask', 'path' and 'mask'. The final 'e' is like the 'a' in 'china'. The word is pronounced 'doo-bl aan-**TAAN**-dre'.

Meaning Double meaning; a word or phrase which can be interpreted in two different ways – one of which is rather sexual in nature.

Examples *The double entendre of the stand-up comedian left the ladies embarrassed.*

The double entendres were lost on Ganesh and Jayanth.

Etymology From an obsolete French expression, which literally meant 'a two-fold meaning'.

Double take

Meaning To react with surprise; to look at something again for the second time because you are surprised by what you saw the first time.

Examples *I did a double take when I saw Hritik walk in with Ramesh.*

The joggers glanced at the tiger in the park and did a double take.

When Satish proposed to Amrit, she did a double take before she burst out laughing.

Double whammy /dʌ-bəl wæ-mɪ/

Pronunciation 'Wham' rhymes with 'ram', 'dam' and 'Sam', and the final 'y' is like the 'i' in 'bit', 'sit' and 'kit'.

Meaning When you put a 'whammy' on someone, you put a curse on them. A double whammy, therefore, is a 'double curse'; they suffer a major setback, a double blow of sorts. Nowadays, the expression is used when good things happen as well.

Examples *My boss tells me that I didn't get the promotion, and you tell me my leave has not been sanctioned. Talk about a double whammy.*

The decision to reduce the frequency of buses and to increase the price of tickets was a double whammy.

Origin The expression was coined by the American cartoonist, Al Capp, in *Li'l Abner*. In this cartoon strip, a character named Evil-Eye Fleegle often put a curse on people. When he did this, he pointed a finger at the person, and kept one of his eyes open. If he wanted to put a double whammy, he kept both eyes open.

Doublespeak

Pronunciation The main stress is on the first syllable of 'double'.

Meaning Deliberately use obscure or ambiguous language. The aim is to make the bad appear good, the simple appear complex, the unpleasant, attractive – using euphemisms.

Examples *I don't think we should call them 'poor people'. Refer to them as 'fiscal underachievers' or 'economically non-affluent'.*

The hospital authorities maintained that the patient did not die; he failed to achieve his wellness potential.

Origin From 'doublethink' and 'doubletalk' – concepts used by George Orwell in his novel, *Ninety Eighty Four.*

Dour /duə/ /dauə/

Pronunciation The word rhymes with 'sure', 'poor' and 'cure'. Some people make it rhyme with 'power' and 'shower'.

Meaning — Normally used to refer to a person's appearance or his manner; to appear very serious and rather unhappy. A 'dour' individual is severe, gloomy and unfriendly.

Examples — *The new teacher's dour look depressed all the students in class.*

Surprisingly, the normally dour Harish became the life of the party.

Etymology — It comes from the Scottish 'dur', meaning 'dull' or 'obstinate'.

Downplay

Pronunciation — The main stress is on 'play' – 'down-**PLAY**'.

Meaning — To make something seem or appear less important than it actually is; to treat an important matter lightly. The word has the same meaning as 'to play down'.

Examples — *The Government tried to downplay the significance of the issue.*

Gayathri always downplays her role in saving the hospital.

To keep his parents from worrying, Shyamraj downplayed the dangers of his job.

Downtime

Pronunciation The stress is on the first syllable.

Meaning Period of time when a machine or a person is not working or not available; to relax.

Examples *What do you normally do in your downtime?*

Sachi is terribly busy negotiating with the workers right now. She hopes to get some downtime next week.

Doyen /dɔi-ən/

Pronunciation The first syllable rhymes with 'toy' and 'boy', while the 'e' sounds like the 'a' in 'china'. The word is pronounced '**DOY**-en'.

Meaning The eldest or the senior-most member of a group who is very knowledgeable about a subject or an area. Politicians frequently use the word when someone senior, who has worked in a particular field for a long time, dies.

Examples *Around these parts, Amar is seen as the doyen of sports journalism.*

The doyen of the Congress party received a standing ovation.

Etymology The French word 'doyen' originally meant 'commander of ten'. It is from this word that we get 'dean'. Derived from the Latin 'decanus', a 'dean' was the head of a group of ten monks in a monastery.

Dragon lady

Meaning A powerful woman who goes about her business in a ruthless manner; a tyrant who bosses over everyone. The term can also be used to refer to a glamorous woman who has a seductive quality about her: a femme fatale.

Examples *The kids refer to Padmini as the dragon lady of our colony.*

Gitesh has been working for a dragon lady for twenty years.

Etymology Milton Caniff, the creator of the *Terry and the Pirates* comic strip, named his villain, a woman of Asian descent, Dragon Lady. This resulted in people calling any powerful Asian woman, a 'dragon lady'. With the passage of time, the term began to be applied to any ruthless woman.

Drama queen

Meaning — Used in informal contexts to refer to a man or a woman who acts overly dramatic in situations; shows disapproval.

Examples — *Juhi made a big fuss when the waiter spilled some water on her. I didn't know she was such a drama queen.*

At the Wimbledon Championships, Virginia Wade accused Andy Murray of being a drama queen.

Droll /drəul/

Pronunciation — The word rhymes with 'role', 'pole' and 'coal'.

Meaning — Being funny or humorous in an odd sort of way. The things the person says may not necessarily have you in splits, but they will keep you amused.

Examples — *The new teacher kept the children entertained with droll stories.*

The several asides he included in his talk were very droll.

Etymology — Perhaps from the Dutch 'drol', meaning 'fat little fellow, goblin'.

Dude

/djuːd/ /duːd/

Pronunciation	The word rhymes with 'rude', 'mood' and 'food'. It is also possible to insert a 'y' sound before the vowel. The word can be pronounced '**DUUD**' or '**DYUUD**'.
Meaning	Mostly used in informal contexts to refer to a man. A woman is usually referred to as 'dudette'.
Examples	*The dude playing the guitar is my boss.* *Who is the dudette in the pink kurta?*
Etymology	According to some scholars, 'dude' is the shortened form of 'doodle' from *Yankee Doodle*.

Dumb-down

Meaning	To make something simple so that many people can understand it or make it more popular. Mostly used to show disapproval.
Examples	*Your article has some wonderful ideas. I strongly feel the ideas need some dumbing down.* *Some of the channels give us a dumbed-down version of what happened in Parliament.*

Dummy up

Meaning — To keep quiet, to stop talking.

Examples — *Whenever a salesman comes home, my father just dummies up and lets my mother do all the talking.*

In our school, students dummy up whenever they see the Principal walk by.

What's wrong with you? Why have you dummied up?

Origin — To keep quiet like the dummy of a ventriloquist.

Dun for

Pronunciation — The word rhymes with 'run', 'gun' and 'sun'.

Meaning — The persistent demand from someone for the repayment of a loan; to harass someone.

Example — *If you don't repay the amount by tomorrow, Nikhil, they will dun you for it day and night.*

Origin — According to one theory, the word comes from Joe Dunn, a London bailiff, who had a reputation for tracking down defaulters.

Ear candy

Meaning Something that is good to listen to – it could be music, someone's voice, accent, etc.

Examples *My father thinks that Richard Burton's voice is ear candy.*

The songs by the Beatles are ear candy.

Of late, I have fallen in love with Jamaican English. It's ear candy.

Eater's coma

Meaning Feeling lazy and sleepy after a heavy meal.

Examples *If I eat everything that is on the table, I'll lapse into an eater's coma.*

I don't think I'll be able to come with you on the walk. It's eater's coma.

Echelon /e̱-ʃə-lɔn/ /e̱-ʃə-la:n/

Pronunciation The 'ech' sounds like the 'esh' in 'mesh' and the final syllable rhymes with 'con' and 'don'. The vowel in the second syllable is like the 'a' in 'china'. Some people pronounce the 'o' like the 'a' in 'path', 'bath' and 'father'. The word can be pronounced '**E**-shi-lon' or '**E**-shi-laan'.

Meaning: The echelons of a business organisation are the people at a particular level in that organisation and the powers and responsibilities associated with that particular level. One usually talks about the higher and lower echelons.

Examples: *The final decision will be made in the higher echelons of the company.*

The new tax cuts will affect only those who are in the lower echelons of the bureaucracy.

The upper echelons of the Government are not in favour of the changes.

Etymology: From the French 'echelon', meaning 'rung of ladder'.

Economical with the truth

Meaning: To lie; to avoid revealing too much.

Examples: *You need to be a little careful with Jaya. She tends to be economical with the truth.*

I didn't tell him everything. I was economical with the truth.

Economically inactive

Meaning: Politically correct way of saying that someone is unemployed.

Examples — *Harini has been economically inactive for six months now.*

The economically inactive members of my family are planning to start their own company.

Edgy

Meaning — A person who is 'edgy' is worried, tense and rather irritable.

Examples — *The soldiers were edgy as they waited for their orders from the Captain.*

The delay was making everyone at the airport edgy.

Eerie

/iə-rɪ/

Pronunciation — The 'ee' in the first syllable is pronounced like the 'ea' in 'fear', 'dear' and 'near', while the following 'ie' sounds like the 'i' in 'sit', 'pit' and 'knit'. The word is pronounced '**IE**-ri'.

Meaning — Strange and frightening in a mysterious way, scary.

Examples — *At night, the sky around the old house on the hill had an eerie glow.*

The eerie sound of the owl scared the children sitting around the campfire.

	The little girl had an eerie feeling that she had seen the stranger before.
Etymology	From the Old English 'earg', meaning 'cowardly'.

Eeyorish /iːjɔr-ɪʃ/

Pronunciation	The 'ee' is like the 'ee' in 'feel', 'peel' and 'heel'; the following 'o' sounds like the 'o' in 'hot', 'cot' and 'dot'. The word is pronounced 'ee-**YOR**-ish'.
Meaning	Gloomy or depressed.
Examples	*I want all of you to stop being Eeyorish. We've been given a wonderful opportunity to make amends.*
	Bala has been Eeyorish all day. But then, that isn't anything new, is it?
Origin	Eeyore is the pessimistic donkey in AA Milne's children's classic, *Winnie the Pooh*. He makes cynical comments about a lot of things, and is seldom happy.

Effeminate /ɪ-fe-mɪ-nət/

Pronunciation	The vowels in the first and third syllables are like the 'i' in 'sit' and 'bit'. The 'fem' rhymes with 'gem', 'them' and 'hem', and the final 'a' is

	like the 'a' in 'china'. The word is pronounced 'i-**FE**-mi-net'.
Meaning	Very unmanly; a male who behaves, looks and sounds more like a woman than a man. Used to show disapproval.
Examples	*The students made fun of the Principal's effeminate walk.* *Tarun's effeminate manner raised eyebrows among the members of the club.*
Etymology	From the Latin 'effeminare', meaning 'make a woman of'.

Efficacy /e̱-fɪ-kə-sɪ/

Pronunciation	The 'e' is like the 'e' in 'set' and 'bet', and the following 'ffic' rhymes with 'sick' and 'pick'. The 'a' is like the 'a' in 'china' and the final 'y' like the 'i' in 'bit' and 'kit'. The word is pronounced '**E**-fi-ke-si'.
Meaning	Attempting to produce the intended or desired result – usually used with medicine.
Examples	*I'm afraid there is little or no information about the efficacy of the drug.* *The company needs to run a few more tests to determine the efficacy of the drug.*
Etymology	It comes from the Latin 'efficacia', meaning 'effectiveness'.

Egalitarian /ɪ-gæ-lɪ-t3ə-ri-ən/

Pronunciation — The vowels in the first and third syllables are pronounced like the 'i' in 'bit', 'hit' and 'chit'. The 'gal' rhymes with 'pal' and 'shall', while the 'tar' in the fourth syllable rhymes with 'bare' and 'share'. The word is pronounced 'i-ga-li-**TARE**-i-en'.

Meaning — Someone who believes that everyone in society is equally important, and therefore, every individual should be given the same rights and opportunities in life. The word can be used as a noun and an adjective.

Examples — *Jayanth's father was a committed egalitarian.*

Rachna wants the newly formed party to adopt egalitarian principles.

Etymology — From the Old French 'égalité', meaning 'equality'.

Ego massage

Meaning — An informal expression, meaning 'to flatter someone'. To stroke someone's ego, telling them nice things to make them feel happy.

Examples — *Sujatha didn't get the ego massage she was hoping for.*

After losing the election, the last thing the candidate wants from her supporters is an ego massage.

Teachers, I am told, need an ego massage every now and then.

Ego-surfing

Meaning To type in one's name to find out how many times it has been included or mentioned in various websites.

Examples *Nagesh was fired because he was caught ego-surfing.*

I wonder if people like Tendulkar and Dravid ego-surf.

Egregious /ɪ-gri:-dʒəs/

Pronunciation The first 'e' is like the 'i' in 'bit', 'hit' and 'sit', and the second like the 'ee' in 'weep', 'sweep' and 'keep'. The 'g' in the final syllable sounds like the 'j' in 'jam' and 'juice', and the final 'iou' like the 'a' in 'china'. The word is pronounced 'i-**GREE**-jes'.

Meaning Shockingly bad, so bad that it stands out. The word has a negative connotation.

Examples *Our politicians tell the most egregious lies and get away with it.*

The documents showed the egregious abuse of power by the police.

Etymology — From the Latin 'egregius': 'ex' means 'out of' and 'greg' means 'herd'. Something that is egregious is prominent; it stands out from the herd.

Either

/ai-ðə/ /iː-ðə/

Pronunciation — The British pronounce the 'ei' in the first syllable like the word 'eye', while the Americans pronounce it like the 'ee' in 'peel' and 'feel'. The word can be pronounced '**EYE**-ther' or '**EE**-ther'.

Examples — *Reshmi doesn't like Harini. She doesn't like Nikita, either.*

Shekar doesn't smoke. He doesn't drink, either.

Etymology — From the Old English 'aghwader', meaning 'each of two'.

Emaciated

/ɪ-mei-sɪ-ei-tɪd/

Pronunciation — The 'e' in the first syllable sounds like the 'i' in 'sit', 'bit' and 'kit'. 'Maci' rhymes with 'racy', 'pacey' and 'lacy'; the final 'ated' rhymes with 'hated', 'dated' and 'fated'. One way of pronouncing the word is 'i-**MAY**-si-ate-id'.

Meaning	Someone who is very weak and thin due to illness or hunger.
Examples	*The emaciated child was unable to walk for more than a minute.* *My grandmother looked very emaciated after her long illness.*
Etymology	From the Latin 'emaciatus', meaning 'make lean'.

Embarrass /ɪm-<u>bæ</u>-rəs/

Pronunciation	The first syllable is like the 'im' in 'him', 'dim' and 'Kim'; the following 'a' is pronounced like the 'a' in 'cat', 'bat' and 'hat'. The final 'a' is like the 'a' in 'china'. The word is pronounced 'im-**BA**-res'.
Meaning	To feel very awkward or ashamed of something.
Examples	*Shantha was embarrassed by her son's rather rude behaviour.* *Sometimes, children do things just to embarrass their parents.*
Etymology	From the Italian 'imbarrare', meaning 'to bar'.

Emeritus

/ɪ-me̲-rɪ-təs/

Pronunciation — The first 'e' and the 'i' in the third syllable sound like the 'i' in 'sit', 'lit' and 'fit', while the 'e' in the second syllable is pronounced like the 'e' in 'set', 'pet' and 'get'. The final vowel sounds like the 'a' in 'china'. The word is pronounced 'i-**ME**-ri-tes'.

Meaning — No longer having a position in the academic institution; retired. Retaining one's title on an honorary basis.

Examples — *When the editor of a newspaper retires, he can call himself 'Editor Emeritus'.*

When Pope Benedict XVI retired, he became 'Pope Emeritus Benedict XVI'.

Etymology — From the Latin 'emereri', meaning 'earning one's discharge by service'. It was first used to refer to veteran soldiers; those who had earned their retirement after having served in the army for many years.

En bloc

Pronunciation — The easiest way to pronounce this expression of French origin is 'on **BLOCK**'.

Meaning — As a whole; all together.

Examples — *The members of the Ethics Committee threatened to resign en bloc.*

The students wanted the VC to adopt the proposed rules en bloc.

Etymology — The literal meaning of this expression is 'in a block'.

Encyclopaedic /ɪn-sai-klə-pi:-dɪk/

Pronunciation — The first syllable is pronounced like the word 'in', and the following 'cy' rhymes with 'by' and 'my'. The 'o' is like the 'a' in 'china', and the 'ae' sounds like the 'ee' in 'bee', 'see' and 'knee'. The word is pronounced 'en-sy-kle-**PEE**-dik'.

Meaning — A person who is like an encyclopaedia; someone who has a great deal of knowledge about many things. An expert.

Examples — *In matters relating to cancer, Suresh's knowledge is encyclopaedic.*

Sushmita has an encyclopaedic knowledge of Carnatic music.

My cousin Anand has an encyclopaedic knowledge of the local restaurants.

Etymology — From the Greek 'enkuklopaideia', meaning 'all-round education'.

Ennui /ɔn-wiː/

Pronunciation: The first syllable is pronounced like the word 'on'; the following 'ui' is like the 'we' in 'weep', 'weed' and 'week'. The word is pronounced 'on-**WEE**'.

Meaning: A literary word, mostly used in formal contexts to mean 'a feeling of boredom'.

Examples: *Since returning home, Ram has experienced a profound sense of ennui.*

Ever since his divorce, Sharath has frequently experienced a profound sense of ennui.

Etymology: It comes from the Old French 'enui', meaning 'annoyance'.

Ensconce /ɪn-skɔns/

Pronunciation: The first syllable is pronounced like the word 'in', and the 'scon' in the second rhymes with 'con' and 'don'. The final 'ce' sounds like the 's' in 'sit', 'sun' and 'swim'. One way of pronouncing the word is 'in-**SKONS**'.

Meaning: Mostly used in formal contexts to mean 'to settle down safely and comfortably'. The word can also be used to mean 'hidden in a safe environment, unseen by others'.

Examples — *I found Sajid watching TV ensconced in my favourite chair.*

Chitra decided to ensconce herself in the small cupboard in the kitchen downstairs.

Ensemble /ɔn-sɔm-bəl/

Pronunciation — The 'e' in the first and second syllables is pronounced like the 'o' in 'pot', 'hot' and 'cot'. The final 'e' is silent and the word is pronounced 'on-**SOM**-bel'.

Meaning — Musicians, actors, dancers, etc. who always perform together can be referred to as an ensemble. Things that combine well can also be called an ensemble.

Examples — *Rahul is a member of a jazz singing ensemble in Hyderabad.*

Prithi bought the whole ensemble – the dress, the matching earrings and the shoes.

Etymology — It comes from the Latin 'insimul', meaning 'at the same time'.

Entourage /ɔn-tʊ-ra:ʒ/

Pronunciation — The first syllable is pronounced like the word 'on', and the second like the word 'to'. The final syllable sounds like the 'rage' in 'garage' and 'mirage'. One way of pronouncing the word is '**ON**-tu-raazh'.

Meaning — The individuals who work for and are constantly with an important or a famous person.

Examples — *The film star and the members of her entourage walked in two hours late.*

The Minister's entourage included several people who were wanted by the police.

Etymology — From the French 'entourer', meaning 'to surround'.

Entrepreneur /ɔn-trə-prə-n3ː/

Pronunciation — The first syllable is like the word 'on', and the 'e' in the second and third syllables sounds like the 'a' in 'china'. The final 'eur' is like the 'ir' in 'dirt', 'bird' and 'shirt'. The word is pronounced 'on-tre-pre-**NE**'.

Meaning — Someone who sets up a business, usually something new. He is a promoter.

Examples — *Yogi calls himself an entrepreneur. If you ask me, he's nothing more than a drug peddler.*

The young entrepreneur retired after selling his small company to Google for 20 crores.

Etymology — This French word literally means 'one who undertakes or manages'.

Epithet /e̲-pɪ-θet/

Pronunciation The first and last 'e' sound like the 'e' in 'set', 'wet' and 'met', and the 'i' is like the 'i' in 'miss', 'kiss' and 'his'. The word is pronounced '**E**-pi-thet'.

Meaning A word or phrase attached to the name of an individual which sums up his most important quality – Solomon the Wise; Mahatma Gandhi, Father of the Nation. Nowadays, the word is used to mean 'term of abuse'.

Examples *Harbajan was accused of hurling racial epithets at Andrew Symonds.*

Please refrain from using such epithets when you are in the company of a lady.

Etymology It comes from the Greek 'epitheton', meaning 'something added'.

Epitome /ɪ-p̲ɪ̲-tə-mi:/

Pronunciation The vowels in the first two syllables are pronounced like the 'i' in 'sit', 'pit' and 'bit'. The 'o' is like the 'a' in 'china', and the final syllable is pronounced like the word 'me'. The word is pronounced 'i-**PIT**-e-mee'.

Meaning A person or a thing that is an ideal example; can be used with both good and bad things.

Examples *I consider him to be the epitome of the crooked politician.*

Rama believes that travelling by AC two-tier is the epitome of extravagance.

Natraj's new driver is the epitome of laziness.

Etymology From the Greek 'epitome', meaning 'abridgement'.

Eponymous /ɪ-pɔ-nɪ-məs/

Pronunciation The 'e' and the 'y' sound like the 'i' in 'bit', 'pit' and 'sit', and the 'pon' in the second syllable rhymes with 'don', 'non' and 'John'. The final 'ou' is like the 'a' in 'china'. The word is pronounced 'i-**PON**-i-mes'.

Meaning An eponymous character in a film or book has the same name as the title of the book or movie. Giving one's name to colleges, schools, cities, etc.

Example *The eponymous hero of the movie* Rocky *is played by Sylvester Stallone.*

Etymology From the Greek 'eponymos', meaning 'giving one's name to' someone or something.

Ersatz /ɜə-zats/

Pronunciation One way of pronouncing this German word is to pronounce the 'er' like the word 'air',

	and the following 's' like the 'z' in 'zip' and 'zoo'. The final syllable, 'atz', sounds like the 'ats' in 'bats', 'rats' and 'cats'. The word can be pronounced '**AIR**-zats'. Some people, however, put the stress on the second syllable.
Meaning	Replace or substitute the original with something very inferior. The word is used to show disapproval.
Example	*I'm told that during the war, my grandmother had to make do with ersatz chocolates and coffee.*
Etymology	The word comes from the German 'ersetzen', meaning 'to replace'.

Erudite /e̠-rʊ-dait/

Pronunciation	The 'e' is like the 'e' in 'set', 'pet' and 'met', and the following 'u' sounds like the 'u' in 'put', 'pull' and 'full'. The final syllable rhymes with 'might', 'kite' and 'fight'. The word is pronounced '**E**-ru-dait'.
Meaning	Formal word, meaning 'scholar' or 'learned'.
Examples	*Sekhar is different from my other cousins. He is very erudite and well informed.* *The old professors were stunned when the young man gave an erudite lecture.*

Etymology — From the Latin 'eruditis', meaning 'learned, well informed'.

Esoteric /iː-səu-te-rik/ /e-səu-te-rik/

Pronunciation — The first 'e' can be pronounced like the 'ee' in 'fees', 'bees' and 'cheese' or like the 'e' in 'set' and 'bet'. The second syllable is like the word 'so'. The word can be pronounced 'ee-so-**TER**-ik' or 'e-so-**TER**-ik'.

Meaning — Something that is difficult to understand; only a select few will be able to comprehend it.

Examples — *Please don't use any esoteric terminology. Tell me in a language I'll understand.*

Usha takes something trivial and turns it into an esoteric philosophical debate.

Etymology — It comes from the Greek 'esoterikos', meaning 'belonging to an inner circle'.

Et al. /et æl/

Pronunciation — The first word rhymes with 'set', 'bet' and 'pet', and the second with 'pal'. The word is pronounced 'et **AL**'.

Meaning — The expression is used after a name or a list of names to indicate that others are also involved.

It is normally used to refer to books and articles written by more than one person.

Examples *For your next class, I would like you to read the article written by Balagopal et al.*

At the concert, they sang the songs of Kishore Kumar, Rafi, et al.

Etymology 'Et al.' comes from Latin, and it is the abbreviated form of 'et alia', meaning 'other people or other things'.

Etiquette /e̱-tɪ-ket/

Pronunciation The 'eti' rhymes with 'petty' and 'Betty', and the final 'quette' sounds like the 'ket' in 'kettle'. The word is pronounced '**E**-ti-ket'.

Meaning Formal rules that determine how we should behave in a social context. These are the rules we observe in our social and professional life.

Examples *There was a time when etiquette was considered important in our country.*

You shouldn't have done what you did. It was a breach of etiquette.

Etymology From the Old French 'etiquette', meaning 'label' or 'ticket'. In the past, these labels had instructions printed on them about how to behave.

Eulogy /ju:-lə-dʒɪ/

Pronunciation: The first syllable is pronounced like the word 'you', and the final 'logy' is like the 'logy' in 'psychology' and 'biology'. The word is pronounced '**YOU**-le-ji'.

Meaning: A highly complimentary speech given at someone's funeral or at the time of his retirement. It praises the individual to the skies. Eulogies can be written about things as well.

Examples: *The eulogy given by the Prime Minister was broadcast live.*

The CEO didn't want any eulogies at the time of his retirement.

I hated the man. How can you expect me to write his eulogy?

Etymology: It comes from the Greek 'eulogia', meaning 'good or fine language'.

Euphemism /ju:-fə-mɪ-zəm/

Pronunciation: The first syllable is like the word 'you' and the following 'ph' is like the 'f' in 'fish' and 'fell'. The second 'e' sounds like the 'a' in 'china' and the final 'mism' rhymes with 'prism'. The word is pronounced '**YOU**-fe-mi-zem'.

Meaning — An indirect or a polite way of referring to something that is embarrassing.

Examples — *The term 'senior citizen' is a euphemism for old people.*

Rani finds it difficult to talk about sex. She always makes use of euphemisms.

Etymology — It comes from the Greek 'euphemos', meaning 'auspicious' or 'sounding good'.

Euthanasia /juːθ-ən-eiʒ-ə/

Pronunciation — The first syllable is pronounced like the word 'youth', while the vowel in the second is like the 'a' in 'china'. The final two syllables are pronounced like the word 'Asia'. One way of pronouncing the word is 'youth-en-**AY**-zhe'.

Meaning — The practice of killing someone who is very ill without causing the person any pain. It is usually done in order to reduce the suffering of an individual or an animal.

Examples — *Many people think that we should have the right to euthanasia.*

Radha doesn't think euthanasia should be considered a crime.

My pet dog was in bad shape, and the vet suggested euthanasia.

Etymology	From the Greek 'eu', meaning 'good', and 'thantos', meaning 'death'.

Exorcism /ek-sɒ-sɪ-zəm/

Pronunciation	The 'ex' is pronounced like the letter 'x', and the following 'or' is like the 'ou' in 'ought', 'sought' and 'fought'. The final 'ism' sounds like the 'ism' in 'prism'. The word is pronounced '**EK**-so-si-zem'.
Meaning	The act of driving away an evil spirit using magic or prayers.
Examples	*The witch doctor tried to exorcise the evil spirit from the library.* *The priest is going to perform an exorcism tonight.*
Etymology	From the Greek 'exorkizein', meaning 'bind by oath'.

Exposé /ek-spəu-zei/

Pronunciation	The first syllable is like the prefix 'ex', and the following 'o' is like the 'o' in 'go', 'so' and 'no'. The 's' sounds like the 'z' in 'zoo', 'zip' and 'zing', and the final syllable rhymes with 'say', 'hay' and 'may'. The word is pronounced 'ek-**SPO**-zay'. It is also possible to have the main stress on the final syllable.

Meaning A story in the mass media – radio, television, newspapers, etc. – which reveals the truth about something to the public.

Examples *The exposé triggered off a debate in Parliament.*

We want an exposé of the shady deals of builders.

The local newspaper relies on exposés to survive.

Etymology It comes from the French 'exposer', meaning 'lay open'.

Eye candy

Meaning Can be used to talk about anything that is pleasing to the eye – a human being or an object.

Examples *Madhuri is not just eye candy. She is very bright.*

Buy the basic model. It's not worth paying five thousand rupees extra for eye candy.

Wadekar walked into the party with an eye candy.

Fait accompli /feit ə-kam-plɪ:/

Pronunciation — The first word is pronounced like the word 'fate'. The 'a' in 'accompli' is like the 'a' in 'china' and the 'i' is like the 'ea' in 'beat' and 'meat'. The second syllable rhymes with 'calm' and 'balm'. The word is pronounced 'fate e-calm-**PLII**'.

Meaning — The decision regarding a matter has already been made, and cannot be changed. There is no point in discussing it or arguing against it.

Examples — *Sunder married a woman his parents disapproved of and presented them with a fait accompli.*

When they realized they were being presented a fait accompli, the members became very angry.

Etymology — This French expression means 'an accomplished fact'.

Fantabulous /fæn-tæ-byu-ləs/

Pronunciation — The first syllable is pronounced like 'fan' and the second like the word 'tab'. The last two syllables are like the 'bulous' in 'fabulous'. The word is pronounced 'fan-**TAB**-yu-les'.

Meaning Mostly limited to informal contexts to mean 'great' or 'excellent'.

Examples *Our captain scored a fantabulous century in the first innings.*

The movie was fantabulous.

Etymology It is a combination of 'fantastic' and 'fabulous'.

Fast talk

Meaning To use deceitful talk to get someone to do something; to lie. Mostly used in informal contexts.

Examples *The Minister tried to fast-talk the Manager into lending him more money.*

My father's boss tried to fast-talk him into becoming the Chairman of the Garden Committee.

Fathead

Meaning Used in informal contexts to refer to a stupid person/plan.

Examples *My friend said Venkat is a fathead.*

The members of the Sports Committee came up with a fatheaded plan.

Origin — A fathead is a person who has fat where his/her brains are supposed to be.

Faux pas /fəu pa:/

Pronunciation — The first word is pronounced like the word 'foe' and the second like the word 'pa'. This French expression is pronounced 'foe **PAA**'.

Meaning — To commit a social blunder, to violate certain accepted social rules and, in the process, end up doing something that is socially embarrassing.

Examples — *The speaker apologized to the audience for his faux pas.*

Mahidhar realized that he'd made a serious faux pas by taking something from Kala's plate.

Etymology — A French expression, meaning 'false step'.

Fecund /fi:-kənd/ /fe-kənd/

Pronunciation — The first syllable can rhyme with either 'peak' or 'peck'. The vowel that follows is like the 'a' in 'china'. The word can be pronounced '**FEE**-kend' or '**FE**-kend'.

Meaning — Used in formal contexts to mean 'highly fertile'; can be used with human beings, animals and plants.

Examples — *The fecund soil enabled them to grow crops throughout the year.*

If we don't control these fecund animals, they will overrun the vegetation.

Ram's fecund imagination enabled him to write four wonderful books.

Etymology — From the Latin 'fecundus', meaning 'fruitful' or 'abundant'.

Feisty /fai-stɪ/

Pronunciation — 'Fei' rhymes with 'hi' and 'bye', and the final 'y' is like the 'i' in 'sick' and 'pick'. The word is pronounced '**FY**-sti'.

Meaning — Someone small who is courageous and determined. Can also describe someone who gets upset or angry very quickly.

Examples — *Don't be fooled by Zeenat's looks. She's a feisty old lady.*

Ashwin said something, and my brother got a bit feisty and slapped him.

Etymology — It comes from the word 'feist', meaning 'small dog'.

Festschrift /fest-ʃrift/

Pronunciation — The first syllable rhymes with 'best' and 'nest', and the second is pronounced like 'shrift'. The word is pronounced '**FEST**-shrift'.

Meaning — A volume of essays or research papers given in honour of someone, usually a scholar or a writer, at the time of his retirement.

Examples — *Prof. Shah was given a Festschrift a week before he retired – articles written by all his former research students.*

Janaki has been with us for 30 years. She deserves a Festschrift.

Etymology — From the German 'fest', meaning 'celebration', and 'shrift', meaning 'writing'.

Fiancée /fɪ-ɔn-sei/

Pronunciation — The first syllable is like the 'fi' in 'fill' and 'fit'. The second is pronounced like the word 'on' and the third like the word 'say'. One simple way of pronouncing this word is 'fi-**ON**-say'. Some people put the stress on the third syllable.

Meaning — The woman a man is engaged to, while fiancé (spelt with a single 'é') refers to the man a woman is engaged to.

Examples *At the party, Mohan introduced me to his fiancée.*

I think Reema's fiancé is an accountant.

Fib /fɪb/

Pronunciation Rhymes with 'nib' and 'bib'.

Meaning To lie about something insignificant; a white lie.

Examples *Mahesh says that he finds it difficult to tell a fib.*

Vikram has been fibbing to everyone about his marks.

Etymology Shortening of 'fible-fable', meaning 'nonsense'.

Finesse /fɪ-nes/

Pronunciation The first syllable is like the 'fi' in 'fit', 'fill' and 'fist', and the following 'nesse' is like the 'nes' in 'nest'. The word is pronounced 'fi-**NES**'.

Meaning To display grace under pressure; to exhibit skill in handling people in delicate or difficult situations. It can also be used to refer to someone's graceful or elegant movements.

Examples *James handled the situation with considerable finesse.*

We must try to finesse our way out of this boring party.

Etymology In Old French, 'fin' meant 'subtle' or 'delicate'.

First night

Meaning In India, the expression is always used to refer to the first night spent together by a newly married couple. For a native speaker of English, it always refers to a premiere; the first public performance of a play.

Examples *The star received a thunderous ovation from the first-night audience.*

The actors didn't get too many laughs on the first night.

Fishwife

Meaning A woman who is very unladylike, someone who is unpleasant and swears loudly.

Examples *When I told Deepa that I wouldn't help her, she swore like a fishwife.*

The two elderly ladies were screaming at each other like fishwives.

Origin From the Old English 'wif', meaning 'woman'; a 'fishwife' was a woman who sold fish. In

England, these individuals frequented the famous Billingsgate market, and they were well known for their foul language and loud voice.

Five o'clock shadow

Meaning: The stubbly growth that a man has on his face at the end of the day.

Examples: *Venkat shaves every day. By the time he comes home, however, he has a five o'clock shadow.*

Please shave before the party. That five o'clock shadow makes you look sick.

Origin: This expression is the brainchild of the advertising company that promoted Gem blades and razors. 'That unsightly beard growth which appears prematurely at about 5 p.m. looks bad' was one of their advertisements.

Flabbergasted /flæ-bə-ga:s-tɪd/ /flæ-bə-gæs-tɪd/

Pronunciation: The English pronounce the first 'a' like the 'a' in 'cab' and 'lab', and the second like the 'ar' in 'park', 'dark' and 'mark'. The Americans, on the other hand, pronounce the second 'a' like the 'a' in the first syllable. The first 'e' is like the 'a' in 'china', and the second like the 'i' in 'bit', 'hit' and 'pit'. The word is pronounced '**FLA**-be-gaas-tid'.

Meaning — Mostly used in informal contexts to mean 'to be astounded, surprised or shocked'; to be confused or dazed about what has just happened.

Examples — *When I told Prema she hadn't got the promotion, she sat flabbergasted.*

I was flabbergasted when I saw Meera's grandmother watching the WWF tournament.

Etymology — Some believe it is a combination of 'flabby' and 'aghast'.

Flavour of the month

Meaning — An individual who is in great demand; someone who has suddenly become very popular.

Examples — *Ever since she won the first prize in the debate, Lina has become the flavour of the month.*

Anil Kumble was the flavour of the month when he took all ten wickets against Pakistan.

Flibbertigibbet /flɪ-bə-tɪ-dʒɪ-bɪt/

Pronunciation — The first three syllables rhyme with 'liberty'. The 'g' sounds like the 'j' in 'jam' and 'juice'. The word is pronounced 'fli-be-ti-**JIB**-it'.

Meaning — An old-fashioned word for a silly or talkative person; it is mostly restricted to women.

Examples — *If it is that flibbertigibbet Janaki, tell her I am not at home.*

Everyone thought that Nandini was a flibbertigibbet, so no one took her ideas seriously.

Flip out

Meaning — To lose control of oneself; to suddenly go crazy – used in informal contexts.

Examples — *When Lina heard that she hadn't been promoted, she flipped out.*

When I asked my boss for a raise, he flipped out.

Flippant /flɪp-ənt/

Pronunciation — The first syllable rhymes with 'clip' and 'slip', while the following 'a' is like the 'a' in 'china'. The word is pronounced '**FLIP**-ent'.

Meaning — Not being very serious about something; attempting to be funny or clever.

Examples — *The committee wasn't impressed with the candidate's flippant answers.*

	Usha was irritated by Shekar's flippant comments.
Etymology	The word originally meant 'nimble in talk'.

Floor it

Meaning	To drive at top speed.
Examples	*When the robber noticed he was being followed, he floored it.*
	We have plenty of time. There is no need to floor it.
Origin	To push the accelerator pedal all the way to the floor.

Flummox /flʌm-əks/

Pronunciation	'Flum' rhymes with 'slum', 'glum' and 'plum'. The 'o' in the second syllable is like the 'a' in 'china'. The word is pronounced '**FLUM**-ex'.
Meaning	To be totally confused about something.
Examples	*The Minister was flummoxed by the reporter's question.*
	During the interview, little Anirudh looked flummoxed.
	Sujatha was completely flummoxed by Adithya.

Foible /fɔi-bəl/

Pronunciation The first syllable rhymes with 'toy' and 'boy', while the 'ble' sounds like the 'ble' in 'double' and 'trouble'. The word is pronounced **'FOY-**bel'.

Meaning A weakness or a minor fault in the character of an individual. It can also be used to refer to a strange habit that someone has that may or may not be annoying.

Examples *Nobody is perfect. Even your new girlfriend has her foibles.*

The newly married couple found it difficult to put up with each other's foibles.

Etymology The French 'foible' was originally used to refer to the weakest part of a sword – the portion from the tip to the middle.

Follically challenged /fɔ-lɪk-(ə)-lɪ/

Pronunciation The 'o' in the first syllable is like the 'o' in 'hot', 'pot' and 'got', and the 'i' in the second and the 'y' in the last syllable are pronounced like the 'i' in 'pit' and 'kit'. The word is pronounced **'FO**-lik(e)-li'.

Meaning Someone who is 'follically challenged' is bald.

Examples *Janaki didn't want to marry someone who was follically challenged.*

Some of my cousins and nephews are follically challenged.

Etymology It comes from the Latin 'folliculus', meaning 'a little bag'.

"It cannot be the Chef's hair in your salad, sir! He is follically challenged."

Follow suit

Meaning To imitate someone; to do what someone does.

Examples *Once I tendered my resignation, I thought the others would follow suit. But they didn't.*

Karthik took his family to Singapore, and his brother followed suit.

Etymology The expression comes from the game of cards. In a game like bridge, if the first player drops a spade, then the others must follow suit. In other words, if the other players are holding a spade, they must play a spade as well.

Foodaholic

Meaning Someone who loves to eat; a compulsive eater.

Examples *Anand, I am told, is a foodaholic.*

Sudha is a foodaholic. She had three large pizzas for dinner last night.

Etymology The suffix 'aholic', meaning 'addicted to', is frequently attached to nouns. For example, we have 'shopaholic' (someone addicted to shopping), 'chocoholic', 'golfaholic', 'workaholic', etc.

Foodie

Meaning Someone who takes great delight in food, and loves to eat different varieties of food.

Examples *A foodie like Sarita would love a place like this.*

The foodies in my college are very unhappy with the hostel menu.

Foot the bill

Meaning To pay the bill; to pay the money that is owed.

Examples *I'm willing to come along if you promise to foot the bill.*

If you think Janani is going to foot the bill, you're out of your mind.

Etymology From the now obsolete expression 'foot up', which meant to 'total or add up'. In the 15th century, when a waiter asked you to 'foot up the bill', he wanted you to to add up the figures and make sure that the total at the bottom or the foot of the bill was correct.

Fork out

Meaning To spend money on something or pay someone rather reluctantly.

Examples *Shyam wasn't willing to fork out ten thousand rupees on some old scooter.*

Ananya had to fork out two thousand rupees for the certificates.

Fortuitous /fɒ-tjuː-ɪ-təs/

Pronunciation — The first syllable is like the word 'for' and the 'tui' is like the 'tue' in 'Tuesday'. The 'i' is like the 'i' in 'knit' and 'bit'. The word is pronounced 'for-**TYUU**-i-tes'.

Meaning — Something that occurs by chance; good fortune.

Examples — *It was a fortuitous meeting.*

The downpour at the beginning of the second set was certainly fortuitous.

The goal that Ronaldo scored was a fortuitous one.

Etymology — From the Latin 'forte', meaning 'by chance'.

Fracas /fræ-kəs/

Pronunciation — The first 'a' is like the 'a' in 'cat' and 'act' and the second is like the 'a' in 'china'. '**FRA**-kes' is one way to pronounce the word.

Meaning — A noisy fight or quarrel in which many people are involved.

Examples — *Two students were injured in the fracas that ensued after the results were announced.*

The fracas over demonetization still continues in Parliament.

Etymology From the Italian 'fracassare', meaning 'uproar, crash'.

Fragile /fræ-dʒail/ /fræ-dʒəl/

Pronunciation The 'a' sounds like the 'a' in 'ant' and 'pants'. The British rhyme the second syllable with 'mile' and 'smile'. The Americans pronounce the 'i' like the 'a' in 'china'. The word can be pronounced '**FRA**-jile' or '**FRA**-jel'.

Meaning Something that can be easily broken; not strong. Can be used with people and things.

Examples *Please don't ask Surendran to handle any of the fragile materials. He's clumsy.*

Don't let Malini's fragile looks fool you.

Etymology From the Latin 'fragilis', meaning 'easily broken'.

Franchise /fræn-tʃaiz/

Pronunciation The 'a' in the first syllable is like the 'a' in 'cat', 'bat' and 'rat'; the second syllable rhymes with 'prize', 'rise' and 'lies'. The word is pronounced '**FRAN**-chize'.

Meaning One meaning is an individual's right to vote in an election. Another is when a company or an organisation gives a person the right to sell its products or services in a particular area using its name.

Examples — *In many European countries, women were not given the franchise until the 20th century.*

Ramesh has been given the franchise to sell our clothing line.

Etymology — From the French 'franchise', meaning 'freedom'.

Frazzle /fræ-zəl/

Pronunciation — The word rhymes with 'razzle' and 'dazzle'. It is pronounced '**FRA**-zel'.

Meaning — Mostly used in informal contexts to mean 'completely exhausted' or 'completely burnt'.

Examples — *Shebani had worn herself to a frazzle looking after her ailing father.*

By the time Veda got off the phone, the curry had been burnt to a frazzle.

Rajesh looked frazzled after his PhD viva.

Etymology — From the Middle English 'facelyn', meaning 'to fray'.

Freebie /fri:bɪ/

Pronunciation — The first syllable is pronounced like the word 'free' and the following 'ie' sounds like the 'i' in 'bit' and 'sit'. The word is pronounced '**FREE**-bi'.

Meaning — Something that is given to you free of cost.

Examples — *The CD that you're listening to right now, I got it as a freebie.*

Last week I got a couple of hand towels and mugs as freebies at the supermarket.

Friendly fire

Meaning — Used by the military to refer to a situation where a solider is accidentally killed by his own troops!

Examples — *My best friend was killed by friendly fire.*

We lost ten of our men to friendly fire.

Frogs

Meaning — Insulting term used by the British to refer to the French.

Example — *I don't want you frogs telling me what to do.*

Origin — The French consider frog's legs to be a delicacy. The English started calling their neighbours 'frog eaters'. This was later shortened to 'frogs'.

Fructuous /frʌk-tyu-es/

Pronunciation The first syllable rhymes with 'truck', and the following 'tu' is like the 'tu' in 'tube' and 'Tuesday'. The 'ou' sounds like the 'a' in 'china'. The word is pronounced **'FRUCK-tyu-es'**.

Meaning Fruitful, productive, highly fertile.

Examples *Let's move on. We need to find fructuous land.*

Our CEO believes that this will be the beginning of a fructuous partnership.

Etymology From the Latin 'fructus', meaning 'fruit'.

Fuddy-duddy /fʌ-dɪ dʌ-dɪ/

Pronunciation The two words rhyme with 'muddy', 'bloody' and 'buddy'. It is pronounced **'FUD**-i dud-y'.

Meaning Someone with very old-fashioned ideas. The word is mostly used to show disapproval.

Examples *Many people think that our new Principal is an old fuddy-duddy.*

It's time that all political parties did away with their old fuddy-duddies.

Fudge /fʌdʒ/

Pronunciation Rhymes with 'judge', 'budge' and 'nudge'.

Meaning When used as a verb, it can mean 'to manipulate or adjust'. As a noun, it refers to a sweet.

Examples *During clinical trials, pharmaceutical companies often fudge their data.*

The shareholder must feel our company is doing great. Fudge figures, if you have to.

Pritha made some fudge this afternoon.

Funny bone

Meaning The bone that extends from the shoulder joint to the elbow. Figuratively used to refer to one's sense of humour.

Examples *Ram was in severe pain as he got hit on the funny bone.*

The movie was a disaster. It failed to tickle my funny bone.

Origin The medical term for the 'funny bone' is 'humerus'; it is pronounced the same way as 'humorous'!

Furore /fjuː-rɒ(r)/ /fjuː-rɒ-rɪ/

Pronunciation: The 'u' can be pronounced like the 'u' in 'pull' and 'full', and the following 'rore' like the word 'roar'. The word can be pronounced '**FYU**-roar'. Some people pronounce the final 'e' like the 'i' in 'it', 'pit' and 'bit'. In such cases, the word is pronounced 'fyu-**RO**-ri'.

Meaning: Widespread anger among people about something; a sudden craze or widespread enthusiasm for something.

Examples: *The Centre's decision has caused a furore among the MPs in Andhra Pradesh.*

The furore over my favourite author's new book is yet to die down.

Etymology: The word comes from the Italian 'furor', meaning 'popular admiration'.

Gabfest /gæb-fest/

Pronunciation: The first syllable rhymes with 'cab', 'tab' and 'jab', while the second rhymes with 'test' and 'pest'. The word is pronounced '**GAB**-fest'.

Meaning: People getting together in order to chat or gossip.

Examples: *Praveen tells me that there's a gabfest going on in the ladies hostel.*

	The two-day conference was nothing more than a gabfest.
Origin	It is a combination of 'gab', meaning 'chatter', and 'fest' – the shortened form of 'festival'.

Game

Meaning	If someone is 'game' for something, then he is eager and willing to do it.
Examples	*Sujatha is game for anything that involves a bit of adventure.* *Prahlad is game for anything that involves eating.* *Manaswini is always game for a movie and dinner.*

Game changer

Meaning	Normally used to refer to people or their ideas; someone who has thought out of the box, and whose new idea has changed the way we have been doing things.
Examples	*The Internet is a game changer as far as gathering information is concerned.* *Online shopping proved to be a game changer for our small company.*

Game face

Meaning The look of concentration and determination on someone's face. Usually used in sports.

Examples *Once he's got his game face on and steps onto the field, Chethan is a completely different person.*

Dravid always had his game face on when he was batting. He seldom smiled.

The candidate had her game face on. We knew we were in for a fight.

Garriage

Meaning Same sex marriage.

Examples *Peter sent photographs of his garriage.*

We've not been invited to their garriage.

Origin It is a combination of 'gay' and 'marriage'.

Gaseous

/gei-sɪ-əs/ /gæ-sɪ-əs/

Pronunciation Some people pronounce the first syllable like the word 'gas', while others pronounce the 'ga' like the word 'gay'. The 'seous' rhymes with 'rious' in 'serious'. The word can be pronounced '**GAY**-si-es' or '**GA**-si-es'.

Meaning — Something that is not in the form of a solid or liquid, but in the form of a gas.

Examples — *The teacher told us that steam is water in its gaseous form.*

On a windy day like today, there's no point in spraying that gaseous mixture.

Gauche /gəuʃ/

Pronunciation — One simple way of pronouncing the word is to pronounce the 'gau' like the word 'go'. The final 'che' is like the 'sh' in 'sheep' and 'shop'. The word is pronounced **'GOESH'**.

Meaning — A clumsy person; someone who is awkward and uncomfortable in the presence of others.

Examples — *Richa is a gauche young woman who dreams of becoming a famous movie star.*

You're so different now, Rahul. What happened to that gauche young man whom I met fifteen years ago?

Etymology — The word comes from the French 'gauche', meaning 'left'. In the past, left-handers were considered to be awkward and clumsy.

Geek /gi:k/

Pronunciation — This rather informal word rhymes with 'peek', 'seek' and 'cheek'.

Meaning — A person with little or no social skills. An individual who is an expert or is very knowledgeable in his limited area of interest (for example, computers) can also be called a geek.

Examples — *I don't want you to invite that geek Harish to our party.*

If it is a computer geek you require, you'd better hire Dravid.

I want to learn everything on my own. I don't want some geek telling me everything.

Etymology — The word comes from the Dutch 'geck', meaning 'fool'. The original 'geek' was someone who entertained his audience by biting off a live chicken's/snake's head! With the passage of time, the word began to be used to refer to anyone who was socially inept; whose interests were very different from those of others.

Gelotology /dʒe-lə-t͟ɔ-lə-dʒɪ/

Pronunciation — The first syllable is pronounced like the word 'gel' and the following 'o' is like the 'a' in 'china'. The word is pronounced 'je-le-**TO**-le-ji'.

Meaning — It is the scientific study of laughter and its effects on the human body.

Examples *According to this gelotologist, we must laugh at least ten minutes every day.*

I wonder how gelotologists react when someone tells them that their research is a laughing matter!

Etymology It comes from the Greek 'gelos', meaning 'laughter'.

Geophagy /dʒɪ-ɔ̲f̲-ə-dʒɪ/

Pronunciation The first and last syllables are pronounced like the 'ji' in 'Jim' and 'Jill'. The 'oph' sounds like the word 'off', and the following 'a' is like the 'a' in 'china'. The word is pronounced 'ji-**OFF**-e-ji'.

Meaning The habit of eating soil, mud and clay – a practice common among people and animals.

Examples *Das tells me some of the tribes in Africa engage in geophagy.*

This article makes it clear that geophagy is quite common among both humans and animals.

Etymology From the Greek 'geo', meaning 'earth', and 'phago', meaning 'to eat'. Animals and humans eat clay, mud, etc. in order to obtain the nutrients they require from the soil.

Get fresh with someone

Meaning To behave rather arrogantly or inappropriately with a person; not showing the respect the individual deserves.

Examples *Don't get fresh with me. Do as you are told.*

The secretary accused the boss of getting fresh with her.

Git /gɪt/

Pronunciation Rhymes with 'sit', 'knit' and 'fit'.

Meaning Used in informal contexts to refer to a man who is annoying.

Examples *How could you have fallen in love with a git like him?*

Tell the git standing over there to stop whistling.

Glitch /glɪtʃ/

Pronunciation Rhymes with 'switch', 'hitch' and 'pitch'.

Meaning A small or minor fault in the working of something. The fault, though minor, usually causes a lot of irritation.

Examples — *The computer has developed a glitch. I would like you to look into it.*

We expected a few glitches, but everything went smoothly.

Etymology — From the Yiddish 'glitsh', meaning 'a slip'.

Glitterati /glɪ-tə-raː-tɪ/

Pronunciation — The first two syllables sound like the word 'glitter', and the 'a' is like the 'a' in 'mask', 'flask' and 'task'. The word is pronounced 'gli-te-**RAA**-ti'.

Meaning — People who generally make the Page 3 of a newspaper – film stars, models, the rich and the famous, etc.

Examples — *The glitterati of Bollywood were present at the premiere.*

As expected, the glitterati showed up in full force for the PM's daughter's wedding.

Etymology — Combination of 'glitter' and 'literati'.

Go ballistic

Meaning — To become very angry about something; to lose your cool with someone for no reason at all.

Examples *When Raju heard that Ganesh was not ready with the report, he went ballistic.*

There are times when Amali goes ballistic for no reason at all.

Origin Ballistic missiles soar to great heights and sometimes go out of control.

Go south

Meaning Used in informal contexts in American English to mean 'to deteriorate in value'; to fail.

Examples *When the election results were announced, the stock market went south.*

In case Plan A goes south, I hope you have Plans B and C.

Go viral

Meaning The expression is mostly used to refer to content that is available on the Internet. It means something that spreads very quickly and becomes extremely popular among the public.

Examples *The video of the Minister slapping her aide has gone viral.*

Some years ago, Dhanush's song 'Why this kolaveri di' went viral.

Gobbledygook /gɔbl-dɪ-gu:k/

Pronunciation The first two syllables sound like the word 'gobble'. The following 'y' is like the 'i' in 'pit' and 'fit', and the final vowel sounds like the 'oo' in 'cool', 'pool' and 'fool'. The word is pronounced '**GOB**-el-di-gook'.

Meaning Limited to informal contexts to mean 'nonsense'; can be used to refer to someone's speech and writing.

Examples *Whenever we asked a question, the answers came back in legal gobbledygook.*

Don't bother reading the article. It is nothing more than gobbledygook.

Origin US Congressman Maury Maverick coined this term to refer to the language used by bureaucrats. In one of his memos, he wrote: "Be short and say what you are talking about. Stop 'pointing up' programs. No more 'finalizing', 'effectuating', or 'dynamics'. Anyone using the words 'activation' or 'implementation' will be shot."

Gobsmacked /gɔb-smækt/

Pronunciation The first syllable rhymes with 'sob', 'cob' and 'Bob', and the second half of the word is pronounced like the word 'smacked'. The word is pronounced '**GOB**-smackt'.

Meaning — Mostly used in informal contexts in British English to mean 'to be totally astonished, to be left speechless'.

Examples — *When the CEO was arrested, we were, like everyone else, gobsmacked.*

Sheba was gobsmacked when she was declared the winner.

Etymology — In British English, 'gob' is often used in informal contexts to refer to the mouth. If someone were to 'smack' or hit you hard on the mouth, your automatic reaction would be to cup your hand over it. You would be rendered speechless for a few seconds.

Goldbricker

Meaning — Used in informal contexts to refer to someone who is lazy; someone who spends his time doing nothing.

Examples — *If you think Madhu is a goldbricker, you should meet his mother.*

Let's not waste our time waiting for those two goldbrickers.

Origin — A gold brick is something that looks valuable, but isn't.

Gonna

/gaː-nə/

Pronunciation The 'o' in the first syllable is like the 'a' in 'path' and 'bath', and the following 'a' is like the 'a' in 'china'. The word is pronounced '**GAA**-ne'.

Meaning Going to. This spelling is not acceptable in formal styles of writing.

Examples *I'm gonna to tell the teacher what you did.*

Malathi is gonna to invest in my company.

Origin 'Gonna', 'wanna' and 'gotta' are all examples of Americanisms. Many Americans in their speech reduce 'going to', 'want to' and 'got to' to 'gonna', wanna' and 'gotta', respectively.

Goose pimples

Meaning When someone gets scared or becomes very excited, the hairs on their skin stand up and the skin develops small bumps – it looks like it is covered by a series of dots. These bumps that one gets when one feels scared, excited or cold are called goose pimples.

Examples *The sinister music brought goose pimples to my arms.*

Just thinking about my final exams gave me goose pimples.

Origin It is called goose pimples because when we get excited or scared and get goose pimples, our skin looks like that of a plucked goose. These pimples are sometimes referred to as 'goose bumps' or 'gooseflesh'.

Grade grubbers

Meaning Someone who flatters teachers in order to get good marks/grades.

Examples *During examination time, the teacher is constantly surrounded by grade grubbers.*

The grade grubbers went to the Professor's house to wish her a happy birthday.

As long as we have human beings teaching, we will definitely have grade grubbers.

Origin In American English, a 'grubber' is someone who begs or pleads for something.

Graduand /græd-ju-ænd/

Pronunciation The first 'a' is like the 'a' in 'ant', 'anti' and 'and', and the following 'du' sounds like the 'du' in 'duty'. The final syllable sounds like the word 'and'. The word is pronounced '**GRAD**-ju-and'.

Meaning Someone who is about to graduate. He has completed all the necessary formalities.

Examples — *Leela hasn't received her certificate as yet. She's still a graduand.*

The angry graduands stormed into the Principal's office.

Etymology — From the Latin 'graduandus', meaning 'to have a degree'.

Gratuitous /grə-tju:-ɪ-təs/

Pronunciation — The 'a' and the final 'ou' are pronounced like the 'a' in 'china'. The 'tu' in the second syllable sounds like the 'tu' in 'Tuesday', and the following 'i' like the 'i' in 'bit', 'hit' and 'pit'. The word is pronounced 'gre-**TYUU**-i-tes'.

Meaning — Nowadays, the word is mostly used to mean 'unwanted' or 'unnecessary'. The word can also be used to mean 'excessive'.

Examples — *Teenagers loved the gratuitous violence and nudity in the film.*

I am sick and tired of Anamika's gratuitous advice.

Etymology — From the Latin 'gratuitus', meaning 'done without pay, voluntary'.

Graveyard shift

Meaning — The shift in a factory from midnight to eight in the morning.

Examples — *We have to cancel our plans. I am working the graveyard shift next week.*

My kids don't want me to do any more graveyard shifts.

Origin — During the Second World War, many factories worked 24 hours a day. When you worked the graveyard shift, you worked at a time when the town was as quiet as a graveyard!

Gravitas /græ-vɪ-tæs/

Pronunciation — The 'a' in the first and third syllables can be pronounced like the 'a' in 'cat', 'bat' and 'sat'. The 'i' in the second sounds like the 'i' in 'bit', 'sit' and 'hit'. The word can be pronounced '**GRA**-vi-tas'.

Meaning — Used to refer to an individual's demeanour; his serious appearance and the way he behaves with others compels them to treat him with respect.

Examples — *The new Vice Chancellor has an air of gravitas about her.*

Vani lacks the gravitas required to become a CEO.

Etymology — From the Latin 'gravitas', meaning 'weight, heaviness'.

Greenhorn

Meaning — A person with little or no experience; someone who can be easily duped or cheated.

Examples — *How could you give a greenhorn like Dilip the job?*

Don't underestimate Sudha. She is no greenhorn.

Origin — When it was first used in the United States, it referred to a young ox or bull – since these animals were inexperienced and their horns hadn't matured, they were called 'greenhorns'. The following century, new army recruits began to be called 'greenhorns'.

Grossed out /grəust aut/

Pronunciation — The 'o' in 'gross' is like the 'o' in 'so', 'no' and 'go'.

Meaning — Used in informal contexts in American English to mean 'to fill someone with disgust'.

Examples *The murder scenes in the movie were very graphic. They grossed me out.*

The smell from the sewage grossed me out.

Ground zero

Meaning Today, the term is used informally to mean 'a place of rapid development or change; a place of violent activity'. It is also used to mean 'elementary level'; a 'starting point'.

Examples *About ten years ago, no one had heard about Vasudeva Nagar. But today, it has become the ground zero from which restaurants and designer shops radiate.*

Many of my students will be starting at ground zero.

My boss didn't like the ad campaign. Looks like I have to return to ground zero.

Origin The site at which an atomic explosion takes place.

Grungy /grʌn-dʒɪ/

Pronunciation 'Grun' rhymes with 'bun' and 'run', and the following 'g' is like the 'j' in 'jam' and 'juice'. The word is pronounced '**GRUN**-ji'.

Meaning Smelly and dirty.

Examples	*Anu tried to put us up in a grungy little hotel.*
	Get your grungy feet off my new sofa.
Origin	Combination of 'grubby' and 'dingy'.

Gubernatorial /gu:bə-nə-tɒ-rɪ-əl/

Pronunciation	'Guber' rhymes with 'uber', and the following 'a' is like the 'a' in 'china'. The next three syllables sound like the 'torial' in 'tutorial'. It is pronounced 'goo-be-ne-**TO**-ri-el'.
Meaning	The word means 'of or relating to the governor'. The Indian media are extremely fond of this word.
Example	*It is difficult to predict which party will win the gubernatorial elections.*
Etymology	From the Latin 'gubernare', meaning 'to steer or govern'. When Arnold Schwarzenegger, the star of the *Terminator* series, was the Governor of California, he was frequently referred to as 'Gubernator'.

Guesstimate

Meaning	To make an educated guess; a rough estimate; to make a prediction without adequate information.

Examples *Vittal's guesstimate is that the share prices will go up by another Rs. 50.*

Bhanu's task is to guesstimate how many will buy the product.

Etymology 'Guesstimate' began to be used by statisticians in the 1930s. It is a combination of two words: 'guess' and 'estimate'.

Guilt trip

Meaning To feel extremely guilty about something. It could be because you have done something wrong, or because you have not done something that you were supposed to have. It can be used as a verb as well.

Examples *Every time my father's aunt visits us, my parents have a guilt trip. I guess it's because they never keep in touch with her or her children.*

If you don't buy these tickets, you'll have a guilt trip.

Don't pay any attention to her disappointed looks. The kid is just trying to guilt-trip you into buying the ice cream.

Gun-shy

Meaning A person who is afraid of guns and tries to keep away from them. Nowadays, it is used to refer to an individual who is very timid and afraid of taking risks.

Examples — *After their last bridge collapsed, the company is gun-shy about building new ones.*

The leaders are worried about the situation and are gun-shy about talking to reporters.

Origin — The word 'shy' is often added to nouns like 'camera', 'gun' and 'publicity' to mean that that an individual is not particularly fond of that thing.

Gung-ho /gʌŋ-həu/

Pronunciation — 'Gung' rhymes with 'sung' and 'rung' and the following 'ho' rhymes with 'so', 'no' and 'go'. It is pronounced 'gung-**HO**'.

Meaning — Mostly used in informal contexts to mean 'enthusiastic or eager' – especially, to fight.

Examples — *The students were gung-ho about the new proposal.*

In Top Gun, *a very young Tom Cruise was a gung-ho fighter pilot.*

Etymology — From the Chinese 'kung ho', meaning 'work together'.

Gymnophobia /dʒɪm-nə-fəu-bɪ-ə/

Meaning — Fear of nudity – it could be the fear of seeing someone else or yourself naked.

Examples — *Mayank doesn't shower at the pool because he's gymnophobic.*

Jaidev refused to come to the nude beach because he has gymnophobia.

Etymology — 'Gym' comes from the Greek 'gumnos', meaning 'naked'. In the past, when an athlete went to the gymnasium, he trained naked. In ancient times, women were not allowed to witness any of the events at the Olympics because all the participants were men, and many chose to perform without a stitch on.

Hackneyed /hæk-nɪd/ /hæk-ni:d/

Pronunciation — The first syllable rhymes with 'back', 'sack' and 'pack', and the following 'neyed' rhymes with the words 'bid', 'did' and 'lid'. One way of pronouncing the word is '**HACK**-nid'. Some people pronounce the second syllable like the word 'need'.

Meaning — A phrase or a word that has been overused; an idea that is trite or unoriginal.

Examples — *The storyline was hackneyed, but the lead actors did a great job.*

You cannot expect the party to win with such hackneyed slogans.

Etymology — 'Hackney' is the name of a village in Middlesex, England.

Half-wit

Meaning — Used in informal contexts to refer to someone who is rather foolish or stupid.

Examples — *The company has hired a bunch of half-wits to do the job.*

I'm not going to let you marry a half-wit like Ravi.

Chalapthi, a notable wit, died in a car accident last night.

Etymology — A 'wit' is someone who has the gift of the gab; he keeps the listener amused with his skilful play on words. The term 'half-wit' was originally used to refer to a writer of mediocre wit; he failed in his attempts to be funny half the time!

Ham actor

Meaning — An actor who is overly theatrical; can be used to refer to people who draw attention to themselves by being overly dramatic.

Examples — *As expected, the acting was pure ham.*

Why did they choose that old ham for the main part?

Origin — Struggling actors made use of pig fat or 'ham fat' to remove their make-up. This practice led to actors being called 'hamfatters'; it was later shortened to 'ham'. Another theory is that the word comes from the title of Shakespeare's play, *Hamlet*. Many of the actors who played the hero were often very theatrical.

Hamburger

Meaning — Ground beef, and not ham, served on a bun.

Examples — *Hamburgers are very popular among college students.*

It's called a hamburger! But the meat inside is beef.

Origin — It was given this name because it first became popular in the city of Hamburg in Germany.

Hand-me-down

Meaning — A piece of clothing or something else that is handed down from one person to another.

Examples — *This shirt is a hand-me-down from my brother.*

Everything that you see in this room is a hand-me-down. Including that TV.

Origin The term was originally used to refer to the clothes that were handed down from the older children to the younger ones.

Hand-me-up

Meaning Gadgets passed on from the younger generation to the older generation – from children to their parents/grandparents.

Examples *The iPod that my grandmother is using is a hand-me-up. My aunt gave it to her.*

I have stopped wasting money on gadgets. I make do with whatever hand-me-ups I get from my grandchildren.

Harass /hæ-rəs/ /hə-ræs/

Pronunciation The British tend to pronounce the first 'a' like the 'a' in 'cat', 'bat' and 'pat', and the second like the 'a' in 'china'. The word is pronounced '**HA**-res'. Americans do the exact opposite. They pronounce the word 'he-**RASS**'.

Meaning To annoy or upset someone; to make a nuisance of yourself.

Examples — *Malini has filed a complaint saying that you've been harassing her.*

The police harassed Vatsala into withdrawing her complaint.

Etymology — From the French 'harasser', meaning to 'vex' or 'tire out'.

Hard sell

Meaning — An aggressive approach to selling a product; using every means available to get the client/ customer to buy the product.

Examples — *The agent gave my father the hard sell, but he refused to buy a new policy.*

I enquired about the price of the scooter and the salesperson gave me the hard sell.

Hard up

Meaning — Mostly used in informal contexts to mean 'not having enough money'; be strapped for cash.

Examples — *Mithun said that he was too hard up to buy his wife a birthday present.*

I am pretty hard up right now. So I have decided to put off my trip to Goa.

Head-hunter

Meaning A term used in the corporate world to refer to someone who goes around trying to persuade people to quit their job and take up another one. The person is usually hired by a company to get top executives from other companies.

Examples *When our General Manager went to Mumbai for a conference, he was approached by several head-hunters.*

I would like to be a head-hunter when I grow up.

"When I said that we need to hire a head-hunter to find the right person, he's not what I had in mind!"

Heads up

Meaning: To warn someone that something is going to happen, and that he needs to be prepared for whatever may come his way. The expression is also frequently used in everyday contexts to refer to someone who is wide awake and alert.

Examples: *We got the heads up about the Chairman's proposed visit.*

Surprisingly, our team played a very heads-up game.

Origin: A person who is wide awake and alert usually keeps his head up to ensure that he is able to see what is happening around him.

Heartsink patient

Meaning: A patient who creates problems for the poor doctor; someone who visits the doctor repeatedly and keeps complaining about his unidentifiable ailments. Whenever the doctor sees such a patient walking into his office, his heart sinks!

Examples: *According to this article, heartsink patients cause anxiety and stress among doctors.*

The surgeon has labelled Sunaina a heartsink patient.

Heebie-jeebies /hi:bɪ-dʒi:biz/

Pronunciation — The 'ee' in both words is like the 'ee' in 'fee', 'bee' and 'see', and the 'ie' sounds like the 'i' in 'it', 'kit' and 'hit'. The final 's' is like the 'z' in 'zip' and 'zoo'. The word is pronounced 'hee-bi **JEE**-biz'.

Meaning — An informal word, meaning 'extremely nervous'.

Examples — *My school Principal gives me the heebie-jeebies.*

There's something about a visit to the dentist that gives me the heebie-jeebies.

Watching scary movies at night gives me the heebie-jeebies.

Origin — The word was coined by the American cartoonist, WB Debeck.

Hegemony /hɪ-dʒem-ə-ni:/

Pronunciation — One way is to pronounce the first syllable like the 'hi' in 'hit' and 'hill', and the second syllable like the word 'gem'. The 'o' sounds like the 'a' in 'china' and the final 'y' like the 'ee' in 'knee' and 'see'. The word can be pronounced 'hi-**JEM**-e-knee'.

Meaning Formal word used to refer to a situation in which one group has more control or power than the others.

Example *India and China are not willing to accept US hegemony.*

Etymology From the Greek 'hegemonia', meaning 'leadership'.

Heinous /hei-nəs/ /hiː-nəs/

Pronunciation There are different ways of pronouncing this rather formal word. One way is to pronounce the first syllable like the word 'hay' or make the syllable rhyme with 'bee', 'fee' and 'see'. The 'ou' that follows sounds like the 'a' in 'china'. The word can be pronounced '**HAY**-nes' or '**HEE**-nes'.

Meaning A 'heinous' crime is one that is evil or wicked; it is the sort of crime that deserves our contempt.

Examples *The soldier was accused of committing heinous crimes during the war.*

I cannot believe that somebody like Shilpa would commit such heinous crimes.

Etymology It comes from the Old French 'hainos', meaning 'hateful, unpleasant'.

Heir /ɜə/

Pronunciation The word is pronounced 'air' and not 'hair'.

Meaning A person who will legally inherit the money, title and property of another when the latter dies.

Examples *The King is without heir.*

Paul is heir to his father's millions.

Etymology From the Latin 'heres', meaning 'successor'.

Heist /haist/

Pronunciation The 'hei' is pronounced like the word 'high'. The word is pronounced **'HIGHST'**.

Meaning A well-organised attempt to steal something very valuable from a place or a person – one usually talks about a 'bank heist' and 'jewellery heist'.

Examples *The bank heist had been meticulously planned.*

The thieves heisted my neighbour's new BMW.

Origin It is American in origin, and according to some scholars, it is a dialectal variation of 'hoist', meaning 'to lift'. The word 'heist' was first used to refer to shoplifters.

Helicopter parents

Meaning — Parents who keep a very close watch on their children and all their activities.

Examples — *Maya's helicopter mother accompanied her to the party.*

Priyanka has never had to deal with problems. Her helicopter parents always solved them for her.

Young man: "I told you that I had helicopter parents."

Young woman: "You did. But I didn't expect them to follow us on our honeymoon."

Origin — They are so called because like the helicopter, they hover, and in the process, become overly involved in their children's life. Some would call this 'over-parenting'.

Hex

Meaning — To put a curse or a spell on someone.

Examples — *Sania has lost in the first round again. I wonder if someone has put a hex on her.*

Tanya is just not eating. She's lost twenty pounds in two weeks. Do you think someone has hexed her?

Every time India plays in this stadium, they lose. Someone has put a hex on it.

Etymology — From the German 'hexe', meaning 'to practice witchcraft'.

Higgledy-piggledy /hɪ-gəl-dɪ pɪ-gəl-dɪ/

Pronunciation — 'Higgle' and 'piggle' rhyme with 'wiggle' and 'wriggle'. The final 'y' is pronounced like the 'i' in 'fit', 'bit' and 'hit'. The word is pronounced 'hi-gel-di **PIG**-el-di'. Some people pronounce the 'y' like the 'ee' in 'see' and 'fees'.

Meaning — Untidy; mostly used in informal contexts to mean scattered.

Examples *When I walked into her room, I found papers higgledy-piggledy on the floor.*

Jewels were scattered higgledy-piggledy about the movie star's bedroom.

Meera's car was piled higgledy-piggledy with suitcases, boxes, pots, pans and buckets.

Origin Some people believe that the messy appearance of a pigsty may have given rise to this expression.

High maintenance

Meaning A woman who is very demanding – a woman who expects a lot of attention and gifts from her partner. The opposite is 'low maintenance'.

Examples *Taranath's new girlfriend is extremely high maintenance.*

Sandeep's high-maintenance girlfriend wants a diamond ring for her twenty-fifth birthday.

Origin It became popular because of the movie, *When Harry Met Sally*.

Highfalutin /hai-fə-lu:-tin/

Pronunciation The first syllable is pronounced like the word 'high', and the following 'a' sounds like the 'a' in 'china'. The 'lut' sounds like the word 'loot'. The word is pronounced 'high-fe-**LOO**-tin'.

Meaning Informal word for pretentious or pompous.

Examples *Some of our Chairman's speeches are written in a highfalutin style.*

I don't like Sujatha's highfalutin ideas.

When writing books for children, don't use highfalutin language.

Origin Could be from 'high-flying' or 'high-flown'.

Hobby-horse

Meaning A subject or an idea that an individual has very strong feelings about. He loves talking about it at great length whenever he gets an opportunity to.

Examples *Corruption is a favourite hobby-horse of my father's.*

Using songs in the language classroom is his favourite hobby-horse.

Origin A hobby-horse was a child's rocking horse. The term was also used to refer to the stick which had a horse's head at one end.

Hogwash

Meaning Nonsense.

Examples *Enough of this hogwash. Now sit down and tell me what really happened.*

I have no time to listen to your hogwash, Seema.

The stuff that was served at the wedding was hogwash.

Etymology — Scraps of food (wash) from the kitchen given to pigs (hogs).

Hoi polloi /hɔi pə-<u>lɔi</u>/

Pronunciation — The 'hoi' and 'loi' rhyme with 'toy' and 'boy'. The 'o' in the first syllable of 'polloi' is like the 'a' in 'china'. The word is pronounced 'hoy pe-**LOY**'.

Meaning — Normally used to refer to the common people – the working class. Some people find this term offensive.

Examples — *The entry fee was kept very high to keep the hoi polloi out.*

Ganesh doesn't particularly enjoy rubbing shoulders with the hoi polloi.

Etymology — In Greek, 'hoi' means 'the' and 'polloi' means 'many'; it literally means 'the many'.

Homage /<u>hɔ</u>-mɪdʒ/

Pronunciation — The 'o' in the first syllable sounds like the 'o' in 'hot', 'pot' and 'got', and the final 'age' rhymes with 'idge' in 'fridge' and 'ridge'. The word is pronounced '**HO**-mij'.

Meaning — When you pay 'homage' to someone, you usually show respect to him and say nice things about him. You have great admiration for the person, and as a result, praise him for his achievements.

Examples — *We must pay homage to the man and his incredible achievements.*

The documentary pays homage to the outstanding athletes of the decade.

Etymology — From the French 'hommage', meaning 'allegiance'.

Hominist /hɔ-mɪ-nɪst/

Pronunciation — The 'o' sounds like the 'o' in 'hot' and 'pot' and the 'i' in the second and third syllables is like the 'i' in 'bit' and 'fit'. The word is pronounced '**HO**-mi-nist'.

Meaning — A man who believes that men should have the same rights as women.

Examples — *They say your friend Bala is a hominist.*

The hominists in the crowd booed the speaker.

Etymology — George Bernard Shaw coined the word in the preface to his play, *Man and Superman*

(1903). Another word that is commonly used now is 'masculinist'.

Honcho

/hɔn-tʃəu/ /hɔn-ʃəu/

Pronunciation: The first 'o' is pronounced like the 'o' in 'stop', 'pop' and 'top', and the second like the 'o' in 'go', 'so' and 'no'. The 'ch' can be pronounced like the 'ch' in 'chips' and 'cheap' or like the 'sh' in 'ship' and 'shoot'. The word can be pronounced '**HON**-cho' or '**HON**-sho'.

Meaning: Mainly used in American English in informal contexts to mean 'the person in charge'. When used as a verb, it means to 'manage or boss something'.

Examples: *Sachi was made the marketing honcho last week.*

The head honcho of the company didn't know a thing.

When Dilip fell ill, Vijay began to honcho his affairs.

Etymology: It comes from the Japanese 'hancho', meaning 'group leader'.

Honeymoon

Meaning: Nowadays, the word is used to refer to the early stages of any relationship where both parties are exceedingly happy with each other.

Examples *The Chief Minister's honeymoon with the media is definitely over.*

Right now, there are no problems. We're still in the honeymoon phase.

Origin In the old days, it was customary in Greece for the newly married couple to drink mead, a fermented drink made from honey, for a period of one month. The 'moon' in the word refers to the thirty days they drank and made merry. After the initial euphoria, the couple realized that their love for each other would not remain constant, but would wax and wane like the moon!

Honey trap

Meaning Mostly used in British English to refer to the strategy of using attractive people to entrap or get information from someone. The expression has a positive meaning as well. It can be used to mean 'something that is most attractive'.

Examples *Our competitors may set up a honey trap to get you to spill the beans.*

The Taj Mahal is a honey trap for most tourists.

Origin — The term was first used in the world of espionage, and now it is frequently used in the world of journalism.

Hooch /huːtʃ/

Pronunciation — The 'hoo' sounds like the word 'who' and the following 'ch' is like the 'ch' in 'which', 'rich' and 'pitch' – '**HUUCH**'.

Meaning — Used in very informal contexts in American English to refer to any alcoholic beverage that has been made illegally.

Examples — *Dilip offered me some hooch, but I turned it down.*

I would like to have some more of that hooch, please.

Origin — It comes from 'Hoochinoo' – the name of a Native American tribe in Alaska who made liquor.

Hors-de-combat /ɒ-də-kɔmːbaː/

Pronunciation — The 'h' and 's' are silent in 'hors'; the word is pronounced like the 'aw' in 'saw', 'jaw' and 'paw'. The vowel that follows is like the 'a' in 'china'. The 'at' in 'combat' sounds like the 'a' in 'path' and 'bath'. One possible way of pronouncing the word is 'aw-de-**COM**-baa'.

Meaning Unable to participate because of an injury.

Examples *Gayathri has hurt her back. She's hors-de-combat as far as tennis is concerned.*

The General spent time with the hors-de-combat at the hospital.

Etymology The French expression literally means 'out of combat'.

Horse sense

Meaning Common sense. Mostly used in American English in informal contexts.

Examples *Malini may be very intelligent. But she has no horse sense.*

Vasundara has too much horse sense to marry someone like Pujara.

Origin The expression was originally used to refer to the plain, unsophisticated mode of thinking that people in the countryside had.

Hotfoot

Meaning Mostly used in informal contexts to mean 'to run or walk quickly to some place'; reaching one's destination without delay.

Examples *When the car broke down, the CEO and his wife were forced to hotfoot it to the airport.*

I got up late yesterday. So I had to hotfoot it to school.

Howled down /haul-daun/

Pronunciation 'Howl' rhymes with 'foul', 'owl' and 'prowl'.

Meaning To prevent someone from talking by shouting or screaming at them.

Examples *The Minister was howled down by the union members.*

As expected, the Principal was howled down by the students.

Hubris /hju:-brɪs/

Pronunciation The 'hu' sounds like the 'hu' in 'huge', 'human' and 'humour', and the 'i' that follows is like the 'i' in 'hit', 'pit' and 'bit'. The word is pronounced '**HYUU**-bris'.

Meaning Nowadays, the word is mostly used in formal contexts to mean 'arrogance or pride'; it is always used to show disapproval.

Examples *The Minister's monumental hubris resulted in the party workers rebelling.*

The hubris that Sanjay demonstrates is totally unwarranted. He is not half as intelligent as he thinks he is.

Etymology — It comes from the Greek 'hybris', meaning 'outrage, insolence'. In Greek literature and mythology, very often it was hubris that ultimately led to a character's downfall.

Hullabaloo /hʌ-lə-bə-lu:/

Pronunciation — The first syllable rhymes with 'dull', 'cull' and 'null'; the 'a' in the second and third syllables is like the 'a' in 'china'. The final 'oo' is pronounced like the 'oo' in 'pool' and 'fool'. The word is pronounced 'hu-le-be-**LOO**'. Some people put the stress on the first syllable.

Meaning — Mostly used in informal contexts to mean a lot of noise made by people who are angry or annoyed. The word suggests disturbance.

Examples — *Deepa Mehta stopped production of her film because of all the hullabaloo it caused.*

The students gathered outside the Vice Chancellor's office and made a real hullabaloo about some of the new courses that were being offered.

Humdinger /hʌm-dɪŋ-ə/

Pronunciation — The first syllable rhymes with 'sum' and 'rum', and the following 'dinger' rhymes with 'singer' and 'ringer'. The word is pronounced '**HUM**-ding-e'.

Meaning — Used in informal contexts to mean 'excellent' or 'marvellous'. It can be used to refer to a person or a thing.

Examples — *The two matches between South Africa and Australia were humdingers.*

Gopal is a humdinger of a guy, all right.

Origin — 'Dinger' was something extraordinary and 'hummer' meant 'full of energy'. This American expression was originally used to refer to a beautiful woman.

Humongous /hju:-mʌŋ-gəs/

Pronunciation — The first syllable rhymes with 'few', 'cue' and 'due', and the following 'mong' with 'rung' and 'dung'. The word is pronounced 'hyuu-**MUNG**-es'.

Meaning — Used in informal contexts to mean 'something that is huge or enormous'.

Examples — *Anita lives in a humongous house in Mumbai.*

Ravi's father-in-law has a humongous nose.

My favourite hero's latest movie is a humongous hit.

Etymology — Combination of 'huge' and 'monstrous'.

Hunky-dory /hʌŋ-kɪ dɒ-rɪ/

Pronunciation 'Hunk' rhymes with 'skunk' and 'punk', and the 'dor' sounds like the word 'door'. The word is pronounced 'hun-ki **DOOR**-i'.

Meaning Used in informal contexts to mean that everything is fine and that everyone is happy with a particular situation.

Examples *Everything was hunky-dory at the party.*

Things weren't exactly hunky-dory during the honeymoon.

Mohan expected fireworks at the meeting. But everything was hunky-dory.

Etymology From the Dutch 'honk', meaning 'home' or 'place of refuge'.

Hydrophobia /hai-drəu-fəu-bi-jə/

Pronunciation The first syllable is like the word 'hi', and the 'o' in the second and third syllables is pronounced like the 'oe' in 'toe', 'doe' and 'Joe'. The word is pronounced 'hai-droe-**PHO**-bi-ye'.

Meaning Fear of water; often a symptom that the person has rabies.

Examples *Dilip is hydrophobic. He can't even get into a bathtub.*

	Three days after the stray dog bit him, Ganesh began to show symptoms of hydrophobia.
Etymology	From the Greek 'hydro', meaning 'water', and 'phobia', meaning 'fear'.

Hymn /hɪm/

Pronunciation	It is pronounced like the word 'him'.
Meaning	A song usually sung in praise of God.
Examples	*The parents were forcing the children to listen to hymns.* *To get the audience involved, we must sing hymns that everyone knows.*
Etymology	From the Greek 'hymnos', meaning 'festive song'.

Hype /haip/

Pronunciation	Rhymes with 'type' and 'pipe'.
Meaning	To attract the attention of others through advertisements, discussions, etc.
Examples	*Before the movie was released, there was a lot of hype.* *There's been a lot of hype surrounding Roy's new book.*

Etymology Some think 'hype' is a short form of 'hyperbole', an exaggerated statement.

Hyperbole /hai-p3:-bə-lɪ/

Pronunciation The word consists of four syllables, not three. The 'hy' is pronounced like the word 'hi', and the following syllable, like the word 'per'. The 'o' is like the 'a' in 'china', and the final 'e' sounds like the 'i' in 'bit', sit' and 'hit'. The word is pronounced 'hi-**PER**-be-li'.

Meaning When you use hyperbole in your speech or writing, you make someone sound much more important than he actually is – you exaggerate the person's importance.

Examples *When you introduce the speaker, please avoid hyperbole.*

One thing that he doesn't believe in is hyperbole.

Etymology From the Greek 'hyperbole', meaning 'exaggeration' or 'extravagance'.

Hypochondriac /hai-pəu-kɔn-drɪ-æk/

Pronunciation The first syllable sounds like 'hi' and the second rhymes with 'so', 'go' and 'Joe'. The 'chon' is pronounced like the word 'con', and the final 'a' like the 'a' in 'ant' and 'pants'.

	The word is pronounced 'hi-poe-**KON**-dri-ak'. Some people pronounce the vowel in the second syllable like the 'a' in 'china'.
Meaning	Someone who constantly worries about his health, even when there is no need to.
Examples	*The movie is about an ageing hypochondriac.*
	We have a few hypochondriacs in our family.
Etymology	It comes from the Greek 'hypo', meaning 'under', and 'khondros', meaning 'cartilage' – false ribs. The ancient Greeks believed that melancholy – the feeling of sadness – was located in this area.

Ibid

/ɪ̱-bɪd/

Pronunciation	The 'i' in the first and second syllables is like the 'i' in 'sit' and 'bit'. The word is pronounced '**I**-bid'.
Meaning	The word is mostly used in formal styles of writing to refer to a source you have quoted or cited. It means that the quote is from the same place/source – it is from the same book, by the same author, etc.
Etymology	It comes from the Latin 'ibidem', meaning 'in the same place'.

Idiosyncrasy /ɪ-dɪ-jəu-sɪŋ-krə-sɪ/

Pronunciation — The first 'i' and the final 'y' are pronounced like the 'i' in 'knit', 'kit' and 'kiss'; the 'dio' is like the 'dio' in 'radio'. The 'sync' is like the word 'sink', and the following 'a' sounds like the 'a' in 'china'. The word is pronounced 'i-di-o-**SIN**-kre-si'.

Meaning — The word can be spelt 'idiosyncracy' or 'idiosyncrasy', and it is normally used to refer to an individual's peculiarities or habits. The word can be used with objects as well.

Examples — *One of his idiosyncrasies was to smell his socks before putting them on.*

Raj didn't like it when his wife made fun of his idiosyncrasies.

Etymology — From the Greek 'idios', meaning 'one's own', and 'synkrasis', meaning 'mixture of personal characteristics'.

Idiot box

Meaning — Television.

Examples — *The children spend too much time in front of the idiot box.*

Let's see what's on the idiot box.

Origin — TV often reduces us to idiots. When we watch television, we become hypnotised; we seldom think. A person who is completely immersed in the programme that he is watching is said to be 'TV stoned'!

Idyllic

/ɪ-dɪ-lɪk/ /ai-dɪ-lɪk/

Pronunciation — The British tend to pronounce the 'i' and the 'y' like the 'i' in 'sit' and 'hit'. The Americans, on the other hand, tend to pronounce the 'i' like the word 'eye'. The word can be pronounced '**I**-di-lick' or '**EYE**-di-lick'.

Meaning — A short piece of prose which describes a happy scene in the countryside is usually referred to as an idyll. Nowadays, the word is used to refer to any pleasant scene or event.

Examples — *This would be an idyllic setting for our school.*

Herbert was hoping that he would have an idyllic marriage.

Iffy

/ɪf-ɪ/

Pronunciation — The first syllable is pronounced like 'if' and the 'y' like the 'i' in 'sit' and 'bit'. The word is pronounced '**IF**-i'.

Meaning — Doubtful, not suitable.

Examples *The weather looked iffy, so we decided not to go on the picnic.*

Remya says that this morning's dhal smells a bit iffy.

I think Achala is still a bit iffy about doing a PhD.

Ignoramus /ɪg-nə-rei-məs/

Pronunciation The 'ig' sounds like the 'ig' in 'pig', 'fig' and 'dig', while the following 'o' and the final 'u' are pronounced like the 'a' in 'china'. The third syllable is pronounced like the word 'ray'. The word is pronounced 'ig-ne-**RAY**-mes'.

Meaning It is mostly used to mean 'a stupid or an ignorant person'.

Examples *How could you hire an ignoramus like Mala for the job?*

The actor called the critic an ignoramus.

Etymology Ignoramus is an example of how the meaning of a word can change over time. It was originally a term used in law to mean 'we don't know'. But when George Ruggle wrote his play *Ignoramus* in the early 17th century, the word acquired its present meaning. The main character in the play was a lawyer named Ignoramus who knew little or nothing about law.

Ilk /ɪlk/

Pronunciation — The word rhymes with 'silk' and 'milk'.

Meaning — The members of one's family; can also be used to mean 'type' or 'sort'. It is mostly used to show disapproval.

Examples — *Ram Mohan and his ilk were present at the wedding.*

I think it's foolish on our part to trust people of that ilk.

Etymology — 'Ilk' comes from the Old English 'ilca', meaning 'same'.

Imbroglio /ɪm-brəu-lɪ-əu/

Pronunciation — The first syllable rhymes with 'him' and 'dim', and the following 'brog' is pronounced like the word 'bro'. The final 'o' rhymes with 'no', 'go' and 'so'. The word is pronounced 'im-**BRO**-li-o'.

Meaning — Literary word, mostly used in formal contexts to mean 'a very confusing, embarrassing or complicated situation'.

Examples — *The imbroglio was the result of the new tax laws.*

Most countries are keen to withdraw their troops from the Afghanistan imbroglio.

Etymology From the Italian 'imbrogliare', meaning 'confuse, tangle'.

Impugn /ɪm-pju:n/

Pronunciation The first syllable rhymes with 'him' and 'rim'; the following 'pugn' rhymes with 'tune' and 'dune'. This formal word is pronounced 'im-**PYUUN**'.

Meaning Calling into question the integrity of an individual.

Examples *When nothing else worked, the candidate started impugning his opponent's character.*

I don't think you should impugn Govind's competence as a teacher.

Etymology The word comes from the Latin 'impugnare', meaning 'to assault, to attack'. The word originally meant 'to beat someone physically'; nowadays, it is used to refer to a verbal assault.

In loco parentis /ɪn ləu-kəu pə-ren-tɪs/

Pronunciation The 'o' in 'loco' is pronounced like the 'o' in 'go', 'so' and 'no'. The 'a' in 'parentis' is like the 'a' in 'china', while the following syllable sounds like 'rent'. The final vowel is like the 'i' in 'bit' and 'sit'. The word is pronounced 'in lo-co pe-**REN**-tis'.

Meaning — To act as the guardian of a child; to take on the responsibilities of a parent.

Examples — *I certainly don't want to stand in loco parentis to Jai's son Harish.*

Since Sujatha was the teacher, she was made in loco parentis.

Etymology — Latin expression, meaning 'in place of a parent'. 'Loco' means 'place' and 'parentis' means 'parent'.

In toto

/ɪn təu-təu/

Pronunciation — The 'to' in both syllables is pronounced like the word 'toe'. The word is pronounced 'in **TOE**-toe'.

Meaning — Latin expression, meaning 'completely' or 'entirely'.

Examples — *The Vice Chancellor rejected the new proposal in toto.*

You can't expect me to accept everything in toto.

In your face

Meaning — Someone who is 'in your face' irritates you and is ready to pick a fight with you; he is very confrontational. Used in informal contexts.

Examples — *I am sick and tired of my boss's in-your-face attitude.*

I like Jamal because he's not one of those in-your-face guys.

I generally don't like people who are always in my face about something.

Inchoate /ɪn-kəu-eit/

Pronunciation — The first syllable sounds like the word 'in', and the second like the prefix 'co'. The final syllable is pronounced like the word 'ate'. It is pronounced 'in-**CO**-ate'.

Meaning — Something that has just begun; it is in its early stages of development, and therefore, not fully formed.

Examples — *As she listened to her father, an inchoate idea formed at the back of her mind.*

The arguments that the Minister put forward were immature and inchoate.

Etymology — It comes from the Latin 'inchoatus', meaning 'to begin'.

Infructuous /ɪn-<u>frʌk</u>-tju:-əs/

Pronunciation: The first syllable is pronounced like the word 'in' and the second rhymes with 'truck'. The following 'tu' rhymes with 'due', 'new' and 'few', and the final 'ou' is like the 'a' in 'china'. The word is pronounced 'in-**FRUCK**-tyoo-es'.

Meaning: Unprofitable; something that does not yield any fruit or result.

Examples: *Gauri made an infructuous appeal to the Chairman to retain the services of Arun.*

Hassan made several infructuous attempts to steal the Nizam's jewels.

Etymology: It comes from the Latin 'fructus', meaning 'fruit'. The word 'infructuous' is not very often used by native speakers of English; it is, however, quite popular among newspaper reporters in India.

Innuendo /ɪn-jʊ-<u>en</u>-dəu/

Pronunciation: The first syllable is like 'in' and the following vowel is like the 'u' in 'full' and 'pull'. The 'en' sounds like the 'en' in 'pen' and 'den' and the final vowel is like the 'o' in 'so' and 'go'. The word is pronounced 'in-yu-**EN**-doe'.

Meaning — Statement in which you indirectly say something uncomplimentary; can be sexual in nature.

Examples — *The women can't stand Jaswant because he's always making sly innuendos.*

The innuendo is meant to tarnish the actor's image.

Both candidates resorted to innuendos during the campaign.

Etymology — From the Latin 'innuendo', meaning 'giving a nod to'.

Insouciance /ɪn-<u>suː</u>-sɪ-ən(t)s/

Pronunciation — The 'i' in the first and third syllables is pronounced like the 'i' in 'bit' and 'kit'. The second syllable is like the word 'sue' and the following 'c' is like the 's' in 'sip' and 'sat'. The final 'iance' is like the 'ience' in 'conscience'. One simple way of pronouncing the word is 'in-**SUE**-si-ens'.

Meaning — Someone who is laid-back; an individual who has a relaxed and easy-going manner, and gives the impression that he does not have a care in the world.

Examples — *There were times when Ram admired his son's youthful insouciance.*

The candidate's insouciance didn't go down well with the members of the interview committee.

Etymology — The word comes from the French 'soucier', meaning 'to care', and 'in', meaning 'not'. Insouciance literally means 'carefree'.

Inter alia

/ɪn-tər ei-liə/ /ɪn-tər æ-liə/

Pronunciation — The first word is like 'inter' and the 'a' in 'alia' can be pronounced like the 'ay' in 'pay', 'say' and 'day' or like the 'a' in 'cat' and 'bat'. The final 'ia' is like the 'ea' in 'dear', 'fear' and 'near'. It is pronounced 'in-ter **AY**-li-e'.

Meaning — Mostly used in formal contexts to mean 'among other things'. It is advisable not to use this expression when you are talking about people.

Examples — *Raju is a collector who has, inter alia, two thousand rare stamps, five hundred cricket cards and five thousand rare coins.*

The paintings lost in the fire include, inter alia, two Picassos and several Ravi Varmas.

Etymology — From the Latin 'inter', meaning 'among', and 'alius', meaning 'other'.

Inveterate /ɪn-v̲e̲t̲-ə-ret/

Pronunciation — The first syllable is like the word 'in' and the second like the word 'vet'. The word is pronounced 'in-**VET**-e-ret'. It can also be pronounced 'in-**VET**-ret'.

Meaning — An inveterate liar is one who has been lying for a long time; someone who is unlikely to stop.

Examples — *Jayanth never believes politicians. He says that all politicians are inveterate liars.*

Being married to an inveterate gambler has taken a toll on Harini's health.

Etymology — 'Inveterate' is from the Latin 'vetus', meaning 'old'. The word 'veteran' also comes from this root.

Invidious /ɪn-v̲ɪ̲-dɪ-əs/

Pronunciation — The 'i' in the first, second and third syllables is pronounced like the 'i' in 'sit', 'pit' and 'kit'. The word is pronounced 'in-**VID**-i-es'.

Meaning — An invidious task is one that is likely to be rather unpleasant; one that could cause resentment or a lot of unhappiness. Mostly used in formal contexts, the word can also mean 'offensively unfair' or 'discriminating'.

Examples *He was given the invidious task of commenting on his boss' work.*

As a mother, she resented the invidious comparison between the two children.

The invidious remarks were attributed to a former member of the club.

Etymology From the Latin 'invidia', meaning 'envy' or 'malice'.

Jejune /dʒə-dʒuːn/

Pronunciation The first vowel is like the 'a' in 'china', and the following syllable is pronounced like the word 'June'. The word is pronounced 'je-**JUNE**'.

Meaning Someone who is rather childish or unsophisticated. When used with things, the word means 'uninteresting'. The word is mostly used in formal contexts to show disapproval.

Examples *I've been listening to jejune lectures all day.*

After deliberating for a couple of days, the committee arrived at jejune generalisations.

Etymology From the Latin 'jejunus', meaning 'fasting or hungry'. When it was first used in English, 'jejune' meant 'going without food'.

Joie de vivre /ʒwa: də vi:vrə/

Pronunciation The 'j' is pronounced like the 's' in 'pleasure' and 'measure'. The sound that follows is like the 'w' in 'wet' and 'wed', and the vowel is like the 'ar' in 'dark' and 'park'. The 'e' in 'de' and 'vivre' sounds like the 'a' in 'china'; 'viv' rhymes with 'weave'. The word is pronounced 'jwa: di **VIIV**-re'.

Meaning A French expression, meaning 'joy of living'; enjoying life.

Examples *For a woman who is nearly 90, she is full of joie de vivre.*

The students were filled with joie de vivre.

Juggernaut

Meaning A massive object that destroys everything in its path; can also be used to refer to huge trucks and buses.

Examples *In the 1980s, no team could stop the West Indies juggernaut.*

I don't understand why you think Rekha is a political juggernaut.

We require juggernauts to carry these pieces of equipment.

Origin Lord Jagannath of Puri gives us this word.

Kafkaesque /kæf-kə-esk/

Pronunciation — The first 'a' is like the 'a' in 'cat' and 'bat', and the second is like the 'a' in 'china'. The final 'esque' is pronounced like the 'esk' in 'desk'. The word is pronounced 'kaf-ke-**ESK**'.

Meaning — Resembling the work of Kafka – a world in which sinister and impersonal forces control human affairs.

Examples — *How did Anand get into this Kafkaesque situation?*

The sense of doom and gloom that pervades the documentary is Kafkaesque.

Origin — In his writings, the Czech–German writer Franz Kafka created a world in which there was little or no sunshine. It was very impersonal, mysterious, and there was always a sense of doom.

Kick-start

Meaning — When used figuratively, the word means 'to start or revive something that has slowed down to a trickle or has stopped completely'.

Examples — *The Finance Minister hopes to kick-start the economy by reducing interest on loans.*

The trouble-shooter failed to kick-start the stalled talks with the union members.

Origin — Starting a motorcycle or scooter.

Kick the habit

Meaning — To give up a bad habit voluntarily.

Examples — *Mukesh smokes like a chimney. He's finding it difficult to kick the habit.*

Sheena has been an addict for over twenty years. There's no way that she can kick the habit.

Kingpin

Meaning — The most important individual in a group or an organisation.

Examples — *After several months of hard work, the police caught the mob kingpin.*

Suresh is one of the kingpins of the movie industry.

Origin — The word comes from the sport of bowling. The single pin that is placed in front of the other nine is called the 'kingpin' or 'headpin'. If one is able to hit this pin hard enough, it will knock down the remaining pins.

Kiosk /ki:-ɔsk/

Pronunciation — The 'ki' is pronounced like the word 'key', and the following 'o' sounds like the 'o' in 'pot', 'hot' and 'got'. One way of pronouncing the word is '**KEY**-osk'.

Meaning — A small structure where newspapers and light refreshments like sandwiches and soda are sold; you usually buy these items through an open window.

Examples — *Thanks to cell phones, telephone kiosks are slowly disappearing.*

Sarita usually buys sandwiches at the station kiosk.

Etymology — From the Persian 'kus', meaning 'pavillion'.

Kiss of death

Meaning — An action which results in the ruin or failure of something; the instrument of a person's downfall.

Examples — *Throwing up on the stage was the kiss of death for Rahul's acting career.*

Asking a nitwit like Moni to make the arrangements was the kiss of death for the party.

Origin	The betrayal of Jesus by Judas in the Garden of Gethsemane. Judas helped identify Jesus to the Roman authorities by kissing him.

Kith /kɪθ/

Pronunciation	The 'ki' is like the 'ki' in 'kill' and 'kiss' and the final 'th' sounds like the 'th' in 'thin' and 'thick'.
Meaning	The word is mostly used nowadays to mean one's friends and acquaintances. It is seldom used independently; it only survives in the expression 'kith and kin'.
Examples	*Ramya had invited all her kith and kin to her wedding.* *I don't think you'd be interested in meeting my kith and kin.*
Etymology	It comes from the Old English 'cythth', which was an umbrella term for everything known – relatives, friends, acquaintances, places, country, etc. In the 14th century, the expression 'kith and kin' was used to refer to one's 'country and relatives'.

Klutz /klʌts/

Pronunciation	The 'uts' rhymes with 'cuts', 'huts' and 'guts'.

Meaning Used in informal contexts to refer to a clumsy, awkward or silly person.

Examples *Don't let Nalini handle the delicate objects. She's a bit of a klutz.*

Aravind is a complete klutz when it comes to making casual conversation.

Pradeep may be a supermodel now. In school, he was a klutz.

Etymology From the Yiddish 'klots', meaning 'clumsy person'.

Knee-jerk reaction

Meaning An automatic or immediate response to something; there is little or no thinking involved.

Examples *Whenever Rahul says 'yes' to something, his wife says 'no'. I think it's a knee-jerk reaction.*

Give the matter some thought. I don't want any knee-jerk responses from senior members like you.

Origin When a doctor taps you on your knee with a reflex hammer (rubber hammer), the leg automatically shoots up. You have no control over this reaction.

Know-it-all/Know-all

Meaning: Someone who thinks he knows everything; unwilling to take advice from others. Attempts to impress others with his knowledge merely succeed in irritating everyone. Usually used to show disapproval.

Examples: *The person heading the Sports Committe is a know-all who has never played a single game in her life.*

Saraswathi, the know-it-all in our family, told us to invest our funds in the stock market.

Nobody really likes Chandra because she is such a know-all.

Kowtow /kau-tau/

Pronunciation: The two syllables rhyme with the words 'how', 'now' and 'vow'. The word is pronounced 'cow-**TOW**'.

Meaning: To do everything to please someone in authority; to obey the individual unquestioningly. Used to show disapproval.

Examples: *Not all bureaucrats in our country kowtow to politicians.*

Our Government has been kowtowing to corporate interests.

Etymology — The word comes from the Chinese 'kotou', meaning 'head knock'. In the past, the Chinese showed their respect for someone by kneeling before the individual and then touching the ground with the forehead.

Kudos /kju:-dɔs/

Pronunciation — The 'ku' is pronounced like the word 'queue' or the letter 'Q'. The 'o' in the second syllable is like the 'o' in 'not', 'hot' and 'got'. The word is pronounced '**Q**-dos'.

Meaning — To get credit for something that you have done; to be praised or congratulated. It is an uncountable noun and is always followed by a singular verb.

Examples — *Rajnikanth enjoys all the kudos that goes with being a successful movie star.*

The soldier received a lot of kudos from the high command for his bravery.

Etymology — From the Greek 'kydos', meaning 'glory or fame'. The students of Oxford and Cambridge Universities made the word popular in the 18th century.

Kvetch /kvetʃ/

Pronunciation — It rhymes with the word 'fetch'.

Meaning	Someone who complains a lot; a complaint.
Examples	*My neighbour, Jayaram, is a kvetch.* *Frankly, I think there's every reason for Kunthala to kvetch.* *Everyone has been kvetching about the new Government policy.*
Etymology	From the Yiddish 'kvetshyn', meaning 'squeeze, press'.

La-di-da /la:-dɪ-da:/

Pronunciation	The 'a' in the first and third words is pronounced like the 'a' in 'bath' and 'ask', while the 'i' in 'di' is like the 'i' in 'sit' and 'it'. It is pronounced 'laa-di-**DAA**'.
Meaning	Mostly used in informal contexts to show disapproval. A 'la-di-da' person is someone who pretends to belong to the upper class, and behaves and speaks in a rather irritating manner.
Examples	*When did Kapil acquire that la-di-da accent?* *Ever since Rakesh became a member of the club, he's become so la-di-dah.*

La-la land

Meaning
To be out of touch with reality; to have no clue as to what is going on.

Examples
I have no idea what's going on with my cousin Ganesh. He seems to be in la-la land.

People who believe that cricket is still a gentleman's game are living in la-la land.

Origin
The city of Los Angeles is usually abbreviated to LA. The people living in this city are thought to be odd or eccentric.

Lackadaisical /læk-ə-dei-zɪ-kəl/

Pronunciation
The first syllable rhymes with 'back' and 'sack', and the third and fourth together sound like the word 'daisy'. The second 'a' is like the 'a' in 'china'. The word is pronounced 'lack-e-**DAY**-zi-kel'.

Meaning
Showing very little enthusiasm or interest in someone or something; putting in very little effort.

Examples
For all the money they make, some of our players are very lackadaisical on the field.

Aditi says that her new boss is annoyingly lackadaisical.

Lacune /lə-kjuː-nə/

Pronunciation — The vowels in the first and last syllables sound like the 'a' in 'china'. The 'cu' is pronounced like the word 'cue'. One way of pronouncing the word is 'le-**CUE**-ne'.

Meaning — Mostly used in formal contexts to mean 'gap' or 'deficiency'.

Examples — *The lawyer argued there was a lacuna in the witness' version of the events.*

In most political parties, there is a lacuna of leadership at the top.

Etymology — From the Latin 'lacuna', meaning 'hole' or 'pit'.

Lagniappe /læn-jæp/

Pronunciation — The 'lagn' is pronounced like the 'lan' in 'land' and 'lance', and the following 'iappe' is like the word 'yap'. The word is pronounced '**LAN**-yap'.

Meaning — Any unexpected gift or benefit; a freebie.

Examples — *Since we had bought so many items, the shopkeeper included a DVD player as lagniappe.*

	When you buy a car during this season, the company usually throws in a langiappe.
Etymology	From the Spanish 'la napa', meaning 'the gift'. The word, used mostly in American English, is not listed in all dictionaries.

Laid-back

Meaning	Someone who is calm and relaxed, does not get flustered.
Examples	*Mythali's laid-back style puts all the guests on her show at ease.* *I like to spend time with my cousin Indu. She's pretty laid-back.* *My cousin Gopal is anything but laid-back. He worries about everything.* *Parthiv has a very lackadaisical approach to his studies.*
Etymology	From 'alack the day', an expression of sorrow or regret.

Laissez-faire /lei-sei f3:/

Pronunciation	The three syllables are pronounced like the words 'lay', 'say' and 'fair', respectively. The word is pronounced 'lay-say **FAIR**'.

Meaning — It means 'non-interference in the affairs of others – individuals, organisations, countries, etc.'

Examples — *I'm afraid your laissez-faire approach is likely to create more problems for the university.*

Unlike most men, my father had a laissez-faire attitude to life.

Etymology — This French expression literally means 'let do' or 'allow to do'.

Lambast(e) /læm-beist/ /læm-bæst/

Pronunciation — The first syllable rhymes with 'ham', 'dam' and 'Sam', while the second rhymes with 'paste', 'haste' and 'taste'. The word is pronounced 'lam-**BASTE**'. It is also possible to pronounce the vowel in the second syllable like the 'a' in the first syllable.

Meaning — Nowadays, the verb is mostly used to refer to a thrashing of the verbal kind. When you lambaste someone, you give him a tongue-lashing; you criticise or scold the individual/thing quite severely.

Examples — *Yadav's first novel was lambasted by all the critics.*

The Vice Chancellor lambasted the students for their irresponsible behaviour.

Etymology The original meaning of this word was to 'assault' or 'thrash' someone.

Leapfrog

Meaning To progress rapidly; to quickly advance in status.

Examples *The school cricket team leapfrogged from the tenth to the third position.*

"If you want to marry my daughter, you have to leapfrog over him."

Kiran leapfrogged two ranks and was made a Major.

John leapfrogged over his colleagues to become a professor.

Origin — Leapfrog is actually the name of a game that many of us played as kids. In this game, one of the kids bends down and the others jump over him.

Leisure /le-ʒə/ /li:-ʒə/

Pronunciation — Some people make it rhyme with 'pleasure', 'treasure' and 'measure'. Others pronounce the 'ei' like the 'ee' in 'fees', 'bees' and 'knees'. In either case, the main stress is on the first syllable.

Meaning — One's free time; time when one is not involved in work of any kind. A 'gentleman of leisure' is someone who is in a position where he does not have to work. He has enough money to live on.

Examples — *In her leisure time, Vandana goes sailing.*

My new job just doesn't give me any time for leisure.

Etymology — From the Latin 'licere', meaning 'to be allowed'.

Leitmotiv/Leitmotif /lait-məu-ti:f/

Pronunciation — The first syllable is pronounced like the word 'light', and the following 'o' is like the 'o' in 'so', 'no' and 'go'. The 'i' sounds like the 'ee' in 'breeze', 'freeze' and 'sneeze'. The final 'v' is like the 'f' in 'fish', 'feel' and 'full'. The word is pronounced '**LIGHT**-mo-tiif'.

Meaning — A term used to refer to any dominant theme that appears repeatedly in something – a book, movie, talk, etc.

Examples — *The leitmotif of the Finance Minister's speech was the need to remain calm.*

The title of his latest movie could serve as the leitmotif for the actor's life.

Etymology — A German word, meaning 'leading motive' or 'leading theme'. It comes from the world of music. In our old films, whenever a wicked person appeared on screen, the snake charmer's music played in the background; it was the director's way of telling the audience that the character was evil. This is an example of leitmotif.

Lemon

Meaning — When you have been tricked into buying something worthless, you have been sold a lemon. When you say that something is a lemon, it implies that it is useless because it fails to work properly.

Examples *I wouldn't borrow Madhavan's car, if I were you. It's a lemon.*

Rajeev bought a radio last month. It's turned out to be a lemon.

Let it ride

Meaning To ignore something for a while; to let it remain as it is.

Examples *Don't worry about making the arrangements for the party right now. Let it ride for another three or four days.*

Sometimes, I don't agree with what my boss says. But I let it ride.

My scooter has been giving me problems. But it's not anything serious. I'm going to let it ride for a while.

Level playing field

Meaning When you give companies or countries a 'level playing field', you provide them an environment in which they are all given an equal opportunity to compete fairly. No one has an advantage.

Examples *If the tax systems are different in each Asian country, how can industries start on a level playing field?*

It's not a level playing field because one of the neighbouring countries is subsidising its steel industry with massive government grants.

The industrialists asked the Minister to provide a level playing field.

Lief /li:f/

Pronunciation It sounds like the word 'leaf'.

Meaning An old-fashioned word, meaning 'gladly' or 'willingly'. When used as an adjective, it means 'dear' or 'beloved'.

Example *I would as lief partner Ramesh as Sameer.*

Etymology 'Lief' comes from the Old English 'leof', meaning 'dear' or 'valued'.

Lieutenant /lef-te-nənt/ /lu:-te-nənt/

Pronunciation The English pronounce the 'lieut' like the word 'left'. The 'e' that follows is pronounced like the 'e' in 'ten', 'pen' and 'hen', and the final 'a' sounds like the 'a' in 'china'. They pronounce the word 'lef-**TE**-nent'. The Americans, on the other hand, pronounce the 'ieu' in the first syllable like the 'oo' in 'pool', 'cool' and 'school'. They pronounce the word 'loo-**TE**-nent'.

Meaning	An officer in the military.

Example	*My cousin is a Lieutenant in the Navy.*

Etymology	It comes from the Old French 'lieu tenant', meaning 'substitute deputy'.

Lilliputian /lɪlɪ-pjuː-ʃən/ /lɪlɪ-pjuː-ʃi-ən/

Pronunciation	The first two syllables are pronounced like 'lily'. The 'pu' rhymes with 'few and 'new', and the 't' sounds like the 'sh' in 'shirt', 'ship' and 'shin'. One way of pronouncing the word is 'li-li-**PYOO**-shen'.

Meaning	Something that is terribly small; intended for very small people. The word is considered literary.

Examples	*We found many Lilliputian figures buried in the sand.*

Harish showed us a Lilliputian chest of drawers and he wanted ten thousand rupees for it.

Etymology	In Jonathan Swift's *Gulliver's Travels*, Lilliput is the country that the hero, Gulliver, finds himself in after he has been shipwrecked. The inhabitants of this country are only six inches tall.

Limbo /lɪm-bəu/

Pronunciation — The first syllable rhymes with 'Tim', 'Jim' and 'Kim', and the following 'bo' with 'so', 'no' and 'go'. The word is pronounced '**LIM**-bo'.

Meaning — When things are in limbo, they are in a state of uncertainty or neglect.

Examples — *Unless the Supreme Court gives its verdict, the various projects will continue to be in limbo.*

Most government projects in India are always in limbo.

The Manager kept Lavanya's promotion in limbo for months.

Etymology — From the Latin 'limbus', meaning 'border' or 'edge'. Originally referred to the region which is believed to exist on the borders of Hell.

Lingua franca /lɪŋg-wə fræŋ-kə/

Pronunciation — The first syllable rhymes with 'sing' and 'ring' and the final 'a' in the two words is like the 'a in 'china'. The 'u' is like the 'w' in 'wet' and 'went'. The first syllable of 'franca' sounds like the word 'frank'. The expression is pronounced '**LING**-gwe frank-e'.

Meaning The language that is used for the purpose of communication by speakers whose mother tongue is different.

Examples *For many educated Indians, English has become the lingua franca.*

Mythreye told me that Swahili is the principal lingua franca in East Africa.

When the four of them get together, Gujarati becomes the lingua franca.

Etymology It comes from the Italian 'lingua franca', meaning 'Frankish tongue'. The mixture of Italian, French, Spanish, Greek and Arabic that was spoken in the Mediterranean ports was called the 'Frankish language'.

Litterateur /lɪ-tə-rə-tə:/

Pronunciation The first two syllables sound like the word 'litter'. The 'a' is like the 'a' in 'china' and the final 'eur' like the 'ir' in 'bird', 'birth' and 'first'. The word is pronounced 'li-te-re-**TIR**'.

Meaning A 'man of letters'; someone who is engaged in literary work and very knowledgeable about literature.

Examples *Publishing a couple of articles in the newspaper doesn't make you a litterateur.*

I tell you, only a great litterateur could have come up with those lines.

Etymology — From the Latin 'littera', meaning 'letter'; a 'litterator' is a 'critic'.

Lobbyist

Meaning — A person who attempts to influence an elected official through legal and illegal means.

Examples — *Nitin has been a lobbyist for some of the biggest companies in our country.*

Environmental lobbyists will ensure that the bill dies a natural death.

Origin — According to the British, the lobby referred to the large entrance hall to the House of Commons. It was possible for the common man to meet Members of Parliament in the 'Lobby' and talk to them.

Logophile

Meaning — Someone who loves words; a lover of words.

Examples — *If you want to know the meaning of the word, talk to Virat. He's a logophile.*

Even Khaja, the confirmed logophile in our class, hadn't heard the word before.

Etymology — It comes from the Greek 'logos', meaning 'word', and 'phile', meaning 'lover of'.

Logorrhoea /lɔg-ɪ-rɪə/

Pronunciation — The first syllable is pronounced like the word 'log', and the 'o' in the second syllable is like the 'a' in 'china'. The final 'ea' rhymes with 'fear', 'dear' and 'near'. The word is pronounced 'log-e-**RIE**'.

Meaning — A communication disorder in which an individual talks for a long time, but rather incoherently. He may talk to himself or to others, but much of what he says will be incomprehensible.

Example — *He suffers from bouts of logorrhoea every now and then.*

Etymology — It comes from the Greek 'logos', meaning 'word', and 'rhia', meaning 'flow'.

Lollapalooza /lɔ-lə-pə-luː-zə/

Pronunciation — The 'o' is like the 'o' in 'hot' and 'pot'; the vowels in the second, third and fifth syllables are like the 'a' in 'china'. The 'oo' is pronounced like the 'oo' in 'cool', 'pool' and 'fool'. The word is pronounced 'lo-le-pe-**LOO**-ze'.

Meaning — A slang word, meaning 'something big, something wondrous'. It can also be used to mean 'a big fat lie'.

Examples — *According to many, Kishore's singing voice is true lollapalooza.*

You should see the bump on Latha's head. It's a lollapalooza.

Our politicians are famous for their lollapaloozas.

Loquacious /lə-kwei-ʃəs/

Pronunciation — The 'o' in the first syllable and the 'iou' in the last sound like the 'a' in 'china'. The 'qua' rhymes with 'sway' and 'way', and the following 'c' is like the 'sh' in 'ship' and 'shape'. One way of pronouncing the word is 'le-**KWAY**-shes'.

Meaning — Someone who loves to talk; formal word for a chatterbox.

Examples — *The loquacious host wouldn't let us leave till we had heard the whole story.*

All the characters in the movie were loquacious.

Etymology — The word comes from the Latin 'loqui', meaning 'to speak'.

Luck out

Meaning	To get lucky; used in informal contexts.

Examples	*Anand really lucked out when he found that house.*

We had no idea what sort of boss Keshav would be, but we really lucked out.

We really lucked out this year – we had no power cuts during the summer.

Lucre /lu:-kə/

Pronunciation	The 'luc' is pronounced like the name 'Luke' and the following 're' is like the 'a' in 'china'. It is pronounced '**LOO**-ke'.

Meaning	Money made through dishonest means.

Examples	*Politicians are in pursuit of filthy lucre.*

Hari earned his lucre by taking bribes from poor farmers.

Etymology	It comes from the Latin 'lucrum', and in Latin, the word had two very different meanings. It meant 'profit' and 'avarice or greed'. In English, only the negative meaning survives.

Lugubrious /luː-guː-bri-əs/

Pronunciation One way is to pronounce the 'u' in the first and second syllables like the 'oo' in 'fool', 'pool' and 'school'. The 'i' sounds like the 'i' in 'it', 'bit' and 'sit', and the final 'ou' is like the 'a' in 'china'. The word is pronounced 'loo-**GOO**-bri-es '.

Meaning The word is mostly used in formal contexts to mean 'sad'.

Examples *I definitely don't wish to see his lugubrious face early in the morning.*

What's wrong? Why are you looking so lugubrious?

I'm in no mood to listen to your lugubrious laments early in the morning.

Etymology From the Latin 'lugere', meaning 'to mourn'.

Magic bullet

Meaning To have the perfect solution to a problem; the perfect medicine.

Examples *Well, I'm afraid there is no magic bullet which can help you lose twenty kilograms in two days.*

According to doctors, there is no magic bullet against cancer or AIDS.

Magnanimous /mæg-næ-nɪ-məs/

Pronunciation — The 'a' in the first and second syllables sounds like the 'a' in 'man', 'tan' and 'fan', while the following 'i' is like the 'i' in 'knit', 'chit' and 'fit'. The vowels in the final syllable sound like the 'a' in 'china'. The word is pronounced 'mag-**NA**-ni-mes'.

Meaning — Someone who is very generous and forgiving; gracious towards those less fortunate than him.

Examples — *Trump was magnanimous in victory; he praised his rival, Hillary Clinton.*

Show the world how magnanimous you can be. Don't press charges against him.

Etymology — From the Latin 'magnum', meaning 'great', and 'animus', meaning 'spirit, mind'.

Magniloquence /mæg-ni-lə-kwens/

Pronunciation — The first syllable rhymes with 'rag', 'tag' and 'bag', and the second with the words 'hill', 'pill' and 'chill'. The 'o' that follows is like the 'a' in 'china', and the final 'quence' is like the 'quence' in 'eloquence' and 'sequence'. The word is pronounced 'mag-**NIL**-e-kwens'.

Meaning	Mostly used in formal contexts to mean pompous speech or writing.
Examples	*Keep it simple. I don't want any trace of magniloquence.* *I didn't complete his latest novel. I just couldn't wade through the magniloquence.*
Etymology	From the Latin 'magniloquent', meaning 'lofty language'.

Magnum opus /mæg-nəm ə͟u-pəs/

Pronunciation	The first syllable rhymes with 'rag', 'bag' and 'sag', while the vowel in the second is like the 'a' in 'china'. The 'o' in 'opus' is like the 'o' in 'no', 'so' and 'go'. The word is pronounced 'mag-nem **O**-pes'.
Meaning	An artist's greatest or most important piece of work. The artist may be a painter, writer or composer.
Examples	*Saritha has finished writing her magnum opus.* The Code of the Woosters *is considered by many to be P.G. Wodehouse's magnum opus.* *Sameer thinks that* Ulysses *is James Joyce's magnum opus.*
Etymology	This Latin expression means 'great work'.

Majorly

Meaning To be 'very' or 'extremely' impressed by something. The word can also be used to mean 'primarily'. Though 'majorly' is considered slang, most standard dictionaries list it.

Examples *Sunita was majorly upset when Ganesh called off the wedding.*

Nandita is majorly a painter. But she does a lot of social work as well.

Make a killing

Meaning To make a lot of money in a short period of time without putting in too much effort.

Examples *According to yesterday's news report, the actors made a killing at the race track.*

Ram believes that he can make a killing on the stock market.

Origin This American expression refers to the killing of a large number of buffaloes in a very short period of time.

Make the grade

Meaning This is an expression mostly used in American English in informal contexts to mean that the work has been done satisfactorily; the required standard has been met. The expression is mostly used in the negative.

Examples *Sarvesh wanted to get into IIT, but he failed to make the grade.*

Sujatha's chocolate cake didn't quite make the grade.

Etymology In the context of the idiom, 'grade' refers to the steep incline a train has to climb. A train that makes the grade is one that is successful in climbing a steep incline or slope.

Mala fide /mei-lə fai-di/ /mei-lə fi:-di/

Pronunciation The 'mal' is pronounced like the word 'male' and 'fid' rhymes with 'tide' and 'side'. The final 'a' is like the 'a' in 'china' and the 'e' is like the 'i' in 'pit' and 'chit'. One way of pronouncing the word is 'male-e **FAI**-di'.

Meaning It means 'in bad faith'. A mala fide action is one that is performed with dishonest intent; a person purposely attempts to cheat or deceive you.

Examples *Most business deals carried out by this Government are mala fide.*

The college is trying to prove that the students acted with mala fide intent.

Etymology In Latin, 'mal' means 'bad' and 'fide' means 'faith'. The opposite of 'mala fide' is 'bona fide', meaning 'in good faith'.

Malaise /mæ-leiz/

Pronunciation The 'ma' is like the 'ma' in 'man' and 'mass' and the second syllable is pronounced like the word 'laze'. The word is pronounced 'ma-**LAZE**'.

Meaning Feeling out of sorts – mentally or physically – but unable to figure out the cause. Feeling ill at ease about things happening around you.

Examples *The rampant corruption is merely symptomatic of a wider malaise in society.*

Aparna could sense there was a serious malaise among the students.

Etymology Malaise comes from the French 'mal', meaning 'bad', and 'aise', meaning 'ease'.

Malevolence /mə-lev-ə-ləns/

Pronunciation The 'a', the 'o' and the second 'e' are pronounced like the 'a' in 'china'. The vowel in the second syllable sounds like the 'le' in 'level', 'lent' and 'less'. The word is pronounced 'me-**LEV**-e-lence'.

Meaning A person who is spiteful; someone keen on harming others.

Examples *The malevolence that was displayed during the debate was frightening.*

The bombing of a school was an act of malevolence.

Etymology From the Latin 'malevolentia', meaning 'ill will, hatred'.

Malfeasance /mæl-fiː-zəns/

Pronunciation The first syllable sounds like the word 'mal', and the following 'feas' like 'fees'. The final 'a' is like the 'a' in 'china' and the 'ce' is like the 's' in 'sip' and 'sit'. The word is pronounced 'mal-**FEE**-zens'.

Meaning A legal term that is mostly used in formal contexts to refer to the dishonest and illegal behaviour of public officials.

Examples *Several cases of malfeasance by the higher ups within the party were never investigated.*

No MP or MLA is going to be removed because of malfeasance.

Etymology From the French 'malfaisant', meaning 'to do badly'.

Malign /mə-lain/

Pronunciation The 'a' is like the 'a' in 'china', and the 'lign' sounds like the word 'line'. The word is pronounced 'me-**LINE**'.

Meaning To speak ill of a person; to deliberately say false or unpleasant things about him.

Examples *The young politician took great delight in maligning his opponent.*

Padma's enemies maligned her by saying she was a spy.

The bleak weather had a malign influence upon his usually cheerful mood.

Etymology From the Old French 'malignier', meaning 'to deceive or plot'.

Manoeuvre /mə-nu:-və/

Pronunciation The 'a' in the first syllable and the 'e' in the final syllable are like the 'a' in 'china'. The 'oeu' is pronounced like the 'oo' in 'cool', 'pool' and 'school', and the final 'r' is silent. The word is pronounced 'me-**NUU**-ve'.

Meaning To move or turn something very skilfully. When you manoeuvre someone into doing something or manoeuvre someone out of something, you use clever, but often illegal methods to get what you want.

Examples *The soldier manoeuvred the tank through the giant trees.*

The election results were achieved through a series of political manoeuvres.

Etymology From the Old French 'manovre', meaning 'manual labour' or 'working with hands'.

Maverick /mæv-(ə)-rɪk/

Pronunciation The first syllable rhymes with 'have' and the following 'e' is like the 'a' in 'china'. The final syllable rhymes with 'sick' and 'brick'. The word is pronounced '**MA**-ve-rik'. Some people drop the second vowel and pronounce the word '**MAV**-rick'.

Meaning A person who does not follow the usual conventions; someone whose ideas and ways of behaviour are very different from that of others.

Examples *Many people think that my friend Bala is a maverick.*

Don't listen to that maverick. He will get you into trouble.

Jaya was always a bit of a maverick.

Origin — Unlike his fellow ranchers, Samuel Augustus Maverick did not brand his cows. His argument was that since everyone was branding their cows, all the cows that were not branded were his!

Mayday

Meaning — A distress signal usually sent from ships and aeroplanes. The word is usually said three times to indicate an emergency.

Examples — *It must have been a bomb. The pilot didn't have time to send out a Mayday.*

The ship's Captain screamed 'Mayday' several times.

Origin — 'Mayday' has been used as an international distress signal in radio communication since 1927. It does not have anything to do with the month of May; it comes from the French 'm'aider', which is the shortened form of 'venez m'aider', meaning 'come help me'. With the passage of time, 'm'aider' became 'Mayday'.

Mea culpa /miːə kʌl-pə/

Pronunciation — One simple way is to pronounce the first syllable 'mea' like the word 'me'. The 'cul' in

	the second word rhymes with 'dull' and 'hull'. The 'a' in the two words is like the 'a' in 'china'. It can be pronounced 'mee-e **KULL**-pe'.
Meaning	An exclamation of apology, meaning 'My fault' or 'I apologize'.
Examples	*Don't blame Sajid for the delay. Mea culpa.* *Our magazine had to issue a mea culpa for getting the facts wrong.*
Etymology	This is a Latin expression, meaning 'through my fault'. The word 'culpa' means 'guilt'.

Mealy-mouthed

Meaning	Someone who is not very frank or direct; not brave or honest enough to say what is on his/her mind.
Examples	*Santosh was too mealy-mouthed to tell Bala that he wouldn't be helping him.* *As usual, the students gave mealy-mouthed excuses for not doing their assignment.*

Meatatarian

Meaning	Someone who strongly prefers meat over vegetables; must have meat with every meal.
Examples	*My friend Anand is a meatatarian.*

The chicken biriyani was so good that Sujatha had three helpings. She is not even a meatatarian.

Etymology Combination of 'meat' and 'vegetarian'.

Medical tourism

Meaning The practice of visiting other countries for medical reasons. Also referred to as 'health tourism'.

Examples *The State makes a lot of money from medical tourism.*

Medical tourism has become a lucrative business for many third-world countries.

Menu /men-ju:/

Pronunciation The first syllable is pronounced like the word 'men' and the second like 'you'. One way of pronouncing the word is '**MEN**-you'.

Meaning Food items that are available in a restaurant.

Examples *It took the waiter ten minutes to get the menu.*

Is there anything interesting on the menu?

Etymology From the French 'menu', meaning 'small, detailed'.

Mickey Mouse

Meaning — A course that is not challenging; where students learn nothing.

Examples — *According to Sujatha, most colleges offer only Mickey Mouse courses.*

Sheba is unable to get a decent job with the Mickey Mouse degree she has.

Milksop /mɪlk-sɔp/

Pronunciation — The second syllable rhymes with 'top' and 'hop'. One way of pronouncing this rather old-fashioned word is '**MILK**-sop'.

Meaning — A pejorative term used to describe a boy or a man who is indecisive; one who is too timid to take decisions on his own. This coward may also be rather effeminate.

Examples — *Don't worry, Manjit won't cause any problems. He's a milksop.*

Marriage seems to have changed Arul. He's no longer the milksop he was.

Origin — A 'sop' is something that is dipped in a liquid before it is eaten; in this context, it refers to a piece of bread dipped in milk. In the old days, milksop was usually given to infants and to grown-ups who were unwell. These individuals were like the milksop – soft and without a backbone.

Mingy

/mɪn-dʒɪ/

Pronunciation: The first syllable rhymes with 'gin', 'tin' and 'bin', and the following 'g' like the 'j' in 'jam' and 'jungle'. The word is pronounced '**MIN**-jy'.

Meaning: Someone who is mean and stingy.

Examples: *You want to know why Sunitha didn't lend you the money? It's because she's mingy.*

You can't be mingy. The money is going to be used for the upkeep of the old building.

Etymology: It is a combination of 'mean' and 'stingy'.

Minutiae

/mai-nju:-ʃɪ-i:/ /mɪ-nju:-ʃɪ-i:/

Pronunciation: The British pronounce the first syllable like the word 'my' and the following 'nu' like the word 'new'. The 't' sounds like the 'sh' in 'ship, 'she' and 'shape'. The second 'i' is pronounced like the 'i' in 'bit', 'pit' and 'sit', and the 'ae' in the final syllable sounds like the 'ee' in 'bee', 'see' and 'knee'. They pronounce the word 'my-**NEW**-shi-ee'. The Americans pronounce the first vowel like the 'i' in 'pit' and 'bit'.

Meaning — The minutiae of someone's daily life are the minute details; the very small and unimportant details of the individual's daily life. The singular of 'minutiae' is 'minutia'.

Examples — *Rangan's latest novel focuses on the minutiae of village life in India.*

Vasundara was too tired to discuss the minutiae of the proposal.

Etymology — From the Latin 'minutia', meaning 'smallness'.

Mischievous /mɪs-tʃɪ-vəs/

Pronunciation — The word consists of only three syllables, and not four. The first syllable is pronounced like the word 'miss'; the following 'ch' sounds like the 'ch' in 'chips' and 'cheat'. The 'ie' is like the 'i' in 'fit', 'bit' and 'kit', while the 'ou' in the final syllable sounds like the 'a' in 'china'. The word is pronounced '**MISS**-chi-ves'.

Meaning — Someone who has fun causing trouble; he usually finds playful and harmless ways of doing this. A 'mischievous remark', on the other hand, is one that is intended to cause serious damage or trouble.

Examples — *There was a mischievous grin on Chethan's face when he answered the question.*

The mischievous rumours about his affair started doing the rounds.

Missent

Meaning — Sent to the wrong person/address. The word is normally used with mail (both email and snail) and text messages.

Examples — *It didn't come as a surprise that the post office had missent the letter.*

A missent text ended his marriage.

Modus operandi /məu-dəs ɔp-ə-ræn-diː/

Pronunciation — The first syllable is like the word 'mode'. The 'op' in 'operandi' rhymes with 'cop', 'hop' and 'top', while 'rand' rhymes with 'band', 'hand' and 'sand'. The vowels in the second syllables of both words sound like the 'a' in 'china'. The word is pronounced 'mode-es op-e-**RAND**-ee'.

Meaning — Mostly used to refer to one's usual method of doing something.

Examples — *The Police Chief was unwilling to discuss the killer's modus operandi.*

If the people are not complaining, keep increasing the price of petrol seems to be the modus operandi of the Government.

Etymology The literal meaning of this Latin expression is 'way of operating'.

Modus vivendi /məud-əs vɪ-ven-di/ /məud-əs vɪ-ven-dai/

Pronunciation For 'modus', see previous entry. The 'i' in the first and last syllables of 'vivendi' are like the 'i' in 'sit' and 'hit'. The second syllable rhymes with 'when' and 'then'. One easy way of pronouncing the word is 'mo-dus vi-**VEN**-di'.

Meaning A practical but temporary arrangement which allows two people who are quarrelling or have a difference of opinion about something, to work or live together while waiting for their dispute to be settled.

Examples *In order to complete the project on time, a modus vivendi was achieved between the two countries.*

Neither country is interested in seeking a modus vivendi.

Etymology It is from Latin, and literally means 'way of living or getting along'.

Mojo /məu-dʒəu/

Pronunciation Both syllables rhyme with 'no', 'go' and 'so'. The word is pronounced '**MO**-joe'.

Meaning: Used in informal contexts to mean 'magic' or 'charm'; something that makes an individual successful or appealing.

Examples: *Federer has got his mojo working again.*

At the party, Sandeep just couldn't get his mojo to work.

If Harish wants to get into the team, he needs to get his mojo back.

Moofer

Meaning: It stands for 'mobile out-of-office worker'. A word coined by Microsoft to refer to people who can get their job done from any location.

Example: *My dad is a moofer. Are you a moofer too?*

Moreish

Meaning: Mostly used in informal contexts in British English to mean that something is so delicious that you wish to eat more of it. The word finds a place in several standard dictionaries.

Examples: *The gulab jamuns are rather moreish, aren't they?*

The laddus you get in that shop are very moreish.

Morgue /mɒg/

Pronunciation — The 'o' sounds like the 'aw' in 'claw' and 'law', and the following 'ue' is silent. The word is pronounced **'MAWG'**.

Meaning — A place where dead bodies are kept; a mortuary. A dull and boring place can also be referred to as a 'morgue'.

Examples — *After living in Mumbai for twenty years, this town is like a morgue.*

The body will remain in the morgue till the son arrives.

Etymology — This French word originally meant 'to look at solemnly'.

Mot juste /məu dʒu:st/

Pronunciation — The 't' in 'mot' is silent, and the word rhymes with 'go', 'so' and 'no'. The 'jus' is pronounced like the word 'juice' and the final 'e' is silent. The word is pronounced 'moe-**JUUST**'.

Meaning — Using the exact or correct word or phrase in a context.

Examples — *Bala wastes a lot of time searching for the mot juste.*

Delicious will not do. I think 'scrumptious' is the mot juste to describe this cake.

Etymology	'Mot' in French means 'word' and 'juste' means 'right'.

Ms /mɪz/

Pronunciation	The word rhymes with 'fizz', 'biz' and 'Liz'.
Meaning	A neutral title used before a woman's name. Unlike 'Mrs' and 'Miss', the title 'Ms' does not indicate whether the woman in question is married or single.
Examples	*There is a Ms Sajida Khan for you on the phone, Sir.* *I would like to introduce you to our new CEO, Ms Madhavi Jose.*
Etymology	Combination of 'Mrs' and 'Miss'.

Mulct /mʌlkt/

Pronunciation	The 'mulc' rhymes with the words 'bulk', 'sulk' and 'hulk'. The word is pronounced '**MULKT**'.
Meaning	A fine imposed on someone as a form of punishment. Nowadays, the word is also used as a verb to mean 'to defraud or swindle'.
Examples	*As expected, Raja mulcted his clients of their hard-earned money.*

We had to pay a mulct of five lakhs for late payment.

Etymology It comes from the Latin 'mulctare', meaning 'to punish or fine'.

Murfing /m<u>ɜ:</u>fiŋ/

Pronunciation The first syllabe rhymes with 'surf'. The word is pronounced '**MURF**-ing'.

Meaning Originally, it meant to surf the Internet mindlessly. Today, it is used in informal contexts to mean to surf the Internet using a mobile phone.

Examples *Like many students, Bhalla wastes a lot of his time murfing.*

Most senior citizens prefer surfing to murfing.

Mythomania /mɪ-θə-<u>mein</u>-iə/

Pronunciation The first syllable is pronounced like the word 'myth' and the 'o' that follows is like the 'a' in 'china'. The word is pronounced 'myth-e-**MAY**-nia'.

Meaning The compulsion to tell a lot of lies; an acute desire to exaggerate. A person who has this compulsion to lie is a mythomaniac.

Examples *Revathi can't help it. She's a mythomaniac.*

I don't think there's any cure for mythomania.

Etymology From the Greek 'mythos', meaning 'anything delivered by word of mouth'.

Ne plus ultra /nei plʌs ʌl-trə/

Pronunciation The 'ne' is pronounced like 'nay'. The expression is pronounced 'nay plus **UL**-tre'.

Meaning Nowadays, it is used to mean 'the highest level of excellence'; something that is close to perfection.

Examples *Rani's career at the university reached its ne plus ultra when she was made Vice Chancellor.*

Since imports have been banned, these local cigars are regarded as the ne plus ultra.

Etymology This Latin expression means 'not further beyond'. The ancient Greeks believed that the expression 'ne plus ultra' was inscribed on the Pillars of Hercules (Strait of Gibraltar) as a warning to ships not to sail any further westward. These Pillars were then the furthest attainable point for any ship; if they ventured any further, they would sail into the uncharted waters of the Atlantic.

Née /nei/

Pronunciation: The word rhymes with 'may', 'say' and 'hay'.

Meaning: Normally used after a married woman's name. When you say 'Padma Srivastav, née Bhalla…', what you mean is that before Padma married Srivastav, her family name was Bhalla.

Example: *Aditi Venkatesh, née Das, was born in Mumbai.*

Etymology: From the French 'naitre', meaning 'born'.

Niche /nɪtʃ/

Pronunciation: The word consists of only one syllable, and it rhymes with 'pitch', 'ditch' and 'stitch'. Some people, however, pronounce the vowel like the 'ee' in 'fees', 'bees' and 'cheese', and the final 'che' like the 'sh' in 'ship', 'should' and 'shin'. They pronounce the word '**KNEESH**'.

Meaning: The word has many different meanings, and one of them is 'finding the perfect job or activity'.

Examples: *Ganeshan is extremely unhappy because he has been unable to find a niche for himself.*

Remya has carved a niche for herself as a social worker.

Etymology According to some scholars, it comes from the Latin 'nidicare', meaning 'nest'.

Nincompoop /nɪŋ-kəm-pu:p/

Pronunciation The first syllable rhymes with 'ring', 'sing' and 'bring'; the following 'o' is like the 'a' in 'china'. The final syllable rhymes with 'hoop' and 'loop'. The word is pronounced '**NING**-kem-poop'.

Meaning Used in informal contexts to refer to a foolish person.

Examples *Who is the nincompoop who forgot to put the butter back in the fridge?*

Tell that nincompoop that I want three and not two plates of dosas.

Etymology Some scholars think that the word comes from the Latin 'non compos mentis', meaning 'not of sound mind'.

Nitpicking

Meaning To examine something very minutely and find fault; to focus on the small and unimportant details in order to find fault.

Examples *At the meeting, the Chairman didn't allow any nitpicking criticism.*

When Devi submitted his report, the boss indulged in a lot of petty nitpicking.

Rahman says he is sick and tired of the nitpicking.

Origin — A 'nit' is actually the egg of a louse or any other parasitic insect. The very demanding job of removing nits from a person's head or an animal's body is called 'nitpicking'.

Noir

/nwa:r/

Pronunciation — The 'oir' sounds like 'are', 'bar' and 'star'. The word is pronounced '**NWAAR**'.

Meaning — The term was first used to refer to a type of detective film made in Hollywood between 1944 and 1954. Everything about these films was dark – the violent characters, the sleazy settings, and the ominous background score. Nowadays, the word is used to refer to a dark kind of fiction as well.

Examples — *James' latest noir thriller has become a bestseller.*

The award-winning director is now planning to make a noir.

Etymology — It comes from the Latin 'niger', meaning 'black'. It is from 'niger' that we get the word 'negro'. The expression 'film noir' literally means 'black film'.

Noisome /nɔi-səm/

Pronunciation The first syllable rhymes with 'toy', 'boy' and 'joy', while the 'o' in the second sounds like the 'a' in 'china'. The word is pronounced '**NOY**-sem'.

Meaning Something that is very disgusting or offensive. The word can also be used to mean 'harmful' or 'dangerous'.

Examples *The noisome odour made quite a few guests throw up.*

The scientists did everything they could to stop the spread of the noisome fumes.

Etymology It comes from the Middle English 'noy', which is the shortened form of 'annoy'.

Nolens volens /nəu-lenz vəu-lenz/

Pronunciation The first syllable in both words rhymes with 'so' and 'go', and the second is like the word 'lens'. The word is pronounced 'no-lenz **VO**-lenz'.

Meaning Willingly or unwillingly; no choice. One is compelled to do something whether one wishes to or not.

Examples *You cannot go anywhere for the time being. You will have to remain here, nolens volens.*

When the market crashed, the CEO was compelled nolens volens to quit his job.

Etymology Latin expression, meaning 'whether unwilling or willing'.

Nomophobia

Meaning The fear that people have that they might be out of cell phone range or that their cell phones may die on them.

Examples *Indu thinks twice about leaving the city. She has nomophobia.*

Dilip is constantly charging his iPhone and iPad. He suffers from nomophobia.

Origin 'Nomo' is the short form of 'no mobile'!

Nonchalant /nɔn-ʃə-lənt/

Pronunciation The first syllable is pronounced 'non'. The 'ch' is like the 'sh' in 'ship', 'shin' and 'sheep'; and the vowels that follow are like the 'a' in 'china'. The word is pronounced '**NON**-she-lent'.

Meaning Someone who is calm and relaxed and not worried about anything; very laid-back.

Examples — *Raju seemed almost nonchalant before the exam.*

The nonchalant manner in which Mahidhar answered the difficult questions angered the teacher.

In most of our movies, during a crisis, it is the hero who remains nonchalant.

Etymology — From the French 'non', meaning 'not', and 'chaloir', meaning 'have concern for'.

Nous /naus/

Pronunciation — The word rhymes with 'house', 'mouse' and 'louse'.

Meaning — The word is used in British English to mean 'intelligence' or 'common sense'.

Examples — *The children had the nous not to turn on the lights when they smelt gas.*

The Minister didn't have the nous to understand the importance of the bill.

Etymology — It comes from the Latin 'nous', meaning 'intellect, mind'.

Nouveau riche /nu:-vəu ri:ʃ/

Pronunciation — The 'ou' sounds like the 'oo' in 'pool', 'fool' and 'cool', and the following 'eau' is like the 'o' in 'so', 'no' and 'go'. The 'i' in 'riche' is like the 'ee' in 'need', 'seed' and 'feed'; the final 'che' is pronounced like the 'sh' in 'ship', 'sheet' and 'sheep'. The word is pronounced 'nuu-voe **RIISH**'.

Meaning — People who have come into a lot of money recently and who want to display their new-found wealth in a crass manner. The expression is mostly used to show disapproval.

Examples — *According to my wife, the new club is extremely popular with the city's nouveau riche.*

Mankad's parents did not approve of his noveau riche lifestyle.

Etymology — 'Nouveau riche' is of French origin, and it literally means 'new rich'.

Nuance

/nju:-a:ns/

Pronunciation — The first syllable is pronounced like the word 'new' and the second rhymes with 'dance', 'chance' and 'glance'. One way of pronouncing the word is '**NEW**-aans'.

Meaning — Refers to the subtle or very small distinctions in meaning, colour or appearance. The word can be used as a noun or an adjective.

Examples — *I am looking for someone who is familiar with the nuances of the local dialect.*

The critic called it a 'complex and nuanced novel'.

Etymology It comes from the Latin 'nubes', meaning 'cloud' or 'mist'.

Nub /nʌb/

Pronunciation The word rhymes with 'pub', 'tub' and 'cub'.

Meaning The most important or essential part of something; it could be an integral part of a story, an argument, a problem, etc. The word can also be used to mean 'a small piece or chunk of something'.

Examples *If you ask me, the nub of the problem is voter apathy.*

Spare me the details. Give me the nub of the story.

The police found a nub of gold inside the victim's pocket.

Etymology From the German 'knubbe', meaning 'knob'.

Numero uno /nju:-mə-rəu u:nəu/

Pronunciation The first syllable can be pronounced like the word 'new' and the following vowel like the 'a' in 'china'. The last syllable in both words rhymes with 'so', 'go' and 'co'. The 'u' in 'uno'

	is like the 'oo' in 'cool', 'pool' and 'fool'. The word is pronounced 'new-me-row **UU**-no'.
Meaning	This Spanish expression means 'number one' or 'the best'. It can also be used to refer to oneself.
Examples	*If you ask me, the coffee that my mother makes is numero uno.* *Tax laws? You'd better talk to Devidas. He is the numero uno in our firm.* *Sure, I will help you. But tell me, what's in it for numero uno?*

Nuptial /nʌp-ʃəl/

Pronunciation	The first syllable rhymes with 'cup', 'pup' and 'cub'; the following 't' is pronounced like the 'sh' in 'sheep', 'ship' and 'show'. The 'ia' in the final syllable sounds like the 'a' in 'china'. The word is pronounced '**NUP**-shel'.
Meaning	Used jocularly to refer to things related to a person's wedding ceremony; considered old fashioned.
Examples	*I had to laugh when the old woman referred to the bedroom as her nuptial chamber.* *The guests yawned as the couple exchanged their lengthy nuptial vows.*
Etymology	From the Latin 'nuptiae', meaning 'wedding'.

Nyctophobia /nɪk-tə-fəu-biə/

Pronunciation The 'nyc' is pronounced like the word 'nick' and the following 'o' like the 'a' in 'china'. One way of pronouncing this word is 'nik-te-**FOE**-bia'.

Meaning Fear of darkness or night.

Examples *I'm nyctophobic, so I don't step out of my house after sunset.*

Prabha's son is exhibiting symptoms of nyctophobia.

Etymoloy In Greek, 'nykto' means 'night'.

Obdurate /ɔb-dju-rət/

Pronunciation The first syllable rhymes with 'sob', 'mob' and 'lob'. The following 'u' is pronounced like the 'u' in 'pull' and 'full'. The 'a' is like the 'a' in 'china', and the final 'e' is silent. The word is pronounced '**OB**-dyu-ret'.

Meaning Mostly used in formal contexts to mean 'stubborn'.

Examples *The Minister found it difficult to implement changes because his department heads were obdurate defenders of the old policies.*

	Raju's obdurate refusal to speak in his mother tongue worried his parents.
Etymology	From the Latin 'obduratus', meaning 'hardened'.

Obsequious /əb-<u>siː</u>-kwɪ-əs/

Pronunciation	The 'o' in the first syllable and the 'ou' in the final syllable sound like the 'a' in 'china'. The 'se' is pronounced like the word 'see', and the following 'qui' sounds like the 'qui' in 'quick', 'quit' and 'quiz'. The word is pronounced 'eb-**SEE**-kwi-es'.
Meaning	A toady; someone who is eager to please others, especially those in power. Mostly used in formal contexts to show disapproval.
Examples	*Ganesh implored Rekha to stop being so obsequious to her husband.* *Anand's obsequious PA stepped into the boardroom wearing a fake smile.*
Etymology	The word comes from the Latin 'obsequiosis', meaning 'compliant, obedient'.

Oeuvre /<u>ɜːv</u>-rə/

Pronunciation	The 'oeuv' in the first syllable sounds like the 'erv' in 'serve', 'nerve' and 'deserve'. The final

'e' sounds like the 'a' in 'china'. The word is pronounced '**ERV**-re'.

Meaning — This rather literary word refers to the complete works of an artist – writer, painter, etc.

Examples — *If it's Wodehouse you are interested in, talk to Bala. He's familiar with his oeuvre.*

The painter's oeuvre will be on display next week.

Etymology — In French, 'oeuvre' means 'work'.

Officious /ə-fɪʃ-əs/

Pronunciation — The vowel in the first and final syllables sounds like the 'a' in 'china'. The second syllable is pronounced like the word 'fish'. The word is pronounced 'e-**FISH**-es'.

Meaning — A meddlesome individual; someone who is eager to offer advice and therefore pokes his nose in other people's affairs. The word is mostly used to show disapproval.

Examples — *It's not surprising that the officious little man has no friends.*

Our officious host spent an hour explaining to us why we should sell the house.

Etymology — It comes from the Latin 'officiosus', meaning 'full of courtesy', 'dutiful'.

Ombudsman /ɔm-budz-mən/

Pronunciation: The 'o' is like the 'o' in 'hot', 'got' and 'not', and the following 'u' sounds like the 'u' in 'put', 'pull' and 'full'. The 's' is pronounced like the 'z' in 'zoo', 'zip' and 'zap', and the final 'a' is like the 'a' in 'china'. The word is pronounced '**OM**-budz-men'.

Meaning: Someone who investigates complaints made by people against the government or any public organisation; an independent official who represents the common man in his fight against the government.

Examples: *All complaints must be made in writing to the banking ombudsman by 3:00 this afternoon.*

Karthik asked the ombudsman what could be done to solve the problem.

Etymology: The word is Swedish in origin and it means 'representative' or 'agent'. I understand that the word was borrowed into English in the 1960s. It is being slowly replaced by 'ombudsperson'.

Omerta /əu-mɜː-taː/

Pronunciation: There are different ways of pronouncing this word. The first vowel sounds like the 'o' in 'so' and 'go', and the following 'er' sounds like the 'ir' in 'bird' and 'shirt'. The final 'a' is like the 'ar' in 'park' and 'dark'. One way of pronouncing the word is 'o-mer-**TAA**'.

Meaning An oath or vow taken by new members of certain criminal organisations that they will remain silent if they are caught by the police. The Mafia practises this code of silence.

Example *As expected, the two men who were arrested remained loyal to the oath of omerta.*

Etymology It is believed to come from the Italian 'umilta', meaning 'humility'.

Onion /ʌn-jən/

Pronunciation The first syllable rhymes with 'sun', 'bun' and 'run'. It is not pronounced like the word 'on'. The following 'i' is like the 'y' in 'young' and 'yes', and the final 'o' is like the 'a' in 'china'. The word is pronounced '**UN**-yen'.

Oust /aust/

Pronunciation The 'ou' is like the 'ou' in 'out', 'shout' and 'bout'; the final 'st' is like the 'st' in 'sting', 'step' and 'stump'.

Meaning To force an individual to leave a position of power; to remove a person from the position he/she has occupied.

Examples — *The three Generals decided that they would oust the Prime Minister.*

There's no way we can oust him now. We must bide our time.

Etymology — From the Old French 'oster', meaning 'remove' or 'take away'.

Out in left field

Meaning — An informal expression, mostly used in American English to mean 'strange, unusual or eccentric'.

Examples — *Some of the ideas that my boss comes up with are way out in left field.*

My cousin Subbu is out in left field. Nobody takes anything he says seriously.

Origin — Behind the left side of the baseball stadium where the Chicago Cubs played, there was a mental institution.

Oven /ʌv-(ə)n/

Pronunciation — The 'ov' sounds like the 'ove' in 'glove', 'love' and 'above'. The word is pronounced '**AV**-en'

Etymology — From the Old English 'ofen', meaning 'furnace'.

Oxymoron

Meaning A phrase in which two words of contradictory meaning are brought together to create an effect. 'Bitter sweet' and 'wise fool' are examples.

Examples *If you ask me, calling our politicians 'public servants' is an oxymoron.*

Groucho Marx thought that the term 'military intelligence' was an oxymoron.

Etymology From the Greek 'oxus', meaning 'sharp', and 'moros', meaning 'foolish'.

Paean /pi:-ən/

Pronunciation The first syllable rhymes with the words 'bee', 'see' and 'fee'. The 'ea' in the second syllable sounds like the 'a' in 'china'. The word is pronounced '**PEE**-en'.

Meaning Originally, a song sung in honour of the Greek god Apollo. Nowadays, the word is used to refer to any work – film, song, piece of writing, etc. – which praises someone or something.

Examples *The song is a paean to love and commitment.*

According to the fans, the movie is a paean to Dhoni's fighting spirit.

Etymology From the Greek 'paian', meaning 'hymn' or 'chant'.

Page 3

Meaning The page in a newspaper which, in addition to including photographs of questionable taste, also provides the local gossip – informs the reader as to who is going out with whom, who is throwing the next big party, etc.

Examples *Narender's parties always become a page 3 item.*

Poor Bakshi has been reduced to a page 3 journalist.

Origin 'Page 3' became famous when Rupert Murdoch bought over *The Sun* in 1969. The following year, every edition of the paper carried a picture of a topless woman on page 3; and as you might expect, the circulation went up dramatically. The bare-breasted women began to be called 'page 3 girls', and many of them became famous. So the original page 3 contained pictures of naked women.

Panache /pə-næʃ/

Pronunciation The word consists of two syllables. The 'a' in the first is pronounced like the 'a' in 'china', while the second syllable rhymes with the words 'cash', 'dash' and 'bash'. The word is pronounced 'pe-**NASH**'.

Meaning — To do something with flair and confidence. Your stylish and skilful ways of doing things – driving, cooking, dressing, etc. – wins you the admiration of many.

Examples — *Richards strode to the crease with great panache.*

I'm told Sathvika used to play the flute with panache.

Etymology — From the Latin 'pinnaculum', meaning 'tuft of feathers'. In Roman times, it was common practice for soldiers to appear distinguished and stylish by wearing colourful feathers on their helmets.

Pandemonium /pæn-də-<u>məun</u>-ɪ-əm/

Pronunciation — The first syllable is pronounced like the word 'pan', while the 'e' in the second and the 'u' in the final syllable are pronounced like the 'a' in 'china'. The 'mon' is like the word 'moan'. The word is pronounced 'pan-de-**MOAN**-i-em'.

Meaning — When there is pandemonium, there is usually a lot of shouting and screaming because people are angry or frightened about something.

Examples *There was pandemonium when the Chairman announced that he was resigning.*

There was pandemonium at the airport when the plane crashed.

Our meetings always end in pandemonium.

Etymology A word coined by John Milton in his *Paradise Lost*. It comes from the Greek 'pan', meaning 'all', and Latin 'daemonium', meaning 'evil spirit'. Milton used the word to refer to a place in the middle of Hell.

Pangram

Meaning A sentence which contains all the letters of the alphabet.

Example *The quick brown fox jumps over a lazy dog.*

Origin Pangrams are very useful in determining how good or bad a particular font is. Since all the letters of the alphabet are in the same sentence, it becomes easy for the font-maker to determine how well the letters contrast with one another.

Panjandrum /pæn-dʒæn-drəm/

Pronunciation The first two syllables rhyme with 'ran', 'fan' and 'ban'; the final 'u' is like the 'a' in 'china'. The word is pronounced 'pan-**JAN**-drem'.

Meaning A pompous individual who believes that he is a powerful and important person. The word is used to show disapproval.

Examples *A panjandrum of the oil industry was present at the party.*

Rahul, our sports channel's panjandrum, will be receiving the award.

Origin The word was coined by the English dramatist Samuel Foote, and it appears in the few nonsense sentences that he wrote to test the memory of an actor who claimed that he had the ability to reproduce anything after hearing it once.

Paparazzi /pæ-pə-ræt-sɪ/

Pronunciation 'Pap' rhymes with 'tap' and 'cap', while the following vowel is like the 'a' in 'china'. The 'razz' is pronounced like 'rats', and the final 'i' is like the 'i' in 'sit' and 'bit'. One way of pronouncing the word is 'pa-pe-**RAT**-si'.

Meaning Photographers who follow famous people wherever they go.

Examples *Once you become famous, you'll be hounded by the paparazzi.*

The ageing star had a wonderful relationship with the paparazzi.

Origin Paparazzi is the plural of Paparazzo – a common surname in Italy. The name became popular thanks to a movie made by Federico Fellini – *La Dolce Vita*. In the film, Paparazzo was the name of a freelance photographer.

Paradigm /pæ-rə-daim/

Pronunciation The first two syllables sound like the word 'para'; the following 'digm' rhymes with 'time' and 'lime'. The word is pronounced '**PA**-re-dime'.

Meaning A model that explains how something works or shows how something is produced. One of the meanings of this formal word is 'typical example of something'.

Examples *For many, the Holocaust is a paradigm of evil.*

The incident that took place yesterday is a paradigm of the destructive side of human nature.

As far as I am concerned, Shantha is a paradigm of all that is good in this world.

Etymology From the Latin 'paradigma', meaning 'example, pattern'.

Parochial /pə-rəu-kɪ-əl/

Pronunciation — The ‘a’ in the first and last syllables is like the ‘a’ in ‘china’; the second syllable sounds like the word ‘row’. The ‘chi’ is like the ‘ki’ in ‘king’, ‘kiss’ and ‘kit’. The word is pronounced ‘pe-**ROW**-ki-el’.

Meaning — To be very limited in one’s outlook; very narrow-minded.

Examples — *Kim has a very parochial attitude. I don’t want him as a team member.*

Many of the political parties are very parochial in their outlook.

Etymology — From the Latin ‘parochialis’, meaning ‘of a parish’ – the small area that a priest looks after.

Party animal

Meaning — Someone who loves parties and other social activities.

Examples — *The party animals next door kept us awake all night.*

Stephen didn’t invite any of the party animals to dinner.

Pastiche /pæs-ti:ʃ/

Pronunciation The 'a' is like the 'a' in 'ant' and 'stamp'; the following 'i' is like the 'ee' in 'seed' and 'deed'. The final 'che' sounds like the 'sh' in 'ship' and 'shoe'. The word is pronounced 'pas-**TEESH**'.

Meaning To deliberately imitate someone's style – artists and musicians often do this.

Examples *The play was a witty pastiche of Shakespeare's* Othello. *The audience loved it.*

The movie was a pastiche of some of the well-known Amitabh films.

Etymology From the Italian 'pasticcio', meaning 'medley, pastry cake'.

Payola /pei-əu-lə/

Pronunciation The first syllable sounds like the word 'pay' and the following 'o' like the 'o' in 'so' and 'no'. The 'a' in the final syllable sounds like the 'a' in 'china'. It is pronounced 'pay-**O**-le'.

Meaning This rather old-fashioned word is mostly used in American English to refer to the bribe paid to someone.

Examples *The Minister was accused of accepting payola from several American firms.*

The CEO of the television company maintained that they had not received any payola for promoting the new film.

Origin In the 1930s, when music became the staple diet of the radio in the US, gramophone companies did everything possible to promote their records/songs. Some of them bribed the disc jockeys working for popular radio stations into playing their records repeatedly. The word is a combination of 'pay' and 'ola': the second half of the word comes from 'Victrola', a gramophone company that was well known in the early 20th century.

Peccadillo /pe-kə-dɪl-əu/

Pronunciation The first syllable is pronounced like the word 'peck' and the following 'a' is like the 'a' in 'china'. 'Dill' rhymes with 'pill', 'chill' and 'fill', while the final 'oe' is like the 'o' in 'go', 'so' and 'no'. The word is pronounced 'peck-e-**DILL**-o'.

Meaning A minor sin or fault.

Examples *The star's latest extramarital peccadillo didn't go down well with his fans.*

The long list of peccadillos finally caught up with the Minister. He was forced to resign.

Etymology From the Latin 'peccatum', meaning 'sin, fault'.

Pejorative /pɪ-dʒɔ-rə-tɪv/

Pronunciation The 'e' in the first syllable and the 'i' in the fourth are pronounced like the 'i' in 'it', 'bit' and 'sit'. The 'o' sounds like the 'o' in 'hot', 'not' and 'lot', while the following 'a' is like the 'a' in 'china'. The word is pronounced 'pe-**JO**-re-tiv'.

Meaning A pejorative word or expression is one which expresses criticism of someone or something. Used in formal contexts.

Examples *Devi made several pejorative comments about the way the matter was handled.*

My teacher thinks that 'Yankee' is a pejorative term.

Etymology It comes from the Latin 'peiorare', meaning 'to make worse'.

Pelf /pelf/

Pronunciation The word rhymes with 'self' and 'shelf'.

Meaning Mostly used in informal contexts to mean 'money made by dishonest means'.

Examples — *The young politician didn't want to share the pelf with anyone.*

Raj isn't interested in serving the people. All he wants is the power and the pelf.

Etymology — From the Old French 'pilfre', meaning 'booty or spoils'; it is from this word that we get 'pilfer'.

Penchant /pen-tʃənt/

Pronunciation — One simple way of saying the word is to pronounce the first syllable like the word 'pen' and the 'a' like the 'a' in 'china'. The word is pronounced '**PEN**-chent'.

Meaning — When you have a penchant for something, you have a strong liking for it; you are in the habit of doing it.

Examples — *Divya has a penchant for wearing jeans and T-shirt.*

Many writers in our country have a penchant for the florid.

Angie has a penchant for adopting babies from different parts of the world.

Etymology — From the Old French 'pencher', meaning 'to incline'.

Peppy

Meaning: Someone who is peppy is lively and full of energy. Can be used with things as well.

Examples: *Why do you have to sing those sad songs? Can't you sing something peppy?*

I like talking to my aunt. She's always peppy and keeps everyone entertained.

Etymology: 'Peppy' comes from 'pep', which in turn is the shortened form of 'pepper'.

Per se /pɜː sei/

Pronunciation: The first word is pronounced like the word 'per', and the second, like the word 'say'. The word is pronounced 'per-**SAY**'.

Meaning: 'Per se' means 'of or by itself'. When you say 'driving per se', you are in no way comparing driving with anything else; you are not considering it in relation to any other thing.

Examples: *Driving, per se, is not something Meera really enjoys.*

My boss, per se, isn't an interesting person to talk to. But he has wonderful contacts.

Uma's job, per se, isn't very interesting, but she manages to make some easy money.

Etymology A Latin expression, meaning 'by itself'.

Percolate /p<u>ɜ:</u>-kə-leit/

Pronunciation The 'perc' is pronounced like the word 'perk' and the following 'o' sounds like the 'a' in 'china'. The final syllable sounds like the word 'late'. The word is pronounced '**PER**-ke-late'.

Meaning When a liquid percolates, it passes slowly through a substance. In the case of coffee, boiling water percolates through ground coffee beans. The word has a figurative meaning as well. When something like an idea or a rumour percolates, it begins to grow or spread slowly.

Examples *Rumours of their romance have begun to percolate through the office.*

Light percolates through those windows early in the morning.

Etymology From the Latin 'percolare', meaning to 'strain through'.

Peripheral /pə-<u>rɪf</u>-ə-rəl/

Pronunciation The 'riph' in the second syllable rhymes with 'stiff' and 'tiff'. The remaining vowels are like the 'a' in 'china'. The word is pronounced 'pe-**RIF**-e-rel'.

Meaning — When you refer to an activity as being peripheral, what you mean is that it is not very important when compared to other activities. This is one of the meanings of the word.

Examples — *As far as I am concerned, cricket should be made peripheral to other activities.*

We have decided to contract out some of our peripheral activities, like training.

In my opinion, history is peripheral to the debate.

Pernickety /pə-nɪk-ə-tɪ/

Pronunciation — The 'er' and the 'e' are like the 'a' in 'china', and the second syllable sounds like the word 'nick'. The final 'ety' sounds like the 'etty' in 'pretty' and 'Betty'. The word is pronounced 'pe-**NICK**-e-ti'.

Meaning — Mostly used in British English in informal contexts to show disapproval. It means 'to focus on the trivial'.

Examples — *Bala is pernickety when it comes to punctuation and formatting.*

Roshni is pernickety about what she eats.

Perspicuous /pə-spɪk-ju-əs/

Pronunciation The 'e' in the first syllable and the 'ou' in the final syllable are like the 'a' in 'china'. 'Spic' rhymes with the words 'stick', 'pick' and 'chick', and the following 'u' sounds like the letter 'u'. The word is pronounced 'pe-**SPIK**-yu-es'.

Meaning Clear and easy to understand.

Examples *The critics say that he was a writer of perspicuous prose. I don't agree at all.*

I'm looking for a perspicuous professor who will create interest among the students.

Etymology From the Latin 'perspicuus', meaning 'transparent'.

Pescetarian /pes-kə-tei-rɪ-ən/

Pronunciation 'Pes' rhymes with 'mess', 'bless' and 'chess', while the following 'e' is like the 'a' in 'china'. The last three syllables are pronounced like the 'tarian' in 'vegetarian'. The word is pronounced 'pes-ke-**TAY**-ri-en'.

Meaning Someone who eats fish, but does not eat meat. The word can also be spelt 'pescatarian'.

Examples *According to this article, Steve Jobs was a pescetarian.*

With the price of fish soaring, pescatarians are being forced to become vegetarians.

Etymology — It comes from the Italian 'pesce', meaning 'fish'.

Phillumenist /fɪ-lu:-mə-nɪst/

Pronunciation — The first syllable sounds like 'fill', and the following 'u' is like the 'oo' in 'cool' and 'pool'. The 'e' is like the 'a' in 'china' and the word is pronounced 'fi-**LOO**-me-nist'.

Meaning — A collector of matchbox labels.

Examples — *Rekha has been a phillumenist since she was eight years old.*

It is an event that all phillumenists look forward to.

Etymology — 'Phil' is from Greek 'philos', meaning 'lover', and 'lumen' is from the Latin 'lumen', meaning 'light'.

Phlegmatic /fleg-mæ-tɪk/

Pronunciation — The 'ph' in the first syllable sounds like the 'f' in 'fish' and 'feel', and the rest of the syllable is pronounced like the word 'leg'. The remaining syllables rhyme with 'static' and 'attic'. The word is pronounced 'fleg-**MA**-tic'.

Meaning	To remain unemotional; someone who remains cool under pressure; does not get easily excited or angry about things.
Examples	*As expected, the champion remained phlegmatic throughout the tense fifth set.* *My boss' greatest asset is his calm, phlegmatic manner.*
Etymology	From the Greek 'phlegmatikos', meaning 'abounding in phlegm'.

Pigeon /pɪdʒ-ən/

Pronunciation	The 'g' is like the 'j' in 'jam', 'juice' and 'jeep', and the following 'eo' is like the 'a' in 'china'. One way of pronouncing the word is '**PIJ**-in'.
Etymology	From the Old French 'pijon', meaning 'a young dove'.

Pigeonhole /pɪdʒ-ɪn-həul/

Pronunciation	The word is pronounced '**PIJ**-en hole'.
Meaning	When you 'pigeonhole someone' or 'put someone in a pigeonhole', you put him in a particular category without really considering all his qualities. The word is mostly used to show disapproval; can be used with both people and things.

Examples *Kunthala's grandson has been unfortunately pigeonholed as a problem child.*

Raju is really strange. It's difficult to put him in a pigeonhole.

Pizzazz /pə-zæz/

Pronunciation The vowel in the first syllable is pronounced like the 'a' in 'china' and the 'a' is like the 'a' in 'cat', 'rat' and 'mat'. The word is pronounced 'pe-**ZAZ**'.

Meaning Something or someone that is full of energy; exceptionally good to look at.

Examples *Everyone agrees that the new President lacks pizzazz.*

The West Indies team of the 1980s had a lot of pizzazz.

The director refused to start shooting because he felt that the script lacked pizzazz.

Origin Coined by Diana Vreeland, the editor of a fashion magazine.

Plethora /pleθ-(ə)-rə/

Pronunciation The first syllable rhymes with 'meth' and 'Beth', and the remaining vowels sound like the 'a' in 'china'. The word is pronounced '**PLETH**-e-re'. Some people drop the vowel in the second syllable and pronounce the word '**PLETH**-re'.

Meaning — A formal word, meaning 'an excess amount of something'.

Examples — *There is a plethora of sycophants in the party.*

Amitabh has won a plethora of awards during his long career.

Etymology — From the Greek 'plethore', meaning 'fullness'.

Poignant /pɔin-jənt/

Pronunciation — The 'poign' rhymes with 'coin' and 'join', and the vowel in the final syllable is like the 'a' in 'china'. A 'y' sound is inserted before the final vowel. The word is pronounced '**POIN**-yent'.

Meaning — Something that is deeply moving and makes you feel extremely sad.

Examples — *The sudden death of the dog was a poignant experience for the entire family.*

The movie brought back poignant memories of his childhood.

Listen, Rama, I have had enough of your poignant stories.

Etymology — From the Old French 'poignant', meaning 'sharp, pointed'.

Potato

/pə-<u>tei</u>-təu/

Pronunciation The first vowel sounds like the 'a' in 'china'. The second syllable 'ta' rhymes with 'say' and 'bay', and the third is pronounced like the word 'toe'. The word is pronounced 'pe-**TAY**-toe'.

Potatohead

Meaning An informal expression used to refer to someone who is stupid.

Examples *The management consists of a bunch of potatoheads!*

You'd better be careful. Anitha is no potatohead.

Listen to me, potatohead. Leave before someone beats you up.

Potpourri

/pəu-pə-<u>ri:</u>/

Pronunciation The 't' is silent; the first syllable rhymes with 'so' and 'no'. The 'ou' sounds like the 'a' in 'china', and the final 'i' is like the 'ee' in 'bees', 'fees' and 'sees'. One way of pronouncing the word is 'po-pe-**REE**'.

Meaning An assortment of dry petals and leaves from different plants and flowers placed in a room

	to give it a pleasant smell. Nowadays, the word is used to mean 'medley' or 'mixed bag': a collection consisting of unrelated things.
Examples	*My favourite author's latest book is a potpourri of essays and short stories.* *Mala sang a potpourri of old Hindi and Tamil songs.*
Etymology	From the French 'pot pourri', meaning 'rotten pot'.

Pounding the books

Meaning	Informal expression meaning 'to study very hard'.
Examples	*My neighbour's son has been pounding the books for over six months now.* *Sandhya had a test on Monday. She spent the entire weekend pounding the books.*

Pre-loved/Pre-owned

Meaning	Buying something second-hand.
Examples	*Would you be interested in buying a pre-loved home?* *Sujatha bought a pre-owned car last month.*

Precocious /prɪ-kəu-ʃəs/

Pronunciation — The 'e' sounds like the 'i' in 'bit', 'kit' and 'pit', while the following 'co' rhymes with 'no', 'so' and 'go'. The 'cious' sounds like the 'cious' in 'precious' and 'gracious'. The word is pronounced 'pri-**KO**-shes'.

Meaning — Mostly used to refer to children who exhibit adult-like maturity. They are far more intelligent and skilled than children of their age. The word can be used as a compliment and to show disapproval.

Examples — *The precocious Leya was admitted to the PhD programme at the age of 15.*

Why have you invited that precocious brat to our son's party?

Etymology — It comes from the Latin 'praecocis', meaning to 'mature or ripen early'.

Professional student

Meaning — Someone who keeps studying for one degree after another, and never takes up a job. He prefers to stay in college for as long as possible and is reluctant to embark on a career of his own. The term can be used as a compliment, as well as an insult.

Examples — *Your father's debts are mounting. I think it's about time you quit being a professional student. Find yourself a real job.*

When Gopi turned 40, he stopped being a professional student.

Profligate /prɔf-lɪ-gət/

Pronunciation — The first syllable sounds like 'Prof.', the abbreviation for 'professor'. The 'i' in the second is like the 'i' in 'bit' and 'sit', and the 'a' in the final syllable is like the 'a' in 'china'. The word is pronounced '**PROF**-li-get'.

Meaning — Someone who is reckless with his money; someone who wastes his resources. It can also be used to refer to someone who has little or no moral values.

Examples — *Rahul accused his former Vice Chancellor of profligate spending.*

According to scientists, our profligate fossil-fuel consumption led to global warming.

The bad company he kept turned Tarun into a profligate.

Etymology — The word comes from the Latin 'profligare', meaning 'ruin' or 'defeat'.

Profundity /prə-fʌn-də-tɪ/

Pronunciation The 'o' and the 'i' are like the 'a' in 'china'. The second syllable sounds like the word 'fund', and the final 'y' is like the 'i' in 'it', pit' and 'sit'. The word is pronounced 'pre-**FUN**-de-ti'.

Meaning Great knowledge or insight. When you talk about the profundity of a statement, you are implying that the meaning of the statement runs deep.

Examples *The committee was impressed by the candidate's knowledge and profundity.*

Some of his lyrics overflow with profundities.

Etymology From 'profound', which in turn is derived from the Latin 'profundus', meaning 'deep'.

Progeny /prɔ-dʒə-nɪ/

Pronunciation The 'o' in the first syllable is like the 'o' in 'hot', 'got' and not'. The 'g' is like the 'j' in 'juice', 'just' and 'jet', and the 'e' is like the 'a' in 'china'. The word is pronounced '**PRO**-je-ni'.

Meaning Mostly used in formal contexts to refer to one's children or descendants.

Examples *The Mafia Don sat behind the desk, and his numerous progeny stood around him.*

For some strange reason, the actor refused to answer questions about his progeny.

Etymology From the Latin 'progenies', meaning 'descendants, family'.

Psephologist /se-fɔ-lə-dʒɪst/

Pronunciation The first 'p' is silent and the 'ph' is like the 'f' in 'fish' and 'fees'. The first vowel is like the 'e' in 'set', sent' and 'sell'. The 'o' that follows is like the 'o' in 'got', 'not' and 'lot'. The last two syllables sound like the 'logist' in 'biologist' and 'geologist'. The word is pronounced 'se-**FO**-le-jist'.

Meaning Psephology is the scientific study of the way in which people vote in elections. A 'psephologist', therefore, is someone who studies how people vote – he comes up with the statistics, trends, etc.

Examples *Several psephologists were interviewed the day before the elections.*

My cousin Mohan wants to be a psephologist when he grows up.

Etymology From the Greek 'psephos', meaning 'pebbles'. The Greeks made use of pebbles to indicate the candidate of their choice.

Psych out /saik aut/

Pronunciation The 'p' in 'psych' is silent'. The word rhymes with 'bike' and 'mike'.

Meaning Mostly used in informal contexts to mean 'to become terribly excited about something'. You get so excited that you lose your ability to think clearly.

Examples *The children psyched out when they saw Dhoni walk onto the stage.*

Raju was so psyched out, he didn't know what to say.

Puerile /puə-rail/

Pronunciation The first syllable is pronounced like the word 'pure' and the second rhymes with the words 'file', 'pile' and 'mile'. The word is pronounced '**PURE**-rile'.

Meaning Being silly or childish.

Examples *The newspapers said that the plot of the new movie was puerile.*

The participants didn't laugh at my joke. They said it was puerile.

Etymology From the Latin 'puerilis', meaning 'boyish, childish'.

Pulchritude /pʌl-krɪ-tju:d/

Pronunciation — The 'pulch' rhymes with 'bulk' and 'hulk', and the following 'i' sounds like the 'i' in 'it', 'bit' and 'fit'. The final syllable is like the 'tude' in 'attitude' and 'aptitude'. The word is pronounced '**PUL**-kri-tyud'.

Meaning — Mostly used in formal contexts to refer to the physical beauty of a woman.

Examples — *The speaker said that it was not the actress' pulchritude that fascinated him.*

The reporter maintained that she had been sacked because she had lost her youthful pulchritude.

Etymology — From the Latin 'pulchritudo', meaning 'beautiful'.

Push the envelope

Meaning — Mostly used in informal contexts to mean 'to go beyond what is currently possible'. As one dictionary puts it, you attempt to 'stretch the boundaries' of something.

Examples — *As a teacher, he is always experimenting – always trying to push the envelope.*

Many believe Apple is a company that is constantly pushing the envelope.

Origin The expression was first used in the 1940s by US Air Force test pilots. Even today, when a pilot tests an aircraft, he usually pushes the envelope; he goes beyond the limits prescribed by the manufacturer in order to determine what the plane can do. The expression became a part of everyday language when Tom Wolfe's novel, *The Right Stuff,* was made into a movie in 1983.

Pusillanimous /pju:-sɪ-l͟æ-nɪ-məs/

Pronunciation The first syllable 'pu' rhymes with 'few', 'new' and 'cue'. The 'i' in the second and fourth syllables sounds like the 'i' in 'bit' and 'sit'. 'Lan' rhymes with 'man' and 'fan', while the final 'ou' is like the 'a' in 'china' One way of pronouncing the word is 'pyuu-si-**LAN**-i-mes'.

Meaning Weak and cowardly; someone who is frightened of taking risks, even very small ones.

Examples *Geetha is too pusillanimous to head a department.*

It's time we stopped being pusillanimous and started exploring the market.

Ashok is too pusillanimous to stand up to his opponents.

Etymology From the Latin 'pusillus', meaning 'very weak, little', and 'animus', meaning 'courage'.

Pussyfoot

Meaning To tread or walk softly like a cat. It can also mean 'to act cautiously'; to be afraid to take a decision or express an opinion.

Examples *The burglar pussyfooted down the stairs.*

Das, will you please stop pussyfooting around and tell us what you want done.

Stop pussyfooting about, and tell me what you think of my painting.

Origin In the early 1900s, the word was frequently used in America to refer to a detective. Theodore Roosevelt, the twenty-sixth President of the United States, popularised the use of the word.

Putative /pjuː-tə-tɪv/

Pronunciation The first syllable rhymes with 'few', 'dew' and 'cue'. The 'a' in the second is like the 'a' in 'china', and the following 'i' sounds like the 'i' in 'it', 'bit' and 'sit'. The word is pronounced '**PYUU**-te-tiv'.

Meaning — Generally believed or accepted to be true. You are not really sure if something is true or not, but you, like others, believe that it is. The word is normally used in formal contexts before nouns.

Examples — *There have been many attempts to capture the putative Abominable Snowman.*

The police shot and killed the putative leader of the terrorist organisation.

Etymology — It comes from the Latin 'putativus', meaning 'supposed'.

Quagmire /kwæg-mai-ə/

Pronunciation — The first syllable rhymes with 'swag' and 'mire' rhymes with 'fire', 'hire' and 'tire'. The word is pronounced '**KWAG**-mire'.

Meaning — The soft wet ground which people sometimes sink into and find very difficult to get out of is referred to as 'quagmire'. Figuratively, it means 'stuck, not making any progress'.

Examples — *After the heavy downpour, the road leading to the forest had become a quagmire.*

Many people in our country feel that we shouldn't get caught in the quagmire of Iraq.

Etymology — The obsolete word 'quag' meant 'marsh'.

Qualm /kwa:m/

Pronunciation — The 'qu' is like the 'qu' in 'quit' and 'quick', and the 'alm' rhymes with 'calm' and 'balm'. The word is pronounced '**KWAAM**'.

Meaning — To have misgivings about something; a feeling of doubt as to whether you are doing the right thing or not.

Examples — *The Minister felt no qualms about lying to the members of the press.*

The man had no qualms about stealing from his own parents.

Etymology — From the Old English 'cwealm', meaning 'death, murder'.

Quasi /kwei-zai/ /kwa:-zai/

Pronunciation — The 'qua' sounds like the 'qua' in 'quake'. The 's' is like the 'z' in 'zip' and 'zoo' and the following 'i' rhymes with 'by' and 'my'. One way of pronouncing the word is '**KWAY**-zai'. The 'a' can also sound like the 'a' in 'dark' and 'park'.

Meaning — Seemingly or partly. When you say that someone's theory is 'quasi-scientific', it means that at first glance it looks like a scientific theory, but it actually isn't. It does not include or contain all the features of such a theory.

Examples — *I was rather disappointed. We were served quasi-Rajasthani food.*

Sameer's quasi-American accent didn't fool anyone.

Etymology — It comes from the Latin 'quasi', meaning 'as it were' or 'almost'.

Que sera sera /kei sə-ra: sə-ra:/

Pronunciation — The 'que' sounds like 'Kay'; the 'e' in 'sera' is like the 'a' in 'china'. The final 'a' sounds like the 'ar' in 'dark' and 'park'. The expression is pronounced '**KAY** se-ra se-ra'.

Meaning — What will be, will be.

Examples — *I warned Amali about Prahlad, but she wouldn't listen. Que sera sera.*

Maria has to delay the submission of her PhD because she's fallen ill. Que sera sera.

Origin — This Spanish expression became popular thanks to a song sung by Doris Day.

Quid pro quo /kwɪd prəu kwəu/

Pronunciation — The 'qu' in the first and last words sounds like the 'qu' in 'quick' and 'quiz'. The 'o' is pronounced like the 'o' in 'so' and 'go'. The expression is pronounced 'kwid pro **KWO**'.

Meaning — This Latin expression literally means 'something for something'. In English, it is mostly used to mean 'to give something to someone in return or exchange for something else'.

Examples — *The Government denied that there was any quid pro quo involved in their decision.*

I don't think there's any company in our country that is immune to quid pro quo.

Quinquennial /kwɪŋ-kwe-nɪ-əl/

Pronunciation — The first syllable rhymes with 'swing', and the second with 'when'. The 'ial' is like the 'ial' in 'burial'. One way of pronouncing the word is 'kwing-**KWEN**-i-el'.

Meaning — The fifth anniversary of any event. The word can also be used to refer to an event that happens every five years or to something that lasts for five years.

Examples — *The Government will be sending a team to carry out the quinquennial inspection.*

Now that the quinquennial reviews are over, we don't have to worry for another five years.

Etymology — From the Latin 'quinque', meaning 'five', and 'annus', meaning 'year'.

Quintessential /kwɪn-tɪ-sen-ʃəl/

Pronunciation: 'Quint' rhymes with the word 'squint', and the syllables that follow are pronounced like the word 'essential'. The word is pronounced 'kwin-ti-**SEN**-shell'.

Meaning: A perfect example of something.

Examples: *According to my wife, John is the quintessential American.*

Nayaz is the quintessential hero: tall, dark and handsome.

Etymology: From the Latin 'quint essentia', meaning 'purest, most essential'.

Qui vive /ki: vi:v/

Pronunciation: 'Qui' is pronounced like the word 'key' and the 'i' in 'vive' sounds like the 'ee' in 'fees' and 'bees'. The expression is pronounced 'key-**VEEV**'.

Meaning: When you say that someone is 'on the qui vive', what you are implying is that he/she is alert; he/she is watching very carefully.

Examples: *Geetha is always on the qui vive for bargains.*

The soldiers were on the qui vive for another assault.

At times like these, we all have to be on the qui vive.

Etymology — This is a French expression, which literally means 'long live, who?'.

Quixotic /kwɪk-s̲ɔ̲-tɪk/

Pronunciation — One way is to pronounce the first syllable like the word 'quick', and the final syllable like the word 'tick'. The 'o' can be pronounced like the 'o' in 'pot', 'got' and 'hot'. The word can be pronounced 'kwik-**SO**-tik'.

Meaning — When you refer to someone's ideas or plans as being quixotic, you mean they are not practical; an idealist.

Examples — *The members of the secret society lived by a quixotic code of honour.*

The Minister is well known for his quixotic ideas.

Origin — The word comes from the title of a satirical novel that Miguel de Cervantes wrote: *Don Quixote*. The main character, Quixote, is an eccentric individual who decides to become a knight in shining armour and save the world. Unfortunately for the ageing hero, the goals he sets for himself are so lofty that they are practically impossible to achieve. After several misadventures, the hero returns to his village a dejected man.

Rambunctious /ræm-bʌŋk-ʃəs/

Pronunciation: The first syllable rhymes with the words 'dam' and 'ham', while the second is pronounced like the word 'bunk'. The 'ct' is like the 'sh' in 'ship' and 'shape', and the 'iou' is like the 'a' in 'china'. One way of pronouncing the word is 'ram-**BUNK**-shes'.

Meaning: Full of youthful energy, and therefore somewhat difficult to control. The word can also be used to mean 'very noisy and disorderly'.

Examples: *The rambunctious entertainer collapsed during the first scene.*

There was a lot of drinking, so it wasn't surprising that the students became rambunctious.

Rapport /ræ-pɒ/

Pronunciation: The first vowel sounds like the 'a' in 'cat' and 'bat' and the second syllable sounds like the word 'pore'. The word is pronounced 'ra-**PORE**'.

Meaning: To understand and have a good relationship with someone; to communicate with the individual easily.

Examples *Lots of people find it strange that I have a good rapport with Bala.*

My physics teacher has an excellent rapport with all his students.

Though Mahesh and I have worked together for several years, we still haven't developed a close rapport.

Etymology From the French 'rapporter', meaning 'to bring back'.

Rara avis /rɜː-rə ei-vis/

Pronunciation The 'rar' sounds like the word 'rare', and the following 'a' is like the 'a' in 'china'. 'Avis' rhymes with the name 'Davis'. One way of pronouncing the expression is 'ra-re **A**-vis'.

Meaning Rare bird; in everyday contexts, the expression is mostly used to refer to a unique person or thing.

Examples *You are lucky to have found someone like Vikram. He's quite the rara avis if you ask me.*

The new professor is both knowledgeable and has a good sense of humour – a rara avis.

Etymology In Latin, 'rara' means 'rare' and 'avis' means 'bird'.

Raucous /rɒ̲-kəs/

Pronunciation The 'rau' sounds like the word 'raw' and the following 'ou' sounds like the 'a' in 'china'. The word is pronounced '**RAW**-kes'.

Meaning A harsh and unpleasantly loud sound, annoying to the ear. Frequently used to mean 'boisterous and disorderly'.

Examples *The infant started crying when he heard Vidya's raucous laughter.*

Although the neighbours complained several times, the raucous party went on all night.

Etymology From the Latin 'raucus', meaning 'hoarse'.

Razzmatazz /ræ̲z̲-mə-tæz/

Pronunciation The 'a' in the first and third syllables is pronounced like the 'a' in 'act', 'pact' and 'fact'. The vowel in the second syllable sounds like the 'a' in 'china'. One way of pronouncing the word is '**RAZ**-me-taz'.

Meaning The pomp, glitter and noise which some shows include to attract the attention of the audience. Slang dictionaries define the word as 'deceptive talk' or 'hype'. The word can also be spelt 'razzamatazz'.

Examples *The razzmatazz of the function amused the foreign delegates.*

As expected, the awards ceremony was filled with razzmatazz.

Don't give me all that razzmatazz, Meera. How much is this going to cost me?

Cut out the razzmatazz, will you? How stupid do you think I am?

Etymology Some believe it comes from 'razzle-dazzle'.

Read you loud and clear

Meaning To understand what someone is telling you.

Examples *You want this job done by next week. I read you loud and clear.*

Of course, I understand what you're suggesting. I read you loud and clear.

Realtor /rɪəl-tə/

Pronunciation The 'real' is pronounced like the word 'real' and the following 'o' like the 'a' in 'china'. The word is pronounced '**REAL**-te'.

Meaning Someone who deals in and is licensed to sell real estate.

Examples *The realtor showed us several houses this morning.*

Chanchala's husband works as a realtor.

Origin — The word was coined by C. Chadbourn in 1916.

Recuse

/rɪ-kjuːz/

Pronunciation — The 'e' is like the 'i' in 'bit', 'fit' and 'hit', and the following 'cuse' is like the 'cuse' in 'accuse' and 'excuse'. The word is pronounced 'ri-**KYOOZ**'.

Meaning — When a judge finds that the defendant is a person who is well known to him, he usually recuses or removes himself from the case. He does this to ensure there is no conflict of interest.

Examples — *The defendant's lawyer requested the Judge to recuse himself.*

The Judge was not willing to recuse herself from the case.

Etymology — From the Latin 'recusare', meaning 'to refuse'.

Red carpet treatment/welcome

Meaning — When you are given a 'red carpet welcome' or the 'red carpet treatment', you are given special treatment on your arrival at some place. You are treated as a guest of honour.

Examples — *When Nelson Mandela visited India, he was given a red carpet welcome.*

The famous film star was rather disappointed that he wasn't given the red carpet treatment.

I was quite surprised that they gave me a red carpet welcome.

Origin — In the old days, the colour red was associated with honour. Important people wore red robes. A red-coloured carpet was always rolled out for royalty.

Red-letter day

Meaning — Important or special days.

Examples — *Preethi says that 21 October is a red-letter day because that's the day she arrived in America.*

Maya considers her wedding anniversary a red-letter day.

Origin — In the old days, the numbers on the calendar were marked either in red or in black ink. The days that were considered 'holy days' were usually marked in red.

Redress /rɪ-dres/

Pronunciation — The first 'e' sounds like the 'i' in 'it', 'bit' and 'hit', and the second syllable is pronounced like the word 'dress'. One way of pronouncing this formal word is 'ri-**DRESS**'.

Meaning — Sometimes, when we injure someone or treat someone badly, we are forced to pay them some form of compensation. This money that we pay the individual is called 'redress'. When used as a verb, the word means to 'to make up for' or 'compensate'.

Examples — *Rama went to court to seek redress for the way the selection committee had discriminated against her.*

The Chief Minister, as expected, refused to redress the grievances of the striking teachers.

Etymology — The word comes from 're', meaning 'again', and 'drecier', meaning 'straighten'.

Regift

Meaning — Giving a gift that you have received and don't like to someone else. The word can be used as a noun and a verb.

Examples — *Geetha is planning to regift the photo frame that she got from Bala.*

I don't have the time to shop. I'll give them a regift.

"I wanted a baby sister. Can we regift him?"

Reminisce /re-mə-nɪs/

Pronunciation 'Rem' rhymes with 'them' and 'gem', and the following 'i' is like the 'a' in 'china'. The final 'nisce' rhymes with 'kiss' and 'miss'. The word is pronounced 're-mi-**NIS**'.

Meaning To dwell on past events; to talk with great pleasure about the good times you had.

Examples *When the two friends met, they reminisced about their college days.*

Sarita says that she doesn't like to reminisce because it makes her feel old.

Etymology From the Latin 'reminiscentia', meaning 'recollection'.

Renaissance /rə-nei-səns/ /re-nə-sa:ns/

Pronunciation One way is to pronounce the vowels in the first and third syllables like the 'a' in 'china', and the 'ai' in the second like the 'ay' in 'ray' and 'bay'. The word, in this case, is pronounced 're-**NAY**-sens'. Some people pronounce the 'e' like the 'e' in 'set' and 'pet' and the following 'ai' like the 'a' in 'china'. They rhyme the final syllable with 'dance' and 'chance' and pronounce the word '**RE**-ne-saans'.

Meaning The period between the 14th and 16th centuries in Europe is usually referred to as the 'Renaissance'. During this period, people began to take an active interest in art, literature, and science. 'Renaissance' is now used to talk about a rebirth of interest in some activity.

Examples *Bhalla believes that letter writing will experience a renaissance soon.*

In many of our cities, traditional music and dancing are experiencing a renaissance.

Etymology This French word literally means 'rebirth'.

Rendezvous /rɔn-dei-vuː/

Pronunciation
The first syllable is pronounced like the name 'Ron' and the second like the word 'day'. The final 'ous' sounds like the 'oo' in 'cool', 'pool' and 'fool'. One way of pronouncing the word is '**RON**-day-voo'.

Meaning
Nowadays, the word is mostly used to refer to the place where a particular group of people usually present themselves or meet. It can also be used to refer to a secret meeting at a particular place or time.

Examples
The coffee shop is a popular rendezvous for the students.

Don't be late for our rendezvous.

Etymology
It comes from the French 'rendez', meaning 'present', and 'vous', meaning 'you'. The word originally meant 'present yourselves'.

Renege /rɪ-niːg/ /rɪ-neig/

Pronunciation
The first syllable is pronounced like 'rin'. The 'ee' can be pronounced like the 'ee' in 'cheese' and 'breeze' or like the 'ay' in 'bay' or 'may'. The word can be pronounced either 'ri-**NEEG**' or 'ri-**NAYG**'.

Meaning
To go back on or break a promise that you had made.

Examples — *If Sunanda reneges on the agreement now, I'll file a case against her.*

Ever since he reneged on the contract, no company wants to do business with him.

Etymology — From the Latin 'renegare', meaning 'deny'.

Repertoire /re-pə-twa:/

Pronunciation — The 'rep' rhymes with 'pep' and 'hep', while the second 'e' sounds like the 'a' in 'china'. The 'o' is pronounced like the 'w' in 'when' and 'what', and the final 'ire' like the 'a' in 'bath', 'father' and 'path'. One way of pronouncing the word is '**RE**-pe-twaa'.

Meaning — Refers to the skills that an individual has which enable him to perform different tasks.

Examples — *Surabhi's repertoire is limited when it comes to cooking.*

The up-and-coming artist has hundreds of old songs in her repertoire.

Etymology — It comes from the Latin 'repertorium', meaning 'inventory'. The word was originally used to refer to the list of plays, songs or dances that an artist or a group was capable of performing.

Requiem /rek-wɪ-əm/

Pronunciation The first syllable rhymes with the words 'deck', 'check' and 'beck'. The following 'ui' sounds like the 'wi' in 'win' and 'wish', and the final 'e' is like the 'a' in 'china'. One way of pronouncing the word is '**RECK**-wi-em'.

Meaning A mass held in church honouring someone who is dead. The word can also be used to refer to any piece of music which is performed to honour someone who has died.

Examples *A requiem was held for the children killed in the shooting.*

The composer wrote the piece as a requiem for his friend.

Etymology The word comes from the Latin 'requies', meaning 'rest'.

Research /rɪ-sɜːtʃ/ /riː-sɜːtʃ/

Pronunciation The British pronounce the vowel in the first syllable like the 'i' in 'sit' and pit', while the Americans pronounce it like the 'ee' in 'feel and 'peel'. The British put the stress on the second syllable ('ri-**SEARCH**'), while the Americans put it on the first ('**REE**-search').

Meaning — A detailed study of something. There was a time when the plural form was 'research'. Nowadays, the word 'researches' has become common.

Examples — *There is some fascinating research going on in the area of aphasia.*

The researches carried out by our team produced unexpected results.

The first chapter of the book summarises his researches.

Etymology — From the Old French 'rececher', meaning 'search closely'.

Rethink

Meaning — The act of thinking about something again; when you 'have a rethink' about a plan, you reassess it. You may make changes to the original or you may choose to discard the plan altogether. It can be used as a noun and a verb.

Examples — *The Minister believes that a fundamental rethink on higher education is needed.*

If you ask me, your proposal needs a rethink.

My boss told me to rethink my strategy.

Righteous /rai-tʃəs/

Pronunciation — The word consists of two syllables. The first syllable rhymes with the words 'hi', 'bye' and 'die'. The 't' sounds like the 'ch' in 'church', 'cheese' and 'chips', and the 'eou' is like the 'a' in 'china'. The word is pronounced '**RYE**-ches'.

Meaning — Morally upright. When you say that someone is 'righteous', you are implying that the individual can be trusted because he will scrupulously follow all moral and religious codes. When such people get angry, their anger is morally justifiable.

Examples — *The villagers do what Ramani wants them to because they regard him as a righteous and holy man.*

Meera's outburst of righteous anger is quite understandable.

Etymology — From the Old English 'rihtwiis' – 'right wise' – meaning 'wise, way'.

Rigmarole /rɪg-mə-rəul/

Pronunciation — The first syllable rhymes with 'pig', 'wig' and 'big', while the 'a' in the second is pronounced like the 'a' in 'china'. The final syllable sounds like the word 'role'. One simple way of pronouncing the word is '**RIG**-me-role'.

Meaning — Any long, foolish, confusing speech or discourse. It can also be used to refer to any long, complicated procedure. Some people spell the word 'rigamarole'.

Examples — *Sneha went through the rigmarole of installing a software package that was already on her computer.*

The speaker went into a long rigmarole about the awards he had won.

Origin — The word comes from 'ragman roll', a game children played in the past.

Riposte /rɪ-pɔst/ /rɪ-pəust/

Pronunciation — The 'i' is like the 'i' in 'bit' and 'hit'. The Americans pronounce the second syllable like the word 'post', while the British rhyme it with 'cost'. In both varieties, however, the stress is on the second syllable.

Meaning — A quick, witty reply to something that someone has said; a retort.

Examples — *It's no fun teasing Madhu. She's incapable of coming up with a suitable riposte.*

Handle Jagdeep with care. He is well known for his biting ripostes.

Etymology — A term used in fencing; comes from the Italian 'riposta', meaning 'reply'. Winston Churchill, the Prime Minister who was sometimes referred to as 'the British bulldog', was well known for his ripostes. Once, a woman told Churchill that if she had been his wife, she would have poisoned his tea. To which Churchill replied, "If you were my wife, I'd drink it!"

Risqué

/rɪs-kei/

Pronunciation — The first syllable is pronounced like the word 'risk', and the final 'ue' like the 'ay' in 'gay', 'bay' and 'may'. The word is pronounced 'ris-**KAY**'.

Meaning — A joke or a story that is 'risqué' is slightly off colour or indecent; something bordering on impropriety.

Examples — *Raju, please remember your dad's warning. No risqué jokes at the party.*

The new director wanted his young actress to wear risqué clothes.

Etymology — The word comes from the French 'risqué', meaning 'risk'.

Roger

Meaning — Message has been received and understood.

Examples — *"You may be cleared to land in another five minutes." "Roger".*

"Stop watching TV and go do your homework." "Roger that, Mom!"

Origin — 'Roger' has been part of pilot lingo since 1927. It was used to let the person they were talking to know that the message had been received. The word 'Roger' was chosen to represent the letter 'r', which of course is the first letter in the word 'received'.

Rotund /rəu-t<u>ʌnd</u>/

Pronunciation — The 'ro' rhymes with 'so', 'no' and 'go', and the syllable that follows sounds like the words 'fund' and 'stunned'. One way of pronouncing the word is 'row-**TUND**'.

Meaning — Someone who is rather plump. The word can be used to describe both people and objects.

Examples — *They made an odd couple. She was tall and slim, and he was short and rotund.*

Several huge, rotund vessels containing pickles were put in the truck.

Etymology — From the Latin 'rotundus', meaning 'circular, round'.

Rubbish (verb)

Meaning — Used in informal contexts to mean 'to severely criticise someone/something'; to dismiss someone/something as being worthless.

Examples — *The teacher took great delight in rubbishing the students' ideas.*

Kanchana's debut film was rubbished by the critics.

Sabotage /sæ-bə-ta:ʒ/

Pronunciation — The first syllable rhymes with 'tab' and 'fab', while the vowel in the second is like the 'a' in 'china'. The final 'age' sounds like the 'age' in 'mirage' and 'garage'. The word is pronounced '**SA**-be-taazh'.

Meaning — To willfully destroy or damage something – machinery, building, equipment, etc. The word can be used as a noun and a verb.

Examples — *Karthika is sabotaging our efforts to find a solution to the problem.*

The rebels have sabotaged everything – railway tracks, dams and water pipelines.

The police believe that it was an act of sabotage.

Etymology 'Sabot' refers to wooden shoes; the French word 'saboter' literally means 'to walk noisily'.

Salad /sæ-ləd/

Pronunciation The first vowel is like the 'a' in 'camp', 'damp' and 'champ', while the second sounds like the 'a' in 'china'. The word is pronounced '**SA**-led'. Many Indians wrongly put the stress on the second syllable.

Meaning A dish containing a lot of raw, cut vegetables.

Examples *Usha usually has a bowl of salad for lunch.*
I would like to have salad to begin with.

Etymology Shortened form of the Latin 'herba salata', meaning 'salted vegetables'.

Sandwich /sæn-wɪtʃ/ /sæn-wɪdʒ/

Pronunciation The first syllable 'sand' rhymes with 'fan', 'ban' and 'can'. Some people pronounce the 'ch' like the 'ch' in 'cheap' and 'chess'; others like the 'j' in 'jeep' and 'juice'. The stress is on the first syllable.

Meaning An item of food consisting of two slices of bread with a piece of meat or a slice of cheese in between. It can also be used to mean 'to be squeezed between two things'.

Examples *Promilla sat there sandwiched between two really fat men.*

I'm sorry, I don't have the time to make you a sandwich.

Origin The name of a village in Kent, meaning 'village of sand'.

Sang-froid /sa:ŋ-fwa:/

Pronunciation One simple way is to pronounce the vowels in the two syllables like the 'a' in 'dance' and 'chance'. The 'r' is like the 'w' in 'wet', 'well' and 'with', and the final 'd' is silent. The word is pronounced 'saang-**FWAA**'.

Meaning The ability to stay composed or calm in a demanding or tense situation.

Examples *Though the crowd was extremely hostile, the visiting team showed remarkable sang-froid.*

Vittal lacks the sang-froid that is expected of a doctor in the ER.

Etymology A word of French origin, meaning 'cold blood'.

Satchel /sætʃ-əl/

Pronunciation The first syllable rhymes with 'hatch', 'catch' and 'patch'; the following 'e' sounds like the 'a' in 'china'. The word is pronounced '**SATCH**-el'.

Meaning A rectangular bag, made of thick cloth, with a long shoulder strap. Before backpacks, children used to carry their books in satchels.

Examples *Somebody should tell Madhavi to discard her old satchel.*

The guard asked me to show him what was inside the satchel before he let me in.

Etymology From the Latin 'saccus', meaning 'bag'.

Savoir-faire /sæv-wa: f<u>ɜə</u>/

Pronunciation The 'a' in the first syllable is like the 'a' in 'fat', 'bat' and 'sat'. The 'o' sounds like the 'w' in 'wet' and 'went' and the following 'ir' is like the 'ar' in 'park' and 'dark'. 'Faire' sounds like 'fair/fare'. The word is pronounced 'sav-waa **FARE**'.

Meaning Having the ability to say and do the right thing in a social situation.

Examples *Meena is famous in diplomatic circles for her savoir-faire.*

I wouldn't hire Bhaskar because he doesn't possess the required savoir-faire.

Javed defused the situation through his savoir-faire.

Etymology A French expression which literally means 'to know how to do'.

Scaremonger

Meaning Someone who spreads rumours or stories that cause panic among the public.

Examples *If you ask me, our reporters are nothing more than scaremongers.*

Scaremongers want us to believe that cell phones will turn our brains to pulp.

Etymology 'Monger' was originally used to refer to someone who sold goods – 'fishmonger', 'cheesemonger', 'ironmonger', etc. Nowadays, 'monger' is usually used with someone who participates in activities which cause trouble.

Schadenfreude /ʃa:-dən-frɔi-də/

Pronunciation The 'scha' sounds like the 'shar' in 'sharp' and 'shark', while the 'e' in the second and final syllables sounds like the 'a' in 'china'. The 'eu' in 'freude' is like the 'oy' in 'boy', 'toy' and 'coy'. The word is pronounced '**SHAA**-den-froy-de'.

Meaning The feeling of delight or joy that we get when terrible things happen to other people.

Examples *The leader of the opposition watched the in-fighting with Schadenfreude.*

Reading about the terrible performance of his replacement was his dose of Schadenfreude.

Etymology In German, 'Freude' means 'joy' and 'Shaden' means 'harm'.

Schedule /ʃedʒ-u:l/ /skedʒ-u:l/

Pronunciation The Americans and the British pronounce this word differently. The English pronounce the 'sch' like the 'sh' in 'ship' and 'sheep', and the following 'd' like the 'j' in 'jam' and 'juice'. The final syllable rhymes with 'pool' and 'cool'. The Americans, on the other hand, pronounce the 'sch' like the 'sk' in 'skill' and 'skin'. The main stress, in both varieties, is on the first syllable.

Meaning One's plans for the day; timetable.

Examples *Anuraag has had to make several changes in his weekly schedule.*

Check the train schedule and let me know when the next one to Mumbai is.

Etymology From the Latin 'schedula', meaning 'strip of paper'.

Schism /ʃɪz-əm/ /sɪz-əm/

Pronunciation — The 'sch' can be pronounced like the 'sh' in 'ship' and 'shape' or like the 's' in 'sit' and 'sin'. The 'ism' sounds like the 'ism' in 'prism'. The word can be pronounced '**SHIZ**-em' or '**SIZ**-em'.

Meaning — Used in formal contexts to refer to a disagreement among a group of people – this rift usually results in a single group breaking up into two.

Examples — *The strike failed because there was a schism within the Union.*

If the controversy continues, it is likely to create a schism within the party.

Etymology — From the French 'scisme', meaning 'split'. The word was first used to refer to the split that occurred within the church in 1054.

Schizophrenia /skɪt-səu-friː-niə/

Pronunciation — The first two syllables are pronounced like the words 'skit' and 'so'. The 'phre' sounds like the word 'free', while the final 'ia' is like the 'ea' in words like 'dear and 'fear'. One way of pronouncing the word is 'skit-so-**FREE**-nie'.

Meaning — A kind of mental illness; one in which a person has all kinds of delusions. As a result, he/she behaves strangely.

Examples — *Several people in Rahul's family have schizophrenia.*

There is a chapter in this book on schizophrenia.

The way some of our politicians behave, one wonders if they have schizophrenia.

Etymology — It comes from the Greek 'skhizein', meaning 'to split', and 'phren', meaning 'heart, mind'.

Schmaltzy /ʃmɔlt-sɪ/

Pronunciation — The 'sch' is pronounced like the 'sh' in 'ship', 'sheep' and 'shin'. The 'malt' sounds like the word 'malt', and the final 'zy' sounds like the 'si' in 'sit', 'sip' and 'sin'. The word is pronounced '**SHMALT**-si'.

Meaning — Mostly used in informal contexts to mean 'excessively sentimental'. When you refer to a piece of music or a work of fiction as being 'schmaltzy', you are suggesting that the work is of no significance; it has no artistic value.

Examples — *The play was so schmaltzy that many people walked out after the first act.*

Your favourite author's latest book is pure schmaltz.

Etymology From the Yiddish word 'shmalts', meaning 'melted fat'.

Schmuck /ʃmʌk/

Pronunciation The 'sch' is like the 'sh' in 'she' and 'sheep', and the following letters rhyme with 'duck' and 'suck'. The word is pronounced '**SHMUCK**'.

Meaning Used in informal contexts to refer to a stupid or silly individual.

Examples *I can't believe that Revathi is going to marry a schmuck like him.*

Who is the schmuck standing there in pink pants?

Scintillating /sɪn-tɪ-lei-tɪŋ/

Pronunciation The first syllable is pronounced like the word 'sin', the second like the word 'till' and the third like the word 'ate'. One way of pronouncing the word is '**SIN**-ti-late-ing'.

Meaning Funny, lively, witty; very skillful or clever.

Examples *The conversation at the party was scintillating.*

My favourite actor gave a scintillating performance on TV last night.

My father tells me that my great grandfather had a scintillating personality.

Etymology Same as 'scintilla'.

Scintilla /sɪn-t̲ɪ̲-lə/

Pronunciation The 'scin' is pronounced like the word 'sin', and the following syllable is pronounced like the word 'till'. The final 'a' is like the 'a' in 'china'. The word is pronounced 'sin-**TILL**-e'.

Meaning An extremely small amount of something; iota.

Examples *According to the lawyer, there isn't a scintilla of evidence against his client.*

I wouldn't worry if I were you. There isn't a scintilla of truth in what he is saying.

Etymology From the Latin 'scintilla', meaning 'spark'.

Scourge /skɜ:dʒ/

Pronunciation The 'sc' sounds like the 'sk' in 'skill', 'skit' and 'skin', and the following 'ourge' is like the word 'urge'. The word is pronounced '**SKURGE**'.

Meaning Someone or something that causes lot of suffering, trouble or destruction. It can be used as a noun or a verb.

Examples *AIDS continues to be a scourge in India and other developing countries.*

The dictator had killed many people. But he wasn't scourged by guilt.

Etymology It comes from the Old French 'escorge', meaning 'to whip'.

Second-guess

Meaning To predict what someone will do; to outguess a person.

Examples *The police tried to second-guess the murderer's next move.*

Charles tried to second-guess what the rules would be five years from now.

Seige mentality

Meaning A person believing that everyone is trying to harm him or is out to get him.

Examples *The findings suggested that many in the police department had a siege mentality that isolated them from the common people whom they were supposed to serve and protect.*

According to the newspaper report, the constant threat of sniper attack is pushing US forces into a siege mentality.

Sepulchre /sep-əl-kə/

Pronunciation — The first syllable rhymes with 'pep', 'rep' and 'hep'. The vowel in the second syllable and the final 're' sound like the 'a' in 'china'. The 'ch' is like the 'k' in 'king' and 'kiss'. The word is pronounced '**SEP**-el-ke'.

Meaning — A burial chamber made of stone; the casket placed in the chamber is also usually made of stone.

Example — *Rohit tries to visit the sepulchre every six months.*

Etymology — It comes from the Latin 'sepulcrum', meaning 'burial place'.

Serendipity /se-rən-dɪ-pɪ-tɪ/

Pronunciation — The first vowel sounds like the 'e' in 'set', 'bet' and 'get', while the 'e' in the second is like the 'a' in 'china'. The 'i' in the third and fourth syllables and the final 'y' are pronounced like the 'i' in 'sit', 'bit' and 'hit'. The word is pronounced 'se-ren-**DI**-pi-ti'.

Meaning — The lucky tendency that some people have in finding interesting or valuable things by chance. The word is considered formal, and is mostly used in literary contexts.

Examples — *According to the artist, some of the best effects in his garden have been the result of serendipity.*

Nutan became a millionaire thanks to a fortunate stroke of serendipity.

Origin — 'Serendip' is the old Persian name for Sri Lanka. In the fairy tale, *The Three Princes of Serendip*, the main characters make wonderful discoveries by chance. Horace Walpole, coined the word 'serendipity' in 1754 in a letter he wrote to his friend.

Severed /se-vəd/

Pronunciation — 'Sever' rhymes with 'never' and 'clever'. The word is pronounced '**SEV**-ed'.

Meaning — When you sever something, you cut it off completely. When you sever a relationship with someone, you abruptly end it.

Examples — *The impact of the collision was such that the driver's head was severed.*

I think we should sever diplomatic relations with China.

Etymology — From the Old French 'sevrer', meaning 'to separate'.

Sew /səu/

Pronunciation It is pronounced like the word 'so'. Many Indians tend to pronounce it like the word 'sue'.

Shake the pagoda tree

Meaning To make money or become rich very quickly.

Example *In the 70s and 80s, many Indians went to Dubai hoping to shake the pagoda tree.*

Origin The idiom, which is seldom heard nowadays, is believed to have been used by the British when they ruled India. According to scholars, the 'pagoda', refers to a coin made either of silver or gold.

Shell-shocked

Meaning The difficult experience which an individual has undergone recently which has left him confused and anxious.

Examples *I think Aparna is a little shell-shocked after the final exam.*

Vinita felt shell-shocked after coping with the boisterous twins all day.

The shell-shocked investors trooped in silently.

Origin — The word 'shell' refers to bombs. The term refers to the gamut of emotions – anger, frustration, confusion, etc. – that one goes through when the city you are living in is constantly bombed.

Shenanigans /ʃə-næ-nɪ-gənz/

Pronunciation — The 'e' in the first syllable and the 'a' in the final syllable are like the 'a' in 'china'. The next two syllables are pronounced like the word 'nanny', and the final 's' is like the 'z' in 'zip' and 'zoo'. One way of pronouncing the word is 'she-**NA**-ny-genz'.

Meaning — The word is mostly used in informal contexts to refer to the dishonest practices or immoral behaviour of an individual.

Examples — *All news channels have focused on the shenanigans of Kalmadi and his associates.*

The police were too scared to look into the Minister's financial shenanigans.

Origin — According to one theory, the word comes from the Irish saying *'Shee nanna gasne'*, meaning 'the Shee are rattling the dishes'. The Irish believed that 'Shee' were spirits that took great delight in moving furniture around in a house!

Shibboleth /ʃɪb-(ə)-leθ/

Pronunciation The first syllable 'shib' rhymes with 'ship' and 'shin'. The 'o' sounds like the 'a' in 'china' and the final 'e' is like the 'e' in 'set' and 'bet'. The word is pronounced '**SHI**-be-leth'. Some people drop the 'o' in the second syllable and pronounce the word '**SHIB**-leth'.

Meaning A word, phrase or custom which one can use to prove that he/she is a true member of a group. It is also used to refer to an old belief or custom which is considered important even today.

Examples *Let's come up with something new. People are sick and tired of listening to our old shibboleths.*

The villagers are unwilling to let go of the shibboleths of child marriage.

Origin It comes from the Hebrew 'sibbolet', meaning 'water' or 'ear of corn'. According to the Hebrew Bible, the Gileadites and the Ephraimites were two tribes that were at war with each other. When the Ephraimites invaded their neighbour, they were soundly thrashed. To prevent the enemy from escaping, the Gileadites set up blockades at various points. Whenever a soldier was caught, the Gileadites made him say the word 'shibboleth'. The

Ephraimites had a problem pronouncing this word because the sound 'sh' did not exist in their language. When a soldier mispronounced the word, he was killed.

Shilly-shally /ʃɪ-lɪ ʃæ-lɪ/

Pronunciation — The first word rhymes with 'silly' and 'hilly', while the first syllable of 'shally' is pronounced like the word 'shall'. The word is pronounced '**SHILL**-i shall-i'.

Meaning — Informal expression, meaning 'being unable to decide or make up one's mind about something'.

Examples — *If you keep shilly-shallying about what to wear, we are going to be late for the concert.*

Anoushka shilly-shallied for two days. Finally, she said no.

Venkatesh never shilly-shallies. He is always sure about what he wants to do.

Origin — It is a repetition of what undecided people normally say: 'shall I, shall I?'

Shoestring budget

Meaning — Given a very small amount of money to spend.

Examples — *My father says we'll be making our next film on a shoestring budget.*

For the next two months, we'll be living on a shoestring budget.

Origin — What we call 'shoelace', Americans call 'shoestring'. As we all know, shoestrings are pretty inexpensive; one doesn't really have to spend too much money to buy a pair.

Shopaholic /ʃɔp-ə-h̲ɔ̲-lɪk/

Pronunciation — The first syllable sounds like the word 'shop', and the following 'a' is like the 'a' in 'china'. The final two syllables sound like the 'holic' in 'alcoholic' and 'workaholic'. The word is pronounced 'shop-e-**HO**-lic'.

Meaning — Someone who is addicted to shopping; a compulsive shopper.

Examples — *Though she denies being one, Rama is a shopaholic.*

Last month's Diwali sale is one that all shopaholics will remember.

Etymology — Combination of 'shop' and 'alcoholic'.

Showboating

Meaning — Showing off in order to attract the attention of others; annoying form of behaviour that players display on the field. A 'showboat' is someone who shows off; an attention seeker.

Examples — *There is too much showboating in cricket these days. It is no longer a gentleman's game.*

When the champion won the title for the sixth time, there was very little showboating.

I don't like the new captain. He's a showboat.

Origin — A showboat was a large boat with a big stage which provided different forms of entertainment for the public.

Shuteye

Meaning — Used in informal contexts in American English to mean 'sleep'.

Examples — *I manage to get twenty minutes of shuteye while I'm on the bus.*

Vikas looks exhausted. Tell him to go get some shuteye.

Sic /sɪk/

Pronunciation — Same as 'sick'.

Meaning — The word is always placed within brackets after someone's quote. It indicates that although the quote contains a mistake, the fault is not

	yours, but that of the person whom you are quoting. The error is in the original quote.
Examples	*The notice read 'Skool (sic) reopens tomorrow'.* *She said she couldn't 'cope up' (sic) with the work.*
Etymology	From the Latin 'sic', meaning 'in this way'.

Silhouette /sɪl-ʊ-et/

Pronunciation	The first syllable rhymes with 'fill', 'pill' and 'bill', and the following 'o' is like the 'u' in 'put' and 'pull'. The final 'ette' is like the 'et' in 'pet' and 'set'. One way of pronouncing the word is 'sil-u-**ET**'.
Meaning	The dark outline that you see of an object or person against a bright background is referred to as a silhouette.
Examples	*As the sun began to rise, one could see the dark silhouette of the fort.* *Silhouetted against the bright lights was the figure of an old woman.* *I want to get a picture of you looking at the dark silhouette of the statue.*
Origin	Etienne de Silhouette was a French author and politician who lived in the 18th century. During

this period, in the world of art, the silhouette portrait had become a rage. While the common man fell in love with the silhouette, art critics took great delight in rubbishing it. When de Silhouette became the Finance Minister, he reduced the budget for the nobility, tripled the taxes on bachelors, and did many other things which made him very unpopular with the powers that be. In order to ridicule the man, the aristocrats began to apply his name to what they believed was meaningless art.

Silver bullet

Meaning Something that provides a very quick solution to a complex or difficult problem. A silver bullet is like a magic wand that makes all problems disappear.

Examples *There is no silver bullet that will solve all the problems of the company.*

The children think they have found a silver bullet for their numerous problems.

Origin Even today, many people believe that creatures like ghosts, vampires and werewolves exist. In the past, the standard belief was that the only way to kill a werewolf was by shooting it with silver bullets.

Sine die /sai-nɪ dai-i:/

Pronunciation: The 'si' rhymes with 'hi' and 'bye', and the following 'e' is like the 'i' in 'kit' and 'sit'. The 'di' sounds like the word 'die' and the final 'e' is like the 'ee' in 'feet' and 'meet'. One way of pronouncing the word is 'sy-ni **DIE**-ee'.

Meaning: Normally used in legal contexts; it means 'indefinitely postponed, without a date being fixed for a future meeting'.

Examples: *The meeting was adjourned sine die.*

As expected, Parliament adjourned sine die.

Etymology: From the Latin 'sine', meaning 'without', and 'dies', meaning 'day'. The expression literally means 'without a fixed day'.

Sine qua non /sɪ-nei kwa: nəun/

Pronunciation: The 'i' in 'sine' sounds like the 'i' in 'pit', 'bit' and 'sit', and the following 'ne' is pronounced like the word 'nay'. The 'a' in 'qua' sounds like the 'a' in 'bath' and 'path', and the final word is pronounced like the word 'known'. One way of pronouncing the expression is 'sin-ay kwa **KNOWN**'.

Meaning: Mostly used in formal contexts to mean 'something that is absolutely essential'.

Examples — *In my opinion, patience is a sine qua non for a teacher.*

Sachi says that a sense of humour is a sine qua non for a job in her company.

Etymology — It is a Latin expression, meaning 'without (sine) which (qua) not (non)'.

Sinister /sɪ̲-nɪs-tə/

Pronunciation — It rhymes with the word 'minister'; the stress is on the first syllable.

Meaning — Threatening; making someone feel that something bad is going to happen.

Examples — *When I heard the sinister music, I knew that something terrible was going to happen.*

In the movie, the villain lives in a sinister-looking place.

A sinister-looking woman sat behind the desk reading a magazine.

Etymology — From the Latin 'sinister', meaning 'left' or 'on the left side'.

Skulduggery /skʌl-d̲ʌ̲g̲-ə-rɪ/

Pronunciation — The first syllable is like the word 'skull' and the second is pronounced like the word 'dug'. The word is pronounced 'skull-**DUG**-e-ri'.

Meaning — Used in formal contexts to refer to dishonest activities that an individual indulges in to get ahead in life. Americans spell the word 'skullduggery'.

Examples — *There is so much skulduggery going on, I don't trust my friends anymore.*

The promising batsman's career was ruined by political skulduggery.

During elections, we expect some skulduggery to go on.

Etymology — From the Scottish 'sculdudrie', meaning 'adultery'.

Skunked

Meaning — Mostly used in American English in informal contexts to mean 'to be completely defeated or routed by someone'.

Examples — *Goran Ivanisevic was skunked by Sampras in the third set.*

In the last election, many of the national parties were skunked by the regional parties.

Sledging /sledʒ-ɪŋ/

Pronunciation — The first syllable rhymes with 'ledge' and 'wedge'. The word is pronounced '**SLEJ**-ing'.

Meaning — This is a word that is mostly used in the context of sports. A player insulting an opponent during a game in order to make him lose his confidence or his concentration is called sledging.

Examples — *There are many people who believe that sledging should be banned.*

After the first set, the newcomer began sledging the champion.

Origin — Ian Chappell believes that the term 'sledge', a shortened form of 'sledgehammer', began to be used in Australia in the early 1960s. (A sledgehammer is a heavy, long-handed instrument which is mostly used to break stones and drive in wedges and stakes). In those days, a player using foul language in the presence of a lady was said to have been as 'subtle as a sledgehammer' – in other words, not subtle at all. Such a person was often nicknamed 'Sledge' because Percy Sledge's song, 'When a man loves a woman', was popular at that time!

Sleepfest

Meaning — When you say that something was a sleepfest, you mean that it was so boring that it put you to sleep. Used in informal contexts.

Examples — *The talk that the Principal gave yesterday was a sleepfest.*

Ratna saw the debate yesterday and she said that it was a sleepfest.

Etymology — Combination of 'sleep' and 'festival'.

Sleuth /slu:θ/

Pronunciation — The 'eu' is pronounced like the 'oo' in 'cool', 'pool' and 'fool', while the final 'th' is like the 'th' in 'thank and 'think'. The word rhymes with 'tooth' and 'booth'.

Meaning — An old-fashioned word for a detective.

Examples — *Hercule Poirot is the famous sleuth created by Agatha Christie.*

The sleuth spent several hours at the crime scene searching for clues.

After reading several Sherlock Holmes stories, my cousin has decided to become a sleuth.

Etymology — From a Norse word, meaning 'trail'.

Slipshod /slɪp-ʃɔd/

Pronunciation — The first syllable sounds like the word 'slip' and the second rhymes with 'god', 'pod' and 'mod'. The word is pronounced '**SLIP**-shod'.

Meaning — It means sloppy or careless.

Examples — *Please don't ask Praveen to write the report. He is a slipshod writer.*

According to the teacher, most students made slipshod presentations.

Etymology — 'Shod' means wearing shoes and 'slip' means 'loose'. The word originally referred to someone who was wearing slippers or shoes that were too big for him.

Slush fund /slʌʃ fʌnd/

Pronunciation — The first word rhymes with 'flush'. It is pronounced '**SLUSH** fund'.

Meaning — Frequently used to refer to the money that political parties and business houses set aside to carry out their illegal activities/practices.

Examples — *Let's use the slush fund to buy the votes of those who are still undecided.*

If you wish to run a successful business, you need to set up a slush fund.

Origin — Several hundred years ago, sailors used the words 'slush' and 'slosh' to refer to the fat or grease that resulted when meat was cooked. During the course of a voyage, this grease was stored; it was sold when the ship reached port. The money that was made was called 'slush fund'.

Smarts

Meaning — The word is used in informal contexts to mean 'intelligence' or 'expertise'.

Examples — *Bala has the smarts to solve the problem.*

They have hired someone with a lot of smarts.

Snitch /snɪtʃ/

Pronunciation — It rhymes with the words 'witch', 'pitch' and 'ditch'.

Meaning — An informer; someone who tattles on others. The word can be used as a noun and a verb.

Examples — *The snitch told the police what the gang was planning to do.*

I'd be careful with Amali. She's the office snitch.

The Registrar wanted Raj to snitch on his classmates.

Soft-pedal

Meaning — The attempt to make something seem less important or less serious than it actually is; to take pains to cover up or downplay the unpleasant aspects of something – for example, a political scandal.

Examples *Is it possible to soft-pedal the Prime Minister's blunder?*

No matter how sensitive the issue is, television channels don't make an attempt to soft-pedal the news.

Etymology The expression comes from the world of music. Pushing down on the soft pedal of a piano enables the pianist to alter the tone quality; the notes sound a lot softer.

Soiree /swa:rei/

Pronunciation The 'soi' in the first syllable is pronounced like the 'swa' in the Indian name 'Swathi'; the second syllable sounds like the word 'ray'. The word is pronounced '**SWAA**-ray'. Americans, on the other hand, tend to put the stress on the second syllable.

Meaning This rather formal word is used to refer to an evening get-together where elegantly dressed individuals eat lots of good food and listen to some wonderful music.

Examples *Our Department will be hosting a soiree on Sunday evening.*

Sorry, I'm really busy this week. There are three soirees that I definitely need to attend.

Etymology 'Soiree' comes from the French 'soir', meaning 'evening'.

Soliloquy

/sə-l̲ɪ̲-lə-kwɪ/

Pronunciation The 'o' in the first and third syllables is pronounced like the 'a' in 'china'. 'Lil' rhymes with 'bill' and 'chill', and the final 'quy' is like the 'qui' in 'quit', 'quiz' and 'quick'. The word is pronounced 'se-**LIL**-e-kwi'.

Meaning A soliloquy is when a character in a play talks to himself or herself and in the process speaks directly to the audience. In this case, the lines are meant for the audience and not for any of the other characters in the play.

Examples *The dramatist employs the soliloquy to let the audience know what the hero is thinking.*

There were far too many soliloquies in the play.

Etymology From the Latin 'solus', meaning 'oneself', and 'loqui', meaning 'speak'. The word means 'speaking to oneself'.

Some

Meaning Can be used in everyday speech to express approval or admiration; wonderful.

Examples *That's some car you've got there.*

That was some movie we saw on TV last night.

Somnambulism /sɔm-<u>næm</u>-bjʊ-lɪzm/

Pronunciation The 'o' is like the 'o' in 'hot', 'got' and 'pot', and the following syllable rhymes with 'Pam', 'dam' and 'jam'. The 'u' rhymes with the words 'put', 'foot' and 'good'; the final 's' is pronounced like the 'z' in 'zip', 'zinc' and 'zoo'. The word is pronounced 'som-**NAM**-byu-li-zem'.

Meaning The word literally means 'to walk in one's sleep'.

Examples *Jai has a history of somnambulism.*

As far as I'm aware, there are no somnambulists in our family.

Etymology In Latin, 'somnus' means 'sleep' and 'ambulare' means 'to walk'.

Soporific /sɔp-ə-<u>rɪf</u>-ɪk/

Pronunciation The first syllable 'sop' rhymes with 'hop', 'top' and 'pop', while the 'o' in the second sounds like the 'a' in 'china'. The 'rif' rhymes with 'stiff' and 'cliff'. The word is pronounced 'sop-e-**RIF**-ic'.

Meaning Things that induce sleep or drowsiness in people – it could be a medicine or drug, the motion of a train, etc. The word can also be used to mean 'tediously boring or monotonous'.

Examples *The summer heat was making Sunita feel soporific.*

Clementine wasn't able to think clearly because her medicine was making her soporific.

Pity the officials who have to listen to the Minister's soporific speeches.

Etymology It is derived from the Latin 'sopor', meaning 'deep sleep or lethargy'.

Sotto voce /sɔ-təu vəu-tʃei/

Pronunciation The first 'o' in 'sotto' sounds like the 'o' in 'hot', 'pot' and 'got'. The second 'o' and the 'o' in 'voce' sound like the 'o' in 'go', 'no' and 'so'. The 'c' is like the 'ch' in 'chick', 'chips' and 'chin', and the final 'e' is like the 'ay' in 'bay' and 'may'. The Italian expression is pronounced 'so-toe **VOE**-chay'.

Meaning To say something under your breath; to speak very quietly so that only those who are near you can hear you.

Examples *The final remark that the Minister made was not for all. It was uttered sotto voce.*

Naveen has the habit of making sotto voce remarks.

Etymology	'Sotto' means 'under' and 'voce' means 'voice'; when you say something 'sotto voce', you say it under your breath or as an aside.

Soul searching

Meaning	Critical examination of our thoughts, feelings and actions; scrutiny of oneself.
Examples	*After much soul searching, Devi decided to report the matter to the police.* *I did a considerable amount of soul searching before turning down the offer.*

Sour

Pronunciation	The word rhymes with 'power', 'our' and 'hour'. Many Indians tend to pronounce it like the words 'pour', 'bore' and 'tore', which is wrong.

Southpaw

Meaning	A left-hander; someone whose dominant hand is his left.
Examples	*We need to have at least one southpaw in our batting line-up.* *Ashwin enjoys bowling to southpaws.*

Origin — A term first used in baseball to refer to a left-handed pitcher.

Spiel /ʃpi:l/

Pronunciation — The 's' sounds like the 'sh' in 'ship' and 'sheep' and the following 'piel' sounds like the word 'peel'. The word is pronounced '**SHPEEL**'.

Meaning — A prepared talk; one that is intended to lure someone into buying or doing something. This talk is usually lengthy, and as a result, rather tedious to listen to. When used as a verb, 'spiel' means 'to reel off'.

Examples — *Jyothi's father gave us the usual spiel about working hard.*

I'm sick and tired of listening to his spiels.

Hari spieled the names of all the Pulitzer Prize winners.

Etymology — From the German 'spielen', meaning 'to play'.

Spin doctor

Meaning — A spokesperson; a person hired by an organisation or individual to provide information to the public in such a way that the person or organisation is seen in a good light.

Examples	*We'll be sending our best spin doctors to ensure that the story dies a natural death.*
	What this country requires are honest politicians. Not spin doctors.
Origin	In journalism, 'spin' is used to refer to the favourable slant given to a story.

Splurge /splɜ:dʒ/

Pronunciation	The 'urge' is pronounced like the word 'urge'.
Meaning	To spend extravagantly; to buy expensive products.
Examples	*Mythili splurged on shoes and clothes yesterday.*
	There is a tendency among Indians to splurge on jewellery.
	Nowadays, young couples splurge on trips to foreign countries.
Etymology	Some people believe it is a combination of 'splash' and 'surge'.

Sponge off /spʌndʒ/

Pronunciation	The 'spon' is pronounced like the word 'spun', and the 'ge' is like the 'j' in 'jam' and 'juice'. The word is pronounced '**SPUNJ**'. The vowel

	is not pronounced like the 'o' in 'on' – the way that many people in our country do.
Meaning	Living off others. When you 'sponge off' others, you take money and food from them without really doing anything in return.
Examples	*Uday, you're nearly 30 years old. It's time you stopped sponging off your parents.* *Till I get a job, I'll be sponging off you, Padma.*

Staccato	/stə-kaː-təu/
Pronunciation	The 'a' in the first syllable is like the 'a' in 'china', and the following 'cca' is pronounced like the word 'car'. The final syllable sounds like the word 'toe'. The word is pronounced 'ste-**KAA**-toe'.
Meaning	In everyday contexts, the word is used to refer to a sudden and short burst of something – sound, speech, movement, etc.
Examples	*Harish's staccato replies failed to impress the committee members.* *The staccato blast of car horns gave Jai a splitting headache.*
Etymology	From the Italian 'staccato', meaning 'disconnected'.

Stamping ground

Meaning A place that someone frequently visits and likes visiting. Americans call it 'stomping ground'.

Examples *The mall and the video parlours have become the stamping ground of most teenagers.*

Jaya was home for just a day. She didn't have time to visit her old stamping grounds.

Statuesque /stæ-tʃʊ-esk/

Pronunciation The first two syllables are pronounced like the word 'statue', and the final 'esque' sounds like the 'esk' in 'desk'. The word is pronounced 'sta-chu-**ESK**'.

Meaning Something that it is well proportioned, like a statue. When you refer to someone as being 'statuesque', what you mean is that the person is attractively tall, graceful and dignified. The word is used to show approval.

Examples *At the press conference, the statuesque actress said she was planning to quit films.*

The young man couldn't take his eyes off the statuesque figure that stood at the doorway.

Stature /stæ-tʃə/

Pronunciation — The 'stat' rhymes with 'catch', 'batch' and 'match', and the following 'ure' is like the 'a' in 'china'. The word is pronounced '**STATCH**-e'.

Meaning — The word can be used to refer to the height of an individual or his reputation.

Examples — *Sunaina's grey hair and short stature made her very easy to recognize.*

I certainly didn't expect such pettiness from a scholar of his stature.

Well-known scientists of international stature will be attending the conference.

Etymology — From the Latin 'statura', meaning 'height'.

Staycation

Meaning — A vacation one spends relaxing at home or a place very close to home.

Examples — *What some of our cricket players really want is a staycation.*

Ranjini's job involves a lot of travel. What she looks forward to is a staycation.

Origin — Coined in the United States, the word is a combination of 'stay' and 'vacation'.

Steadfast

Meaning	Unchanging, unwavering; remaining loyal.
Examples	*Vijay has been my steadfast friend since childhood.* *Russia has been India's steadfast ally for several decades.*
Etymology	One of the meanings of 'fast' is 'steady' or 'fixed'. The word literally means 'fixed place'.

Stealth /stelθ/

Pronunciation	The word rhymes with 'health' and 'wealth'.
Meaning	To move cautiously, for you do not wish to be seen or heard; secretive.
Examples	*The audience watched in awe the stealth of the tiger as it neared its prey.* *The terrorists used stealth to get into the prison compound.*
Etymology	From an Old English word, meaning 'steal'.

Stealth call

Meaning	To ring someone at a time when you know they will not be able to take your call. This is usually done to avoid talking to the individual.

Examples | *I knew Veda had an early morning class. I stealth-called him then.*

Bhanu had left several messages. So I stealth-called her at a time when I knew she would be in a meeting.

Stockholm syndrome /stɔk-həum sɪn-drəum/

Pronunciation — The first syllable is pronounced like 'stock' and the second like 'home'. The expression is pronounced '**STOCK**-home sin-drome'.

Meaning — The feeling of trust and affection that a hostage develops towards his captors.

Examples — *Maya was with her captors for two months. It's not surprising that she developed Stockholm syndrome.*

During the hostage crisis, Preetam was the first victim of the Stockholm syndrome.

Origin — This was first noted in the case of the people who were taken hostage during a bank robbery in Stockholm, Sweden in 1973.

Stonewall

Meaning — When you accuse someone of 'stonewalling', what you mean is that the individual is being obstructive, uncooperative or evasive.

The person is delaying taking a decision about something or refusing to answer your questions because there is something he wishes to hide. The word is normally used to show disapproval.

Examples *The incompetent Minister tried his best to stonewall the questions posed by angry students.*

The Principal stonewalled when the reporter asked him about the scandal on campus.

Etymology Since walls made of stones were difficult to break through, the word 'stonewall' began to be used to refer to anything that presented a formidable obstacle. The term is also used in cricket. When a batsman 'stonewalls', he spends a lot of time at the crease without really attempting to score runs.

Stooge /stu:dʒ/

Pronunciation The 'oo' is pronounced like the 'oo' in 'fool', 'pool' and 'cool'. The final 'ge' sounds like the 'j' in 'jam' and 'jump'. The word is pronounced **'STOOJ'**.

Meaning A person who is completely under someone's control; a pawn.

Examples *Kishore says he's sick and tired of being the Chairman's stooge.*

Leya maintains that she's no one's stooge. But nobody believes her.

Etymology — Some people believe that it is a corruption of the word 'student'.

Stove

/stəuv/

Pronunciation — The word rhymes with 'stole' and 'stone'. The vowel is not pronounced like the 'u' in 'cut' and 'but'.

Etymology — From the Dutch 'stove', meaning 'heated room'.

Straight arrow

Meaning — An honest individual who follows all rules.

Examples — *Straight arrows like Ganpat never make good businessmen.*

Your friend Raja is not a straight arrow. I just don't trust him.

I'm voting for Mankad. Unlike the other candidates, he's a straight arrow.

Origin — From the expression, 'straight as an arrow'.

Straw poll

Meaning — Informal way of gathering information to understand which way the people will be voting. The term can be used with regard to everyday matters as well, not necessarily elections.

Examples — *The students had a straw poll as to whether the working hours of the library should be extended.*

I took a straw poll of the immediate members of the family. Not many were interested in going to Goa during summer.

Origin — In the 19th century in the US, when straw polls were conducted, a potential voter was given an actual piece of straw. He was then asked a question. If the individual returned the straw without bending it, it meant that his answer to the question was 'yes'. In order to signify a 'nay' vote, the voter returned the straw bent.

Study animal

Meaning — A term mostly used in informal contexts by students to refer to someone who studies very hard.

Examples — *People tell me that my friend Madhu is a study animal.*

My sister Lisa has always been a study animal. I wish I could be one too.

Stymie /stai-mɪ/

Pronunciation The first syllable rhymes with 'my', 'by' and 'hi', and the 'ie' in the second syllable is like the 'i' in 'bin', 'fin' and 'tin'. The word is pronounced '**STY**-mi'.

Meaning To stand in the way of someone doing or achieving something; to be an obstacle and prevent something from happening – either intentionally or unintentionally.

Examples *Some of the policies adopted by the present Government have stymied the growth of small towns and villages.*

Our attempts to get the city parks cleaned have been stymied by the lack of volunteers.

Origin Stymie is a term used in golf. When you are stymied, you really do not know what to do because your opponent's ball is between yours and the hole.

Suave /swa:v/

Pronunciation The 'su' is like the 'sw' in 'swim' and 'swan', while the following 'a' sounds like the 'a' in 'path', 'bath' and 'ask'. The final 'e' is silent.

This monosyllabic word is pronounced '**SWAAV**'.

Meaning — Mostly used to refer to men who are charming and sophisticated; someone who is rather smooth. Frequently used to show disapproval.

Examples — *The seasoned actor, as expected, gave his usual suave performance.*

Yuktha was bowled over by the suave and sophisticated gentleman.

Etymology — The word comes from the Latin 'suavis', meaning 'agreeable'.

Sub rosa /sʌb rəu-zə/

Pronunciation — The 'ros' is pronounced like the word 'rose' and the 'a' sounds like the 'a' in 'china'. The word is pronounced 'sub **ROZ**-e'.

Meaning — Done secretly or done in private.

Examples — *As expected, the Chairperson held the crucial meeting sub rosa.*

Ganeshan wants transparency. No more sub rosa meetings.

Etymology — This Latin expression literally means 'under the rose'. During the Middle Ages, at important council meetings, a single rose was usually hung from the ceiling. This was a signal to all those sitting/standing under the flower (sub rosa) that they were sworn to secrecy.

Subaltern /sʌb-əl-tən/ /sə-bɒl-tən/

Pronunciation — In British English, the first syllable is pronounced like the word 'sub', and the following vowels like the 'a' in 'china'. The word is pronounced '**SUB**-el-ten'. In American English, on the other hand, it is the 'u' and 'e' that are like the 'a' in 'china'. The 'bal' in the second syllable is pronounced like the word 'ball'. The word is pronounced 'se-**BALL**-ten'.

Meaning — It means 'subordinate'. Nowadays, the term is used to refer to the underprivileged or the disadvantaged.

Example — *As a young subaltern, you are expected to speak only when spoken to.*

Etymology — The word was originally a term used in the army to refer to any commissioned officer below the rank of captain.

Subterfuge /sʌb-tə-fju:dʒ/

Pronunciation — The first syllable rhymes with the words 'cub', 'tub' and 'hub'. The following 'er' sounds like the 'a' in 'china', and the final syllable rhymes with the word 'huge'. The word is pronounced '**SUB**-te-fyuuj'.

Meaning — When you trick someone or employ dishonest means in order to achieve your goal, you are making use of subterfuge. Very often, the deception is employed to hide one's real intentions.

Examples — *I don't care how you get the information. Obtain it by subterfuge if you have to.*

Everyone knew the Minister wasn't sick at all. It was only a subterfuge.

Etymology — From the Latin 'subterfugium', meaning 'to evade, escape'.

Succinct /sək-siŋkt/

Pronunciation — The 'u' is like the 'a' in 'china', and the first 'c' is like the 'k' in 'kiss' and 'keep'. The syllable that follows sounds like the word 'sink', and the final 't' is like the 't' in 'table' and 'tin'. The word is pronounced 'sek-**SINKT**'.

Meaning — Used in formal contexts to indicate approval. A person who is succinct, speaks clearly and concisely; he is to the point.

Examples — *The reporters were rather happy with the Mayor's succinct reply.*

It's about time you learnt to express your ideas succinctly.

Etymology — It comes from the Latin 'succintus', meaning 'prepared, short'.

Succour /sʌ-kə/

Pronunciation — The word is pronounced like the word 'sucker'.

Meaning — The help that is given to someone who is desperately in need of it. In American English, the word is spelt 'succor'.

Examples — *Raja went to the hospital every week to give succour to the terminally ill.*

Our job here is to give succour to those who need it.

Etymology — The word comes from the Latin 'succurrere', meaning 'run to help'.

Succulent /sʌk-jʊ-lənt/

Pronunciation — The 'succ' is pronounced like the word 'suck'. The sound that follows is like the 'y' in 'yes' and 'yellow', and the following 'u' is like the 'u' in 'pull', 'full' and 'bull'. The 'e' sounds like the 'a' in 'china'. The word is pronounced '**SUCK**-yu-lent'.

Meaning — Food that is 'succulent' is very juicy and good to eat.

Examples — *Shalini placed the succulent fruit on top of the ice cream and served it to the guest.*

When I saw him dip pieces of succulent chicken in ketchup, it made me hungry.

Etymology — From the Latin 'succulentis', meaning 'juicy'.

Suite

/swi:t/

Pronunciation — Sounds like the word 'sweet'.

Meaning — A set of rooms in a hotel or a set of furniture. These are just two of the meanings.

"The Minister's family is full of crooks. I'm told they have a permanent suite in Tihar jail."

Examples — *We have booked the Honeymoon Suite at the Taj.*

Mala wants to buy a new suite of furniture.

Etymology — From the Old French 'suite', meaning 'act of following, attendance'.

Sumptuous /sʌmp-tʃʊ-əs/

Pronunciation — The first syllable rhymes with the words 'pump', 'lump' and 'bump', and the following 't' sounds like the 'ch' in 'chew' and 'cheese'. The 'u' is like the 'u' in 'put' and 'full', and the final 'ou' is like the 'a' in 'china'. One simple way of pronouncing the word is '**SUMP**-chu-es'.

Meaning — Mostly used to refer to expensive things that can be consumed or enjoyed. The word is not used with people.

Examples — *We went to the new restaurant and had a sumptuous meal.*

Prema decided to buy herself a sumptuous dress for her son's wedding.

Etymology — The word comes from the Latin 'sumptuosus', meaning 'costly, expensive'.

Superb /sʊ-pɜ:b/

Pronunciation — The first vowel is like the 'u' in 'put' and the following 'er' is like the 'ir' in 'bird' and 'shirt'. The word is pronounced 'su-**PERB**' and not '**SUU**-perb'. Remember, it is '**SUU**-per' but 'su-**PERB**'.

Supine /su:-pain/ /sju:-pain/

Pronunciation — The 'u' sounds like the 'oo' in 'cool', 'pool' and 'school', and the following syllable rhymes with the words 'dine', 'mine' and 'shine'. Some people rhyme the first syllable with the words 'due', 'few' and 'cue'. In either case, the stress is on the first syllable – '**SUU**-pine' or '**SYUU**-pine'.

Meaning — Looking up while lying flat on one's back. The word can also have a negative connotation; it can mean a spineless individual who is willing to be bossed around by others.

Examples — *Ranjit walked past a row of supine bodies snoring in unison.*

The Vice Chancellor flouted all the rules, and there was little opposition from the supine staff.

Etymology — From the Latin 'supinus', meaning 'lying on one's back'.

Sycophancy /sɪk-ə-fən-sɪ/

Pronunciation — The 'syc' is like the word 'sick', and the following 'o' and 'a' sound like the 'a' in 'china'. The final 'y' is like the 'i' in 'bit', 'sit' and 'kit'; the word is pronounced '**SICK**-e-fen-si'.

Meaning — A 'sycophant' is someone who flatters others, especially those in power, in order to get something from them. Such insincere behaviour is referred to as 'sycophancy'.

Examples — *At the party, the well-known cricket player was surrounded by sycophants.*

Please, we do not want any of your sycophancy here.

Etymology — It comes from the Greek 'sykophantes', meaning 'false accuser'.

Syrupy /sɪ-rə-pɪ/

Pronunciation — The 'y' sounds like the 'i' in 'knit' and 'kit' and the 'u' is like the 'a' in 'china'. The word is pronounced '**SI**-re-pi'.

Meaning — Thick and sweet. Figuratively, the word is used to mean 'extremely sentimental'. Used to show disapproval.

Examples — *The girls in my class generally go gaga over syrupy love stories.*

I hate it when they make books into movies. The movie always turns out to be syrupy.

At our farewell, the Principal was matter of fact. Not at all syrupy.

Etymology — From the Old French 'sirop', meaning 'sugared drink'.

Tagged along

Meaning — To accompany someone even though he has not asked you to; like an uninvited guest, you force yourself on him.

Examples — *Whenever Raman took Laxmi to a movie, her brother tagged along with them.*

When I went out with my friends, I made it very clear to my parents that I didn't want my younger brother tagging along with us.

Wherever Shilpi went, the cute puppy tagged along.

Tailspin

Meaning — A situation that is completely out of control; things falling apart at an alarming rate.

Examples — *After the divorce, Govind's life went into a tailspin. It took him a year to get it back in order.*

When Satish wasn't given a promotion, his life went into a tailspin.

The fall in interest rates sent the stock market into a tailspin.

Origin — When a pilot loses control, and the plane dives quickly to the ground, and spins its tail in wide circles.

Take a hike

Meaning — Informal way of telling someone to get lost. Other expressions which have the same meaning are 'beat it', 'go jump in a lake' and 'take a walk'.

Examples — *The Chinese have been making too many demands of late. It's about time our PM told them to take a hike.*

Some of my cousins were beginning to irritate me. I told them to take a hike.

Take a rain check

Meaning If someone invites you to dinner, and you are unable to go, you can always ask for a 'rain check'. What you mean by this is that circumstances do not permit you to accept the invitation; you are, however, willing to go out with the person some other time.

Examples *I can't go to the beach with you this weekend. How about a rain check?*

Sridhar wanted to give me a treat this weekend. I've asked for a rain check.

"Oh, do I have to come right now? Can't I take a rain check?"

Origin — The expression comes from the world of baseball. Whenever a ballgame had to be cancelled because of rain, spectators who had paid to get in were given a ticket stub as they left the stadium. This stub was called 'rain check', and it allowed a person to see another game at the same stadium on some other day.

Tally ho

/tæ-lɪ <u>həu</u>/

Pronunciation — The first word rhymes with 'rally' and 'pally', while the second rhymes with 'so', 'no' and 'go'. The expression is pronounced 'tally **HO**'.

Meaning — What a hunter shouts when he sees his prey; this expression was used to alert the hounds (dogs) which had been brought along to chase and kill the prey – usually a fox.

Etymology — It is a corruption of the French expression 'ty-hillaut a qui forheur': hunters in France shouted this when they spotted a deer.

Tanked

Meaning — Used in informal contexts to mean 'defeated'.

Examples — *The moment I walked onto the field, I knew that our team would get tanked today.*

I didn't expect Nadal to get tanked by some unknown player.

Tantamount /tæn-tə-maunt/

Pronunciation: The first syllable rhymes with 'pan' and 'ban', and the vowel in the second is like the 'a' in 'china'. The final syllable sounds like the word 'mount'. The word is pronounced '**TAN**-te-mount'.

Meaning: When you say that one thing is 'tantamount' to another, you mean that the two are equivalent; they are likely to be equal in terms of effect and value.

Examples: *You need to understand that my boss' request is tantamount to a command.*

They want us to believe that any criticism of the Prime Minister is tantamount to treason.

The superstar's statement was tantamount to saying that actors and politicians are above the law.

Etymology: From the Anglo-French phrase 'tant amunter', meaning 'to amount to as much'.

Tchotchke /tʃɔtʃ-kə/

Pronunciation: The 'tch' at the beginning and end of the first syllable is pronounced like the 'ch' in 'cheese',

	'cheat' and 'cheap'. The 'o' is like the 'o' in 'hot', 'got' and 'pot', and the final 'e' is like the 'a' in 'china'. The word is pronounced '**CHOCH**-ke'.
Meaning	Refers to the inexpensive toys or trinkets sold on the roadside or in small shops; items of cheap quality and of little value. The word is mostly used in American English to show disapproval.
Examples	*Whenever Ravi went on vacation, he always brought back a few tchotchkes.* *Sunanda is more interested in buying tchotchkes than a Rolex watch.*
Etymology	According to one dictionary, it comes from the Polish 'czaczko', meaning 'trinket'. Nowadays, the word is used to refer to the souvenirs or promotional items which companies hand out at trade shows. These items usually have the company's name or logo on them.

Teeming

Teeming	/ti:m-ɪŋ/
Pronunciation	The first syllable sounds like the word 'team'.
Meaning	Full of; in great numbers.
Examples	*During summer, most hill stations are usually teeming with tourists.*

Sujatha says her mind is teeming with ideas.

Hema took me to a spot where the river was teeming with fish.

Etymology — From the Old English 'tieman', meaning 'give birth to'.

Teflon

/tef-lɔn/

Pronunciation — The first syllable rhymes with 'chef' and 'Jeff', and the second vowel sounds like the 'o' in 'got', 'not' and 'pot'. The word is pronounced '**TEF**-lon'.

Meaning — A coating given to a pot or a pan to prevent food from sticking to it. Nowadays, the word is used with people as well. Someone whose reputation remains untarnished despite all the allegations levelled against him. Like a Teflon-coated pot, nothing sticks to the individual.

Examples — *Jimmy Carter called Ronald Reagan a 'Teflon President'.*

I call my cousin 'Teflon Suma' because she is impervious to all criticism.

Janaki is one of those Teflon politicians I have absolute contempt for.

Telegenic /te-lɪ-dʒen-ɪk/

Pronunciation 'Tele' rhymes with 'jelly' and 'belly'; the 'g' is like the 'j' in 'jam' and 'juice'. The word is pronounced 'tel-i-**JEN**-ic'.

Meaning Someone who looks good on television.

Examples *Some of our newsreaders are not very telegenic.*

The producers are on the lookout for young girls who are telegenic.

Etymology Combination of 'television' and 'photogenic'.

Teller

Meaning To count.

Examples *The bank teller wouldn't give me the change I needed.*

It took nearly an hour to get the money because the usual teller was on leave.

Etymology From the Old English 'tellan', meaning 'to calculate or count'. Over a period of time, 'tellan' acquired another meaning – to narrate. This gave us the verb 'tell'. With the passage of time, the original meaning ('to count') fell out of use, and the second one ('to narrate') became the principal meaning of the word.

'Teller' meaning 'count' survives in a limited number of terms: bank teller, ATM, etc.

Tete-a-tete

/teit-a:-teit/

Pronunciation 'Tete' rhymes with 'date', 'hate' and 'late', and the following 'a' sounds like the 'a' in 'bath', 'path' and 'mask'. It is pronounced 'tate-aaa-**TATE**'.

Meaning A private conversation between two individuals.

Examples *The Principal had a tete-a-tete with the Head of the English Department.*

I am not interested in having a tete-a-tete with that pompous Ganguly.

Rahul has regular tete-a-tetes with Shoba.

Etymology A French expression, meaning 'head to head'.

Texter's thumb

Meaning The injury that results to the thumb due to constant texting on the cell phone.

Examples *Many kids I know have texter's thumb.*

Sujatha's texter's thumb is keeping her from contacting us.

Textually challenged

Meaning: Someone who finds it difficult to send messages on his cell; takes time to type out a simple message.

Examples: *My grandfather never responds to my messages. He's textually challenged.*
Many of the senior citizens I know are textually challenged.

Textual satisfaction

Meaning: The satisfaction a person gets when he realizes that he has a missed call and several new messages.

Example: *I had textual satisfaction on my birthday. My friends were sending me messages all day long.*

Thanatology /θæ-nə-tɔ̲-lə-dʒɪ/

Pronunciation: 'Than' rhymes with 'tan' and 'fan', while the vowel in the second syllable sounds like the 'a' in 'china'. The final 'ology' sounds like the 'ology' in 'biology' and 'zoology'. The word is pronounced 'tha-ne-**TO**-le-ji'.

Meaning: The scientific study of death; looks at both the physical and social aspects.

Example — *There are some universities that offer a course in thanatology.*

Etymology — The word comes from the Greek ‘thanatos’, meaning ‘death’. In Greek mythology, Thanatos was the personification of death.

Thesaurus /θɪ-sɒ-rəs/

Pronunciation — The first vowel is like the ‘i’ in ‘chit’, ‘knit’ and ‘wit’. The second syllable is pronounced like the word ‘saw’ and the final ‘u’ is like the ‘a’ in ‘china’. The word is pronounced ‘thi-**SAW**-res’.

Meaning — A kind of a dictionary in which synonyms or words which have similar meaning are grouped together.

Examples — *Ahmed insists that when we write, we should always have a dictionary and a thesaurus by our side.*

I went to the thesaurus and figured out which was the appropriate word to use.

Etymology — The word comes from the Greek ‘thesauros’, meaning ‘treasure chest’ or ‘storehouse’. It was originally used to refer to any dictionary or encyclopaedia. When Roget published his thesaurus in 1852, the word acquired its current meaning.

Thoroughfare

Meaning — A road/street that the public can use to get from one place to another; a route between two places.

Examples — *Traffic has come to a halt on all major thoroughfares in the city.*

We need to find a way to stop people from using our colony as a thoroughfare.

Etymology — One of the meanings of 'fare' is 'passage', and till the 14th century, it was possible to use 'thorough' and 'through' interchangeably. 'Thoroughfare' originally meant 'through passage'.

Tier /tiə/

Pronunciation — The word rhymes with 'fear', 'cheer' and 'dear'. It is not pronounced like the word 'tyre' or 'tire' as many people do in our country.

Meaning — The word has several meanings and one of them is 'different levels or layers'.

Examples — *The AC two-tier compartment caught fire.*

Javed had a great view because he was sitting in one of the top tiers of the stadium.

Etymology — From the Old French 'tire', meaning 'rank, order'.

Tiff

Meaning — Used in informal contexts to refer to a minor or a petty quarrel between two individuals who know each other well.

Examples — *My parents have a tiff every now and then.*

As a Manager, Moushami didn't want to get involved in the employees' tiffs.

Tinderbox

Meaning — Any material like dry grass, wood, straw, etc. that can be used to start a fire quickly. Figuratively, it can be used to refer to an explosive situation; one that can turn violent very quickly.

Examples — *The tension on campus makes it a tinderbox where riots could break out at any moment.*

During the hot summer months, the huts in these villages become a potential tinderbox.

Etymology — From the Old English 'tynder', meaning 'to ignite or kindle'. In the old days, every home had a tinderbox; this small metal box contained tinder and all the other things required to light a fire.

Tinseltown

Meaning — An uncomplimentary term used to refer to Hollywood and the glamour associated with it.

Examples — *The Bollywood director wanted to make it big in Tinseltown.*

One of the biggest stars in Tinseltown committed suicide last night.

Origin — The word 'tinsel' has been used for several centuries to describe something that is rather showy and gaudy. When you refer to Hollywood as Tinseltown, what you mean is that although the place glitters, like the people in it, it does not have any substance.

Etymology — From the French 'estincelle', meaning 'spark'.

Tittle-tattle /tɪ-t(ə)l tæ-t(ə)l/

Pronunciation — The first word rhymes with 'little' and 'brittle', and the 'a' in 'tattle' is like the 'a' in 'cat', 'bat' and 'sat'. The word is pronounced '**TIT**-el ta-tel'.

Meaning — An old-fashioned word for gossip. When you tittle-tattle, you speak unkindly about someone behind the person's back; you are indulging in meaningless chatter.

Examples *The editor knew that tittle-tattle about the up-and-coming star would help sell the magazine.*

The good thing about Maria is that she's not interested in office tittle-tattle.

Origin 'Tattle' comes from the Flemish 'tatelen', meaning 'stutter' or 'chatter'. 'Tittle', on the other hand, comes from the world of printing. It is mainly used to refer to the diacritic or the small marks that are used when writing. For example, the small dot that appears on the letter 'i' and on the letter 'j' is a 'tittle'. Since the 'tittle' was something very small, the word was added to 'tattle' to underline the insignificance of the talk/chatter.

Toast

Meaning When you propose a toast to someone, you are wishing him happiness and success in life. This is one of the meanings of the word.

Examples *Let us raise our glasses and propose a toast to the bride and groom.*

Vimal and his wife toasted the success of their friend.

Origin In 17th century Europe, at parties and on special occasions, a piece of bread or toast was dropped into a bottle of wine or ale. The bottle was passed around among the guests and they each drank a little bit of the brew. The last person to get the bottle was the guest of honour. When he poured out the contents, the toast came out too. So, in the old days, when somebody was toasted, he was actually given a piece of toast!

To go postal

Meaning — To become extremely angry or violent with one's colleagues.

Examples — *When Harish didn't get promoted, he went postal. He punched his boss.*

Jane went postal when her Head accused her of being the VC's mouthpiece.

Origin — The expression owes its origin to a number of incidents that took place in post offices in the United States in the 1980s and 1990s. Several postal workers, who were apparently under a lot of stress, shot and killed many of their colleagues in the workplace – before turning the gun on themselves. So when you go postal, you go ballistic, like a worker in the mailroom.

Toothsome

Meaning — Something that not only tastes great, but also looks great. 'Tooth' is being used figuratively to mean 'taste'.

Examples — *The restaurant didn't look great. But all of us enjoyed the toothsome sandwiches and fruit salad they served us.*

Last night, we had toothsome gulab jamuns for dessert.

Those pastries may be toothsome, but you're likely to end up with a stomach ache if you eat any more.

Top-drawer

Meaning — Belonging to high society; top quality.

Examples — *The company is putting Revathi up in a really top-drawer hotel.*

Mithun is on the lookout for a teacher who is top-drawer.

Naila claims to be out of the top-drawer, but nobody believes her.

Origin — People generally kept their valuables in the top drawer.

Topiary /təup-jə-rɪ/

Pronunciation — The 'top' rhymes with the words 'hope', 'soap' and 'dope'. The 'i' is like the 'y' in 'yes', 'yet' and 'you', and the following 'a' sounds like the 'a' in 'china'. One way of pronouncing the word is '**TOPE**-ye-ri'.

Meaning — The clipping of shrubs and trees in the shapes of animals.

Examples — *The children enjoyed looking at the topiary.*

We wish to hire someone who has specialised in topiary art.

Etymology — From the Latin 'topiarius', meaning 'ornamental gardener'.

Tortoise /tɒ-təs/

Pronunciation — The first syllable rhymes with 'nor' and 'for', and the second is like the words 'miss', 'hiss' and 'kiss'. The word is pronounced '**TOR**-tis'. The second syllable is not pronounced like the word 'toys', the way many Indians do.

Touch base with someone

Meaning — This is an informal expression meaning 'to get in touch with or stay in contact with someone'.

Examples — *My sister touches base with her kids every day.*

I think something is wrong. Lina hasn't touched base in a week.

Origin — It comes from the world of baseball.

Touché

/tu:-ʃei/

Pronunciation — The 'tou' is pronounced like the word 'two'. The following 'ch' sounds like the 'sh' in 'ship', 'shin' and 'sheep', and the final 'e' is like the 'ay' in 'bay', 'day' and 'may'. The word is pronounced 'two-**SHAY**'.

Meaning — During an argument, when your opponent says something and you respond by saying 'touché', you are admitting that the individual has made a very good point – one that deserves to be acknowledged.

Examples — *That was a brilliant counter-argument, Nalini. Touché!*

Politicians keep saying English should be banned. But when it comes to their own children, they send them to the best English medium schools.
Touché!

Etymology — From the French 'toucher', meaning 'to hit'. Used in the sport of fencing.

Tour de force /tuə-də fɒs/

Pronunciation The first word is pronounced like the word 'tour' and the last like the word 'force'. The 'e' in 'de' is like the 'a' in 'china'. The expression is pronounced 'tour-de-**FORCE**'.

Meaning When you call someone's speech or performance a 'tour de force', what you mean is that it was outstanding; it was very well done. It is something that is unlikely to be equalled by others.

Examples *According to critics, my favourite author's latest novel is a tour de force.*

The ageing actor's performance as the drunken father is a tour de force.

Etymology This French expression literally means 'feat of strength'.

Tout /taut/

Pronunciation It rhymes with the word 'doubt', 'bout' and 'shout'.

Meaning When you tout someone as something, you deliberately praise the individual in order to convince people that he is important or good. It can also mean 'to sell something'.

Examples *Shailender is being touted as the next boxing champion.*

Nayaz is being touted as the ideal candidate for the job.

Now that Ganguly is back in the team, many multinationals will use him to tout their products.

Etymology From the Old English 'totian', meaning 'peep, peer'.

Townterview

Meaning Originally, the term was used to refer to the members of the public interviewing a politician in a town hall. This gathering in a relatively small place was meant to provide a sense of intimacy.

Examples *Hillary Clinton is famous for her townterviews.*

The townterview with the Prime Minister will be next week.

Etymology This word is a combination of 'town' and 'interview'.

Trailblazer

Meaning Someone who has done somcthing that no one has done before; someone who has discovered or developed a new method of doing something.

Examples — *Jambu will always be remembered as a trailblazer in cancer research.*

Padma was a trailblazer in the field of AIDS research.

The company has blazed a trail in developing new medicines for curing AIDS.

Origin — The expression came into being in the late 18th century when American settlers were pushing further and further west – towards Oregon, California, etc. Since they were exploring uncharted territory and didn't want to get lost along the way, they used to mark the trail that they had taken. One of the ways that they used to do it was to remove the bark from some of the trees. This method of marking trees was known as 'blazing'.

Trenchant /tren-tʃənt/

Pronunciation — The first syllable rhymes with the words 'French', 'drench' and 'wrench'. The following 'a' is like the 'a' in 'china'. The word is pronounced '**TRENCH**-ent'.

Meaning — A trenchant argument is a forceful or vigorous argument. The word can also be used to mean 'caustic' or 'critical'.

Examples	*Geetha's trenchant wit didn't go down well with the members of the Board.* *Vikram's trenchant argument for a unified state made interesting reading.*
Etymology	It comes from the Old French 'trenchier', meaning 'to cut'.

Trypanophobia /trɪ-pæ-nəu-fəu-biə/

Pronunciation	The 'y' in the first syllable is like the 'i' in 'bit', 'hit' and 'sit', and the following syllable is pronounced like the word 'pan'. It is also possible to pronounce the 'a' in the second syllable like the 'a' in 'china'. The 'o' is like the 'o' in 'go', so' and 'no', and the final syllables are pronounced like the word 'phobia'. One way of pronouncing the word is 'tri-pan-o-**FOE**-bia'.
Meaning	The extreme and irrational fear of injections or needles.
Etymology	From the Greek 'trypano', meaning 'auger', a device used for boring holes in wood.

Tryst /trɪst/ /traist/

Pronunciation	Some people pronounce the 'y' like the 'i' in 'sit', 'bit' and 'fit', while others pronounce it

like the 'y' in 'my' and 'by'. The word can be pronounced '**TRIST**' or '**TRYST**'.

Meaning — The meeting of two lovers at an appointed time is called a 'tryst'; the word is considered literary. There is a tendency nowadays to use the word to mean 'appointment'.

Examples — *Kapil, if you don't hurry you'll be late for the tryst. Never keep a girl waiting.*

"Ladies and gentleman, we have a tryst with destiny", said the speaker.

Etymology — From the Old French 'tristre', meaning 'waiting place'.

Tsetse

/<u>tet</u>-sɪ/

Pronunciation — The first 's' is silent. 'Tset' rhymes with words like 'set', 'bet' and 'met'. The 'e' in the second syllable is like the 'i' in 'sit', 'knit' and 'bit'. The word is pronounced '**TET**-si'.

Meaning — An African fly which feeds on the blood of animals.

Turncoat

Meaning — People who switch allegiances or change their opinion radically whenever convenient; mostly used to show disapproval.

Examples *Why would you want that political turncoat to preside?*

Priya was a fool to trust a turncoat like Yogesh.

Origin The Duke of Saxony lived very close to the French border, and therefore, made it a point to keep both the Saxons and the French in good humour. The Duke's reversible coat was blue on one side, and white on the other. Whenever a Frenchman visited his place, the Duke was seen wearing a white coat. When he wanted to please the Saxons, the Duke turned the coat inside out, and wore the blue side.

TV stoned

Meaning A person immersed in his favourite television show and being totally unaware of the world around him. He is like someone who is under the influence of drugs.

Examples *I was TV stoned and that's why I didn't hear the phone ring.*

Sangeetha's father is usually TV stoned when he watches the evening news.

Uber

/u:bə/

Pronunciation — The first vowel sounds like the 'oo' in 'cool', 'pool' and 'school', while the following 'er' is like the 'a' in 'china'. The word is pronounced '**OO**-be'.

Meaning — The word is frequently used in English before nouns to mean 'extremely' or 'super'. When used with a person, it means he is a great example of something.

Examples — *Uberbatsman Virat Kohli will score at least three centuries in the series.*

For their first anniversary, Rajiv wants to buy Nanda an uberexpensive car.

Where did you get those sandals, Waheeda? They're ubercool.

Etymology — From the German 'uber', meaning 'over'.

Ubiquitous

/jʊ-bɪk-wɪ-təs/

Pronunciation — The first vowel is like the 'u' in 'pull' and 'full', and the following 'i' rhymes with 'pick' and 'tick'. The 'quit' sounds like the word 'quit', and the final 'ou' is pronounced like the 'a' in 'china' The word is pronounced 'yu-**BIK**-wi-tes'.

Meaning	Something that seems to be present everywhere; mostly used in formal contexts.
Examples	*During the picnic, the ubiquitous little ants made our lives miserable.* *Many people find the ubiquitous hoardings in the city very distracting.* *Some people feel threatened by the ubiquitous spread of English.*
Etymology	From the Latin 'ubique', meaning 'everywhere'.

Umpteen /ʌmp-ti:n/

Pronunciation	The first syllable rhymes with 'bump', 'pump' and 'lump'; the second is pronounced like the word 'teen'. The word is pronounced 'ump-**TEEN**'.
Meaning	Many or a lot of.
Examples	*I emailed Janani umpteen times, but she never responded.* *Bhaveen revised the paper umpteen times before submitting it.* *Naila has seen the movie umpteen times.*
Etymology	Combination of 'umpty', meaning 'an indefinite number of', and 'teen'.

Uncouth /ʌn-<u>kuːθ</u>/

Pronunciation The first syllable sounds like the 'un' in 'bun', 'fun' and 'sun', while the following 'couth' rhymes with the words 'youth' and 'tooth'. The word is pronounced 'un-**KUUTH**'.

Meaning Someone who is lacking in manners; this unsophisticated individual is often rude, and frequently says things that embarrass those around him.

Examples *There is no way I'll let you marry Sanjay. He is uncouth.*

Mithali is uncouth, brash and hated by all her colleagues.

Etymology The word comes from the Old English 'un', meaning 'not', and 'cunnan', meaning 'know'. 'Uncouth' originally meant 'not known'; later, it acquired the meaning 'strange'. With the passage of time, 'uncouth' began to mean 'uncultured'.

Unctuous /<u>ʌŋk</u>-tʃʊ-əs/

Pronunciation The 'unc' in the first syllable is pronounced like the 'unc' in 'uncle'. The 't' sounds like the 'ch' in 'cheat', 'chap' and 'cheap', while the following 'u' is like the 'u' in 'put', 'pull' and 'full'. The final 'ou' is like the 'a' in 'china'. The word is pronounced '**UNK**-chu-es'.

Meaning — A formal word meaning 'being insincere' or 'faking it' – pretending to be interested in what someone is saying or saying nice things about people you do not like.

Examples — *After my accident, Saroja came to see me oozing unctuous sympathy.*

I can't stand Shalini and Kapil. There is something unctuous about them.

Etymology — From the Latin 'unctuosis', meaning 'greasy'.

Urban legend

Meaning — A frightening or funny story told and retold so many times that it becomes a part of popular mythology; people believe it to be true.

Examples — *One of the popular urban legends in the US is that there are alligators in the sewers.*

The story that Suraj keeps insisting is true is nothing more than an urban legend.

Uxoricide /ʌk-sɒ-rɪ-said/

Pronunciation — The first syllable sounds like the 'uck' in 'buck' and 'tuck', and the second like the 'aw' in 'paw', 'saw' and 'raw'. The word is pronounced 'uk-**SAW**-ri-side'.

Meaning A husband killing his wife.

Example *The police think that it is a case of uxoricide.*

Etymology From the Latin 'uxor', meaning 'wife'.

Valet /væ-lei/ /væ-lɪt/

Pronunciation The 'a' is pronounced like the 'a' in 'cat', 'bat' and 'hat'. Some people pronounce the 'let' like 'lay' and others like the word 'lit'. The word can be pronounced '**VA**-lit'. Some people put the stress on the second syllable.

Meaning In American English, the word is normally used to refer to someone who has been hired to clean or park cars. In British English, it is used to refer to a male attendant; someone who takes care of the needs of his employer. He is like a butler.

Examples *In his next birth, Bala wishes to be P.G. Wodehouse's valet.*

Most restaurants in the city have valet parking.

Vanilla /və-nɪl-ə/

Pronunciation The vowel in the first and last syllable is pronounced like the 'a' in 'china', and the second syllable sounds like the word 'nil'. The word is pronounced 've-**NIL**-e'.

Meaning — Used in informal contexts to refer to the basic model of an electronic gadget – the one without the bells and whistles. It can also be used to mean 'dull' or 'ordinary'.

Examples — *My grandmother wants a cell phone. I'm planning to get her a vanilla model.*

After having been in the limelight for nearly fifteen years, the star found the vanilla domestic life rather depressing.

Origin — When it comes to ice cream, vanilla is believed to be the most basic flavour.

Vase /va:z/ /veis/

Pronunciation — In India, most people tend to make this word rhyme with 'face', 'lace' and 'case'. This is how the Americans pronounce the word! The British, on the other hand, pronounce the 'a' like the 'a' in 'ask', 'mask' and 'task', and the 's' like the 'z' in 'zoo' and 'zip'. They pronounce the word '**VAAZ**'.

Meaning — A container mostly used to hold flowers.

Examples — *Priyanka hit the robber on the head with a vase.*

Where is the vase Naveen gave us last week?

Etymology — From the Latin 'vas', meaning 'container, vessel'.

Verbiage /v<u>ɜ:</u>-bɪ-ɪdʒ/

Pronunciation — The word consists of three syllables, and not two. The first syllable is pronounced like the word 'verb', and the following 'i' is like the 'i' in 'pit', 'kit' and 'bit'. The final 'age' is pronounced like the 'idge' in 'fridge', 'bridge' and 'ridge'. This rather formal word is pronounced '**VERB**-i-ij'.

Meaning — Mostly used to refer to the manner in which someone writes or speaks. He is difficult to understand because he uses too many words or complicated sentences.

Examples — *The chapter needs to be edited. Spend some time removing the verbiage.*

Madhav's talk contained too much technical verbiage.

Etymology — From the French 'verbier', meaning 'to chatter'.

Vibes /vaibz/

Pronunciation — The first vowel sounds like the 'y' in 'my' and 'by', and the 's' is like the 'z' in 'zip' and 'zoo'. The word is pronounced '**VYBZ**'.

Meaning — Mostly used in informal contexts to refer to the good or bad feelings that you sometimes get when you meet a new person or when you walk into a strange place; sensing something intuitively. Short form of 'vibrations'.

Examples — *Whenever I see Venkat, I get really bad vibes.*

I don't think you should buy this house. I don't like the vibes I get here.

Meera doesn't want to work with Pramod. She says she gets strange vibes from that guy.

Vide

/vai-dɪ/ /vi:-dei/

Pronunciation — The word consists of two syllables, and not one. The 'i' sounds like the 'y' in 'my', 'shy' and 'by'. The following 'e' is like the 'i' in 'pit', 'bit' and 'sit'. Some people, however, pronounce the first vowel like the 'ee' in 'see', 'bee' and 'ghee', and the second like the 'ay' in 'day', 'bay' and 'say'. The word can be pronounced '**VY**-di' or '**VEE**-day'.

Meaning — The word is mostly used in academic articles. When the author uses this word, he means that he would like the reader to refer to a particular book, document or page for additional information.

Examples — *The comic has also played a serious role in films – vide* The Truman Show.

The dissertation needs to be rewritten for there are far too many mistakes – vide pages 31, 32, 33, 36 and 40.

Etymology — 'Vide' is a Latin word, meaning 'look at' or 'refer to'. Formal letters referring to an earlier correspondence always make use of this word.

Vidiot

Meaning — Someone who plays video games all the time and loses touch with reality or someone who is constantly glued to the TV or video.

Examples — *Most of the students in my class are confirmed vidiots.*

The vidiot didn't realise his house was on fire.

Etymology — It is a combination of 'video' and 'idiot'.

Vigilante /vɪ-dʒɪ-læn-tɪ/

Pronunciation — The vowels in the first and the final syllables are pronounced like the 'i' in 'hit', 'it' and 'sit'. The second syllable sounds like the name 'Jill' and the third like the word 'ant'. The word is pronounced 'vi-ji-**LAN**-ti'.

Meaning — Someone who takes the law into his own hands and punishes those who have committed crimes; the word has a negative connotation. One frequently talks about 'vigilante groups' and 'vigilante justice'.

Examples *The vigilante is believed to have killed the Don's right-hand man.*

A vigilante group shut down the gambling den next to the school.

Some believe Batman is nothing more than a vigilante.

Etymology It comes from the Latin 'viglantem', meaning 'watchful' or 'careful'.

Vignette /vɪn-jet/

Pronunciation The 'g' and the final 'e' are silent. The first syllable rhymes with the words 'win', 'bin' and 'sin', and the 'ett' in the second syllable is pronounced like the word 'yet'. The word is pronounced 'vin-**YET**'.

Meaning It can be used to refer to a short piece of writing, a photograph or a drawing which captures the typical characteristics of a person or thing; an episode.

Examples *You certainly don't expect a city-bred girl to write a vignette of small-town life.*

The director has made use of several vignettes to weave the story together.

Etymology — The word comes from the Old French 'vigne', meaning 'vine'. Originally, the term was used to refer to the drawings of vines that one found at the beginning of every chapter of a printed book.

Villain /vɪl-ən/

Pronunciation — The first syllable rhymes with 'will', 'bill' and 'pill', and the final 'ai' is like the 'a' in 'china'. The word is pronounced '**VIL**-en'.

Meaning — A criminal; the 'baddie' in films. Can also be used to refer to someone or something.

Examples — *Shabana played the role of the villain with panache.*

A group of young villains have been targeting the elderly.

According to this researcher, it is not cholesterol, but sugar that is the villain.

Etymology — The Latin word 'villa' originally meant 'country house' or 'farm'; someone who stayed in a villa was referred to as a 'villain'. He was usually a poor farmer and since the conditions in which he lived were bad, he often had to resort to crime to make ends meet. With the passage of time, 'villain' began to be used to refer to people with antisocial tendencies.

Virago /vɪ-ra:gəu/

Pronunciation: The vowel in the first syllable is like the 'i' in 'sit', 'knit' and 'bit', while the following 'a' is like the 'a' in 'bath', 'mask' and 'dance'. The final syllable sounds like the word 'go'. The word is pronounced 'vi-**RAA**-go'.

Meaning: A woman who is ill tempered and rather bossy. Someone who shouts and screams a lot.

Examples: *This job requires someone with tact. You are out of your mind to ask a virago like Deepa to do it.*

I'd think twice before marrying Anil. His mother is a foul-mouthed virago.

How Sanjay fell in love with a virago like Meena is beyond me.

Etymology: The word comes from the Latin root 'vir', meaning 'man' or 'virile'. Virago was first used as a compliment; when you referred to a woman as being a virago, you meant she had great strength and courage.

Vis-a-vis /vi:z-a:-vi:/

Pronunciation: The 's' in the first 'vis' is like the 'z' in 'zip' and 'zoo'; the second 's' is silent. The 'i' sounds like the 'ee' in 'feel', 'peel' and 'heel', and the

	'a' is pronounced like the 'a' in 'bath' and 'path'. The word is pronounced 'viiz-aa-**VII**'.
Meaning	Face to face. It is also used to mean 'in relation to' and 'in comparison with someone or something'.
Examples	*My salary vis-a-vis the other accountants in the firm is very low.* *Revathi looked poor and shabby vis-a-vis her well-dressed cousin.* *Vidya and Shyam chatted vis-a-vis after many years.*
Etymology	In French, 'vis' means 'face'. 'Vis-a-vis' means 'face to face'.

Vitiate /vɪ-ʃɪ-eit/

Pronunciation	The 'vit' rhymes with 'wish' and 'mish', and the following 'i' is like the 'i' in 'hit' and 'sit'. The final syllable rhymes with 'fate' and 'late'. The word is pronounced '**VI**-shi-ate'.
Meaning	The word has different meanings. One of them is 'damaged' or 'made defective'; something that is imperfect. Mostly used in formal contexts.
Examples	*Scientists believe that moisture in the cave had vitiated the once beautiful paintings.*

A few MPs are convinced that our culture has been vitiated by pop and rock music.

Etymology — It comes from the Latin 'vitium', meaning 'fault, vice'.

Vivacious /vɪ-veɪ-ʃəs/

Pronunciation — The 'i' is like the 'i' in 'sit' and 'kit', and the following 'a' is like the 'ay' in 'day' and 'may'. The 'cious' sounds like the final syllable in 'precious' and 'anxious'. The word is pronounced 'vi-**VAY**-shes'.

Meaning — Something that is full of life and energy. The word is generally used with women.

Examples — *Sarita's daughter is a vivacious little thing.*

Malini's vivacious manner put some life into the drab meeting.

Not many people consider Patna to be a vivacious city.

Etymology — From the Latin 'vivax', meaning 'lively'.

Volkswagen /fəuks-wa:gən/

Pronunciation — The first syllable is pronounced like the word 'folks'. The following 'a' is like the 'a' in 'bath', 'path' and 'carpet'; the final 'e' is like the 'a' in 'china'. The word is pronounced '**FOLKS**-waagen'.

Meaning — Name of a German auto maker.

Etymology — In German, 'volks' means 'people's' and 'wagen' means 'car'. The name literally means 'the people's car'. Guess who came up with the idea of a people's car? Adolf Hitler!

Volte-face /vɔlt-fæs/

Pronunciation — The 'o' in 'volte' is like the 'o' in 'hot', 'pot' and 'not'. Some people pronounce it like the 'o' in 'go', 'so' and 'no'. The 'a' in 'face' is like the 'a' in 'act' and 'fact'. The final 'e' in both words is silent. The word is pronounced 'volt-**FAS**'.

Meaning — To face in the opposite direction; to do a complete turnaround. A total change in attitude towards something or someone.

Examples — *The Chairman's speech represents a complete volte-face in company thinking.*

Some of the Ministers didn't go along with the party's volte-face on education.

Etymology — From the Italian 'volta faccia', meaning 'turn face'.

Voluminous /və-l<u>ju:</u>-mɪ-nəs/

Pronunciation: The first 'o' and the final 'ou' sound like the 'a' in 'china'. The second syllable rhymes with 'few', 'due' and 'new', while the following 'i' is like the 'i' in 'it', 'pit' and 'sit'. The word is pronounced 've-**LYOO**-mi-nes'.

Meaning: When you say that something is voluminous, you are implying that it is large; it contains many things. Something that is very lengthy and detailed.

Examples: *Sangeetha requires time to go through the voluminous file.*

Jaideep went to sleep on the voluminous sofa.

Etymology: From the Latin 'volumen', meaning 'that which is rolled'.

Vouchsafe /vautʃ-<u>seif</u>/

Pronunciation: The first syllable 'vouch' rhymes with 'couch', 'pouch' and 'ouch', and the second is pronounced like the word 'safe'. The word is pronounced 'vouch-**SAFE**'.

Meaning: When you vouchsafe something to someone, you tell or give the person something – sometimes, in a rather condescending manner. The word is mostly used in formal contexts.

Examples *The Prime Minister refused to vouchsafe a reply to the members of the press.*

The eccentric billionaire vouchsafed his driver three bars of gold.

Etymology The word literally means 'vouch as safe'.

Vox populi /vɔks pɔp-ju-li:/

Pronunciation 'Vox' rhymes with 'pox', 'fox' and 'box'. The 'u' in 'populi' sounds like the 'u' in 'university' and 'unit', while the final 'i' is like the 'ee' in 'bee', 'fee' and 'see'. Some people pronounce the final 'i' like the 'ie' in 'tie', 'die' and 'pie'. The word is pronounced 'vox **POP**-yu-lee'.

Meaning A technique normally used in radio and television broadcasting. Reporters ask people on the street to give their opinion about something – who they will be voting for, what the new budget will look like, etc. The term is often abbreviated to either 'vox pop' or 'vox pops'.

Examples *Sai Prasad likes to make use of vox pop in his radio programmes.*

Sneha's film made use of vox pop.

Can you get me some vox populi by six this evening?

Etymology This is an expression borrowed from Latin, meaning 'voice of the people'.

Voyeur /vɔi-j3:/

Pronunciation: One simple way of pronouncing the word is to make the first syllable rhyme with 'boy', 'toy' and 'joy'. The second syllable begins with the sound 'y' and the final 'ur' sounds like the 'ir' in 'shirt' and 'dirt'. The word is pronounced 'voy-**YE**'.

Meaning: A 'voyeur' is a peeping Tom; someone who takes great pleasure seeing other people naked.

Examples: *The voyeur had placed several hidden cameras in the shower room.*

Peeping through the window to see if anyone was home made me feel like a voyeur.

Etymology: From the French 'voyeur', meaning 'one who views'.

Walk the talk

Meaning: The full expression is 'talk the talk and walk the walk'. When you tell someone to 'walk the talk', you are asking him to do what he has said he would do. In other words, you want the individual to stop talking about what he intends to do, and just do it.

"You've always said that you're not afraid of sharks. Now walk the talk."

Examples *You've been telling all my friends that you will beat me in straight sets. Now, walk the talk.*

Politicians forget about the promises they had made during the campaign. Once they are in power, they don't walk the talk.

Walking disaster area

Meaning A clumsy individual; someone who causes or is involved in many accidents.

Examples *When he was young, my cousin Suresh was a walking disaster area.*

Our previous maidservant was a walking disaster area.

Wannabe /wɔ-nə-bɪ/

Pronunciation The first syllable is pronounced like the word 'want' without the 't'. The second vowel is like the 'a' in 'china' and the final 'e' is like the 'i' in 'sit' and 'wit'. The word is pronounced **'WA**-ne-bi'.

Meaning Someone who apes or imitates others in order to become famous – usually, unsuccessfully. Aspiring to become like someone.

Examples *Don't pay any attention to Nandu. He's just another wannabe writer.*

As a coach, I have met many wannabe Tendulkars.

Etymology 'Want to be' when said very quickly sounds like 'wannabe'.

Watchdog agency

Meaning People who come together to ensure that our rights and interests are being protected; they make sure that companies, governments, etc, follow the letter of the law, and do not cheat the public.

Examples *We are hoping to set up an anti-drug watchdog agency soon.*

For the watchdog committee to do good work, we need more funding.

Watershed moment

Meaning In everyday contexts, the word is used to mean 'important changes' or the 'turning point' in a situation or event.

Examples *For most cricket enthusiasts, 1983 was a watershed year.*

A watershed moment came in her life when she was admitted to Harvard.

Etymology The word comes from the German 'wasserscheide', meaning 'water divide' or 'water parting'. A 'watershed' is the point where a flowing body of water – river, stream, etc. – separates or parts. The word 'shed' was used in the past to mean 'partition' or 'separation'. The parting in one's hair is also called a 'shed'.

Webinar

/web-ɪ-na:/

Meaning A 'webinar' is a seminar transmitted over the web; it involves a lot of interaction between the participants. The term can be used to refer to a presentation, lecture or workshop that is broadcast over the web.

Examples *I'm afraid I won't be able to come. I'm taking part in a webinar.*

Jaswanth refuses to participate in webinars.

Etymology The word is a combination of 'web' and 'seminar'.

Webtrovert

Meaning Someone who in real life is extremely shy, but on social media – Facebook, Twitter, etc. – comes across as being an extrovert.

Examples *In real life, Hema is very boring to talk to. She's a webtrovert.*

Quite a few people I know are webtroverts.

I thought Maria would speak up at the meeting. But it turns out, she's a webtrovert.

Etymology A combination of 'web' and 'extrovert'.

Wee hours

Meaning Used in informal contexts to refer to the early hours of the morning; the time between midnight and sunrise when it is still relatively dark outside. Also possible to say 'small hours'.

Examples *Shaheen didn't go to bed till the small hours of the morning.*

We got up in the wee hours to watch the closing ceremony on television.

Some of my cousins who work in the software industry return home in the wee hours.

Etymology In Middle English, 'we' or 'wei' meant 'small'.

Weird /wiəd/

Pronunciation The word rhymes with 'feared', 'neared' and 'beard'.

Meaning When you say that something is weird, you mean that it is rather strange or unusual. This word, which is mostly used in informal contexts, can be used with people and things.

Examples *I met Sadhana's husband yesterday. The guy is really weird.*

My boss has some weird ideas about how an organisation should be run.

Wetware

Meaning — The human brain; human being.

Examples — *Who is the wetware your company will be using to test our software?*

If we get someone with experience, then all we'll need to do is upgrade his wetware.

Etymology — Combination of 'wet' and 'software'.

Wherewithal /w3ə-wɪð-ɒl/

Pronunciation — The first syllable is pronounced like the word 'where', the second like the word 'with', and the final like the word 'all'. The word is pronounced '**WHERE**-with-all'.

Meaning — The funds or money required for a particular purpose. The word is usually used with the definite article.

Examples — *I am sorry to say that we don't have the wherewithal to complete the renovation.*

The wherewithal was sent to our factory in Hyderabad to produce spurious drugs.

Jasmine has the wherewithal to buy two houses.

Etymology A combination of 'where' and 'withal', meaning 'means by which'.

Whistle-blower

Meaning Someone who informs his superiors of the illegal activities that are going on in an organisation. By doing this, he hopes to put an end to the wrongdoing. If the powers-that-be do not take action, then the whistle-blower may choose to take matters into his own hands and inform the media.

Examples *There is a need to protect whistle-blowers in our country.*

Someone is leaking information to the media. I want to know who the whistle-blower is.

Origin The expression comes from the practice adopted by 'Bobbies', English policeman. In the old days, every policeman carried a whistle with him, and he would blow on it whenever he saw a crime taking place. This was to alert the other Bobbies who were in the vicinity.

Willing to take his/her medicine

Meaning The individual is willing to accept punishment because he believes he deserves it. He is willing to submit himself to something unpleasant.

Examples — *Whenever I do something wrong, I am usually willing to take my medicine.*

Reema thought it was excessive, but Gopal took his medicine like a man.

Willy-nilly /wɪlɪ nɪlɪ/

Pronunciation — The first syllables sound like 'will' and 'nil', respectively. The final 'y' in both cases is pronounced like the 'i' in 'bit' and 'sit'. The word is pronounced 'will-y **NILL**-y'.

Meaning — When you do something 'willy-nilly', you do it under compulsion. The expression can also be used to mean 'doing something in a careless or disorganised manner'; doing it without any prior planning.

Examples — *The boss' wife is organising the show. So we all have to contribute, willy-nilly.*

Be careful. Otherwise, you will be dragged, willy-nilly, into the fight.

The students rushed in and threw their bags willy-nilly into the storeroom.

Etymology — The expression is a contraction of 'will ye, nill ye'. 'Nill', a word that we no longer use, meant 'to be unwilling'.

Wimpy

Meaning — When you call someone a 'wimp', you mean that he is a very weak and timid individual; he is spineless.

Examples — *Don't be such a wimp, Raju. Just go ahead and take the plunge.*

How can you ask someone wimpy like Karthik to be the next President?

Origin — According to some scholars, 'wimpy' comes from the word 'whimper'. Others believe that it comes from the name of a character in a well-known cartoon show, *Popeye*. J. Wellington Wimpy, affectionately called 'Wimpy', is Popeye's friend. He is spineless and never participates in any of the fights that Popeye is constantly getting himself into.

Winning ugly

Meaning — To win even though you did not play your best; to fight and scrape and manage to find a way to win.

Examples — *Brijesh's aim is to win. He doesn't care if he wins ugly.*

Champions like Federer and Nadal don't seem to mind winning ugly once in a while.

W00t /wu:t/

Pronunciation Rhymes with 'boot', 'suit' and 'root'.

Meaning Frequently used in everyday conversation as an expression of joy and excitement.

Examples *Believe it or not, the bank has decided to give us the loan we'd asked for. W00t!*

I've got an A in the exam! W00t!

Origin The Internet has given us many words, and 'w00t' is one them. It originated in 'competitive online gaming', and was used as an acronym by players for 'we owned the other team'. Meaning, they were much better than the other team and beat them easily. The word can also be spelt 'woot', and was included in the list of 'Merriam-Webster's Words of the Year' for 2007.

Wordrobe

Meaning An individual's vocabulary; the number of words he knows.

Examples *Shreya has added nearly 500 words to her wordrobe.*

You have a long way to go, Prakash. Your wordrobe is very limited.

Etymology Combination of 'word' and 'robe' – like 'wardrobe'.

Worrywart

Meaning Someone who worries excessively. He worries even when there is no reason to. Mostly used in American English in informal contexts.

Examples *When I went to the library, I unfortunately ran into that worrywart, Sonba.*

After spending some time with worrywarts, I end up feeling depressed.

Wrap rage

Meaning The anger that you sometimes feel trying to unwrap something – usually a gift.

Examples *The video game that my parents had bought was so tightly packed that it took me nearly twenty minutes to open it. That was the first time I ever experienced wrap rage.*

I understand wrap rage is quite common in the US and Britain during Christmas.

Wuthering /wʌ-ðə-rɪŋ/

Pronunciation The first two syllables rhyme with the words 'mother' and 'brother', and the final syllable is pronounced like the word 'ring'. The word is pronounced '**WU**-the-ring'.

Meaning — A strong wind that makes a loud noise when it blows.

Examples — *Seema couldn't sleep because of the eerie noise the wuthering wind made.*

We didn't bring the right clothes for this wuthering weather.

Etymology — It comes from the Scottish 'whithering', meaning 'rushing, blustering'.

Xenophobia /zen-ə-fəu-biə/

Pronunciation — The first syllable is pronounced like the word 'zen', and the following 'o' is like the 'a' in 'china'. The word is pronounced 'zen-e-**FOE**-bie'.

Meaning — The extreme fear or dislike of people from other countries – foreigners. If you hate foreigners, then you could say that you are xenophobic.

Examples — *The current government is adding to the xenophobia already existing.*

Malathy is too xenophobic to go abroad.

Bala's xenophobia prevented him from meeting some interesting people.

Yada yada yada /jæ-də/

Pronunciation The first 'a' is like the 'a' in 'act' and 'pact' and the second like the 'a' in 'china'. It is pronounced 'ya-de ya-de **YA**-de'.

Meaning Used in informal contexts to mean boring talk; blah blah blah.

Examples *Bharath had to listen to a lot of yada yada yada about plagiarism.*

It was a typical evening. Came home, had coffee, read the paper, yada yada yada.

Yap /jæp/

Etymology Rhymes with 'tap', 'rap' and 'sap'.

Meaning To talk for a long time in an annoying manner.

Examples *Like most teenagers, Kavita spent a lot of her time yapping on the phone.*

The last time Renu came here, she just couldn't stop yapping about her kids.

Yellular /jel-jʊ-lə/

Pronunciation The first syllable is pronounced like the word 'yell', and the following two sound like the 'ular' in 'cellular'. The word is pronounced '**YELL**-yu-le'.

Meaning — Shouting into the cell phone in order to be heard when the signal is bad.

Examples — *Some idiot on the train went yellular at three in the morning.*

Everyone stopped what they were doing and stared at the man who had gone yellular.

Etymology — It is a combination of 'yell' and 'cellular'. Not listed in any standard dictionary.

Yes-man

Meaning — Someone who says 'yes' to everything that his boss/leader says because he wants to be in his good books; a weak individual.

Examples — *The Minister had the sense not to surround herself with yes-men.*

The 'yes-men' looked very nervous when the police questioned them about the missing CEO.

Young Turks

Meaning — Frequently used in politics to refer to a person or a group of people who are keen on making some radical changes in a well-established organisation. These young individuals are bubbling with ideas and are rather impatient to implement them; they are keen to usurp power from the old conservatives who have been running the show till now.

Examples *At the meeting, it was only the Young Turks that spoke against the Director.*

The Young Turks in the teaching faculty want the VC to apologise to the students.

Etymology The term was first used to refer to a nationalist party that was keen on bringing about changes in the political system in Turkey. The members of the party were called 'Young Turks' because the founding members were all very young – most were in their early 30s, while a few were in their late 20s. In 1908, the party succeeded in overthrowing Sultan Abdul Hamid II.

You're nuts

Meaning Mostly used in informal contexts to mean 'you are crazy'.

Examples *Naresh wants to invest all his savings in the stock market. The guy is nuts, I tell you.*

I wouldn't go out with Kamal if I were you. My friends tell me he's nuts.

Origin

During the 19th century, the word 'nut' began to be used to refer to an individual's head. Soon the word replaced the word 'head' in the expression 'off one's head', meaning 'crazy'.

Zeitgeist

/zait-gaist/ /tsait-gaist/

Pronunciation

There are several ways of pronouncing this word of German origin. The 'z' can be pronounced like the 'z' in 'zip' and 'zero' or like the 'ts' in 'cuts', 'huts' and 'puts'. The 'ei' in the first and second syllables is like the 'i' in 'fight', 'might' and 'tight'. The word is pronounced '**ZAIT**-gaist' or '**TSAIT**-gaist'.

Meaning

Normally used to refer to the spirit of the age. Zeitgeist has been defined as 'the general set of ideas, beliefs, feelings, etc. which is typical of a particular period in history'.

Examples

The movie successfully captured the Zeitgeist of the 1990s.

According to this article, Virat is the Zeitgeist of the modern cricket captain – brash and aggressive.

Etymology

'Zeit' in German means 'time' and 'Geist' means 'spirit'. The word literally means 'spirit of the time'.

Zenith

/<u>zen</u>-ɪθ/ /<u>zi:</u>-niθ/

Pronunciation — There are two ways of pronouncing this word. Some people pronounce the 'e' like the 'e' in 'set', 'bet' and 'pet', while others pronounce it like the 'ee' in 'fees', 'bees' and 'knees'. The final vowel sounds like the 'i' in 'pit', 'kit' and 'hit'. The word can be pronounced '**ZEN**-ith' or '**ZEE**-nith'.

Meaning — Generally used to refer to the high point or the most successful phase of one's life. It can also mean the highest point reached by an object – ball, missile, rocket, etc.

Examples — *Naveen's career reached its zenith when he was just thirty.*

The missile exploded much before it reached its zenith.

Etymology — It comes from the Old French 'cenith', which some people say is a corruption of the Arabic 'samt-ar-ras', meaning 'the way over the head'.

Zephyr

/<u>zef</u>-ə/

Pronunciation — The first syllable 'zeph' rhymes with 'deaf', 'ref' and 'and 'chef'. The 'y' sounds like the 'a' in 'china' and the final 'r' is silent. The word is pronounced '**ZEF**-e'.

Meaning	A soft gentle breeze can be referred to as 'zephyr'; the word is mostly used in literary contexts.
Examples	*Mukund watched the branches sway as a gentle zephyr passed through them.* *The forecast was for heavy winds, but it was only a gentle zephyr.*
Etymology	From the Greek 'Zephyros', meaning 'the west wind'.

Zero in on

Meaning	To focus one's attention on something or someone. It can also be used to mean 'to aim at'.
Examples	*Pratibha picked up the binoculars and zeroed in on the parrots sitting on the tree.* *As expected, the Opposition has zeroed in on the problem of unemployment.* *The missiles were zeroing in on their targets.*

Zing

Meaning	To add life to something, to make it interesting or exciting.
Examples	*In this year's auction, we need to take someone who will bring some zing to the team.*

As a teacher, Madhu does not have the zing her mother had.

The soup is rather bland. You need to put some zing in it.